TWAYNE'S WORLD AUTHORS SERIES

A Survey of the World's Literature

Sylvia E. Bowman, Indiana University

GENERAL EDITOR

SPAIN

Gerald E. Wade, Vanderbilt University
Janet Winecoff Díaz, University of North Carolina

EDITORS

Agustín Moreto

(TWAS 308)

Agustín Moreto

Agustín Moreto

By JAMES A. CASTAÑEDA

Rice University

Twayne Publishers, Inc.   ::   New York

Library of Congress Cataloging in Publication Data

Castañeda, James A
  Agustín Moreto.

  (Twayne's world authors series. TWAS 308. Spain)
  Bibliography: p. 173
  1. Moreto y Cavana, Agustín, 1618–1669.
PQ6417.C34   862'.3   73–22007
ISBN O–8057–2633–0

$\mathcal{C}$

To my Mother and Dad

Preface

There is no single treatise which deals with Moreto's biography and all phases of his literary production. Since the nature and scope of a volume of the Twayne series preclude any pretension to a truly comprehensive study, the modest goal of this book is to provide an up-to-date synthesis of available information on the life and works of this Golden Age dramatist whose talent and literary importance are far greater than indicated by the surprisingly scant scholarly comment which has been devoted to him. Most students of Spanish Golden Age theater agree upon the convenient division into two cycles: that of Lope de Vega (1562–1635) and his school, or followers, and that of Calderón (1600–1681) and his. There is also general agreement on a classification of quality and importance which groups Lope de Vega, Tirso de Molina (1584?–1648), Juan Ruiz de Alarcón (1581–1639), and Calderón as the undisputed principal figures in Golden Age theater. There exist extensive bibliographies and several monographic studies on each of these four dramatists but, quantitatively, scholarly treatment of the next line of dramatists falls off very sharply. Critical assessment of the dramatists of the seventeenth century often classifies Rojas Zorrilla (1607–1648) and Moreto (1618–1669) as the sole members of a group superior to all but Lope, Tirso, Alarcón, and Calderón. It is thus in the context of his acceptance as one of the six most important Spanish Golden Age dramatists that we lament the paucity of scholarship which has been devoted to Moreto.

Owing both to a dearth of documentary biographical data and to a tendency not to reveal himself autobiographically in his plays, we are not able to reconstruct the life of Moreto with the completeness that has been attained in the cases of Lope de Vega and several other contemporary literary figures. Perhaps this very absence of documentary biographic evidence invited the forging of spurious legends, including the belief, not discredited until the mid-nineteenth century, that Moreto specified in his will that he be buried in ground reserved for criminals in order to atone for the murder of a friend of Lope de Vega's, or the unfounded foppish character ascribed to Moreto by Lesage in *Gil Blas*. The area in which Moreto has been most maligned is that in which, at times, a difficult distinction must be made between dramatic originality and plagiarism. Superficial criticism summarily denies Moreto a considerable portion of the value merited by his dramatic works because he is thematically indebted to contemporary dramatists or members of the immediately preceding cycle of Lope de Vega. One important aim of this volume is a continuation of work initiated in recent years on the subject of literary creativity as the concept was known to playwrights of the Golden Age. As in the case of the author treated in this volume, our pretensions are not to originality, but rather to clarity in a presentation which could never avoid extremely heavy indebtedness to the studies, impressive in nature if not in number, which have paved the way. The principal contributions to Moretian scholarship are the edition of thirty-three plays, with valuable prefatory material, published by don Luis Fernández-Guerra y Orbe in 1856 in volume XXXIX of the *Biblioteca de Autores Españoles*, Ruth Lee Kennedy's invaluable volume, *The Dramatic Art of Moreto* (1931–1932), and her several important subsequent articles. Other substantial contributions to Moreto studies are Cotarelo y Mori's *La bibliografía de Moreto* (1927), Ermanno Caldera's *Il teatro di Moreto* (1960), and Frank P. Casa's *The Dramatic Craftsmanship of Moreto* (1966). A great debt of gratitude is expressed to all of the scholars who have contributed insights to the understanding and appreciation of Moreto and his art. To echo a famous phrase, the critical work on Moreto which we have consulted truly constitutes *una brava mina* (a rich mine). Like the playwright whom we treat, if we can convey to our readers with faithfulness and clarity the wealth of insight available in the works we have consulted, our efforts will not have been in vain.

Special thanks are in order to the respective staffs of Rice University's Fondren Library, the British Museum, the Institut Hispanique of Paris, and Madrid's Biblioteca Nacional. Miss

Preface

Patti Jo Allen typed the first draft of this book, which was begun in Madrid during a sabbatical leave generously granted by Rice University. The final text was typed by my wife, and the bibliography by Christine Womack. The translations to English are the author's. To all of the institutions and individuals, named and unnamed, who have so kindly collaborated in this project through cooperation, advice, encouragement, and criticism go the deep appreciation and heartfelt gratitude of the author, who holds himself exclusively responsible for whatever shortcomings may be present in this volume.

JAMES A. CASTAÑEDA

Rice University

Contents

Preface

Chronology

Chronology

1618   Agustín Moreto y Cavana is born in Madrid; baptized April 9 in the parish of San Ginés.

1621   Death of Philip III, ascension to the throne of his son, Philip IV.

1627   Death of the controversial baroque poet Góngora.

1634   October 18: Moreto enrolls at the University of Alcalá to study logic.

1635   Death in Madrid of the creator of the modern Spanish theater, Lope de Vega.

1639   December 11: Moreto receives the degree of *Licenciado* (Licentiate). Death of the Mexican-born dramatist, Ruiz de Alarcón, in Madrid.

1640   February 4: inauguration of the *Coliseo*, court theater in the Buen Retiro.

1642   Moreto, already a priest of minor orders, takes possession of a benefice in Santa María Magdalena, in Mondéjar, diocese of Toledo.

1643   Death of Moreto's father.

1644   October 6: Spanish theaters are closed in mourning for the death of the Queen, Isabel of Bourbon, first wife of Philip IV (reopened in the spring of 1645).

1646   October 9: theaters closed again in mourning for the death of Prince Baltasar (reopened probably in 1650).

1648   January 23: death of the dramatist Rojas Zorrilla in Madrid. Death of Tirso de Molina in Almazán.

1649   Moreto already a member of the Academia Castellana.

1652   April 25: Moreto signs the autograph manuscript of *El poder de la amistad* (*The Power of Friendship*).

1654   Publication of the *Primera parte* (First Volume) of Moreto's plays, printed by Diego Díaz de la Carrera, called *el maldito* (the accursed) because of the scant care with which he did his work.

1656   Moreto composes the *loas* and *sainetes* for the festival of Corpus Christi in Seville.

1657   Moreto enters the service of don Baltasar de Moscoso, Cardinal

Archbishop of Toledo. He is assigned quarters in the *Hospital del Refugio*, administered by the Brotherhood of San Pedro.

1658   Death of Baltasar Gracián.

1669   October 25: Moreto draws up his last will and testament before Cristóbal Ramírez. Antonio Fernández has to sign for him, Moreto being incapable of doing it himself. October 28: Agustín Moreto passes away in Toledo.

CHAPTER 1

A Biographical Sketch

THE parents of our playwright, don Agustín Moreto and doña Violante Cavana,[1] were both native Italians, probably from Milan.[2] There is documentary evidence,[3] dated December 11, 1625, that the senior Agustín Moreto owned seven houses on the Calle de San Miguel, in Madrid. The source of the family's apparent affluence has been variously stated to be a secondhand shop[4] and trade in grain,[5] but both Entrambasaguas[6] and Ruth Lee Kennedy[7] report failure in their attempts to discover any documentary support for these allegations concerning the father's business activity. Suffice it to say that every indication points to a comfortable economic situation, one which Miss Kennedy postulates to explain the attitude toward money which she detects in Moreto's theater: "Moreto's profound contempt for money ... is hardly the characteristic attitude of one who has felt its need."[8]

In one of the family's seven houses, our author was born early in 1618. He was baptized on April 9 in the parish of San Ginés. References are found to two older sisters: Ana and Tomasa, and four brothers and two sisters younger than he: Gregorio, Julián, Juan Francisco, Antonio, Angela María, and Margarita.[9]

The facts available on Moreto's life are few. We have little documentary evidence to show any court involvement other than the staging there of an occasional play and nothing to reveal anything concerning his personal life other than his university education, literary production, and ecclesiastical appointments. Neither does Moreto reveal his own personality or overtly carry his life and problems to the stage in autobiographic roles such as Lope de Vega's Belardo. The vacuum created by this dearth of fact may well explain the large proportion of spurious, imaginative accounts which have been perpetuated under the false pretense of biographic comment.

In 1724, Lesage, in his *Histoire de Gil Blas de Santillane*, makes the following incidental reference: "Look at that gallant young gentleman who is whistling as he walks up and down the room, and who rests his weight first on one foot and then on the other. That is Don Agustín Moreto, a young poet not without talent, but whom the flatterers and the ignorant have driven almost crazy [with vanity]."[10] Few readers have taken at face value Lesage's passage, which also contains the historical inaccuracy of making Moreto a contemporary of the unfortunate royal favorite, Rodrigo Calderón, who died before Moreto's birth. To most students of Moreto, the most logical assumption would be a confusion in Lesage of the author Moreto with his foppish creation, the protagonist of *El lindo don Diego* (*Don Diego the Dandy*).

Other apocryphal biographic items were propagated in 1842 by Mesonero Romanos,[11] who claims to have found in the archives of Simancas a document which proves that Moreto served as a soldier in Flanders and that he was responsible for the death of Baltasar Eliseo de Medinilla, disciple and great personal friend of Lope de Vega. When this story was examined critically, it was discovered that the assassination had taken place in 1620, when Agustín Moreto was two years of age, much too young to be even the most precocious of assassins. The discrediting of this legend made necessary the revision of another biographic detail, erroneously linked to Moreto's alleged heinous crime. Some biographical accounts report that Moreto asked to be buried in the *Pradillo de los ahorcados* (The Field of the Hanged) in penance for his crime. Historically, where Moreto asked to be buried was in the *Pradillo del Carmen*; his certificate of burial declares that he was interred in the Church of San Juan Bautista, under the vault of the *Escuela de Christo* (School of Christ).[12] The foregoing is a case purely and simply of misinformation forged into an account which several succeeding generations accepted at face value.

Some of the more spurious biographic accounts were provided in 1855 by don Juan Guillén y Buzarán,[13] who cites Mesonero as a source and claims to have found in Salamanca,[14] late in

1848, a document which provided many hitherto unknown details concerning Moreto's life. The tale he weaves rests heavily on a suggested mutual enmity shared by Moreto and the Count– Duke of Olivares, powerful favorite of Philip IV. Guillén y Buzarán publishes copies of correspondence purported to have been exchanged by the two, including a bitter and insulting letter from Moreto, dated March, 1638. These items, along with several allusions to a tempestuous and adventuresome youth, should be taken as the product of nothing more than Guillén y Buzarán's fertile imagination.

From 1634 to 1637 Agustín Moreto studied logic and physics at the famous University of Alcalá de Henares, where he graduated as Licentiate on December 11, 1639. His first known literary work is a eulogistic poem which he composed a few months prior to his graduation for the poet Montalbán's funeral. It is probable that his initial dramatic efforts date from this period.[15] A document dated May 30, 1642, reveals that Agustín was, by that time, a cleric of minor orders in the Church of Santa María Magdalena, in the town of Mondéjar, diocese of Toledo, a benefice which was obtained only after being contested legally.[16]

Moreto is reputed to have participated as an actor before King Philip IV in an impromptu allegorical enactment of the creation of the world. If the report is true, the event took place before 1644, the year of the death of another illustrious participant, Luis Vélez de Guevara. The cast also included Calderón de la Barca. Moreto, playing the role of Abel, concluded a couplet with lines so scandalous that Fernández-Guerra spares his readers their transcription.[17]

Moreto's father died on January 26, 1643. In 1649 Agustín was already a member of the *Academia de Madrid o Castellana*, whose secretary was the witty Jerónimo de Cáncer, one of Moreto's most frequent dramatic collaborators. In 1654 Moreto published the *Primera parte* (First Volume) of his plays, a collection of twelve *comedias*. This is the only volume of the author's plays published during his life.

According to a document dated May 28, 1652,[18] a certain Bartolomé de Lara rented a room on Madrid's Calle del Clavel to don Agustín Moreto Cavana, *vecino de Madrid* ("resident of Madrid"), the first biannual payment period to begin on

June 1. Another reference, dated May 5, 1654, to the performance in Madrid of a play of Moreto's leads Ruth Lee Kennedy[19] to suppose that Moreto was probably in Madrid when the *Primera parte* of his plays was published, and not away from the court, as Fernández-Guerra speculated,[20] possibly to explain the innumerable shortcomings of that volume.

Barrionuevo, in a letter dated February 21, 1657, refers as follows to our poet: "They say that Don Agustín Moreto became a Carthusian or a Capuchin in Seville, in order to escape from the Biscayans who were looking for him to kill him. He has probably done the right thing if he has done this, unless he hangs up his habit upon returning to Madrid."[21] Cotarelo remarks that "Although we don't yet know the year of Moreto's ordination as a priest, Barrionuevo's *Aviso* indicates that early in 1657 it had not yet been accomplished."[22] Although the turbulent life implied by Barrionuevo's *Aviso* finds no documentary support, Moreto's presence in Seville in 1656 is attested by a document dated June 8, 1656, which states that Moreto wrote the *loas* and *sainetes* for the Corpus Christi celebrations of that year.[23] Moreto's entering the priesthood is also attested by Fray Antonio de Jesús María in his treatise on the illustrious Cardinal Archbishop of Toledo, don Baltasar de Moscoso y Sandoval.[24]

According to Fray Antonio, when don Baltasar reorganized the Brotherhood of San Pedro, in Toledo, by adding to it the Hospital of San Nicolás, "he named to care for it don Agustín Moreto, his *chaplain* ... who, renouncing the deserved applause that the theaters gave to him, devoted his pen to divine praise, his enthusiasm or poetic fervor converted into a spirit of devotion. And, in order for his presence to be more permanent, he provided lodgings for him in the hospital."[25] Don Agustín entered the Brotherhood on December 28, 1659. According to La Barrera,[26] he never held, as has been believed, the post of rector, nor of principal chaplain; there is evidence only that he once substituted for the secretary in a meeting of March 22, 1662, when the latter, probably because of sickness, was unable to attend.

In the midst of his duties and charitable exercises, Moreto was not abandoned by his dramatic muses. Some of his plays can be assigned to the period of ten or twelve years which he spent in the hospital, and when a final illness attacked him in October of 1669, he was in the process of writing *Santa Rosa del Perú* (*St. Rose of Peru*).

Moreto died in Toledo on the twenty-eighth of the same month, leaving all of his possessions to the poor, and designating as executors his brother Julián and the licenciado Francisco Carrasco Marín, secretary of the brotherhood.

Nicolás Antonio (1617–1684), erudite contemporary of Moreto, concurs with Fray Antonio in 1672 that Moreto ceased to write for the stage following his entry into the Church.[27] Ruth Lee Kennedy argues convincingly, however, that Moreto did continue to compose plays, although he probably wrote no secular drama after the death of Philip IV in December, 1665.[28]

The following biographical incident is intimately connected with Moretian criticism and, by and large, is responsible for the denial of much of the literary acclaim which is due Moreto.

In September of 1649, Jerónimo de Cáncer y Velasco, incoming secretary of the *Academia Castellana,* was required to read to the members on the occasion of his assumption of his new duties, a *vejamen,*[29] a burlesque literary composition of his own invention. Cáncer's theme was a feigned dream, in which Latin and Italian poets were laying siege to Mount Parnassus and Apollo was begging for the aid of the Castilian poets. Cáncer then reports that, in the midst of the otherwise total compliance of the group, his eye was caught by one member who had not hastened off to help: "In the midst of this danger I noticed that Don Agustín was still seated, going through papers which seemed to be old forgotten plays." Moreto is reported to have been saying to himself: "This one isn't worth anything. Something can be taken from this, changing it somewhat. This scene can be used." Upbraided for this activity at a time when everyone else was bearing arms, Moreto responds: "I'm fighting here more than anyone, because I'm undermining the enemy." To Cáncer's observation that it looked more as if he were just looking for things to take from those old plays, Moreto replied: "That's just what obliges me to say that I'm undermining the enemy—you can see that in this stanza:

> Consider that I'm mining
> when you complain about me;

> for in these old plays
> I've found a rich mine."[30]

It is interesting to note that the passage devoted to Moreto was only one of twelve joking references made by Cáncer in this same *vejamen* to contemporary poets and friends. Rojas Zorrilla's baldness was also an object of his jest, as was the extreme ugliness of Juan de Zabaleta, and the extraordinary size of the nose of Juan Vélez, son of the famous playwright Luis Vélez de Guevara. In short, Cáncer's reference to Moreto's use of old plays was most assuredly but one of several more or less affectionate jibes made in a jovial setting. He would be surprised to see the transcendence attained through the years by this reference to Moreto, for the innocent passage from which we have quoted represents the cornerstone of a systematic indictment of plagiarism leveled against our playwright. But the effects of this moment of Moreto's biography comprise the material for subsequent chapters.

CHAPTER 2

The Spanish Stage in Moreto's Day

NOTHING approaching full comprehension of the Spanish Golden Age theater can be attained without adequate knowledge of the vital context in which the plays were produced. The printed texts bequeathed to us by the seventeenth century will remain but pale and esoteric reflections of an unknown age as long as we ignore such important factors as the physical structure, administration, and limitations of the theaters themselves, the composition, nature, and number of theatrical companies in existence, historical events which made their impact felt in the theater, royal and governmental edicts which affected and controlled the theatrical world and, last but not least, the composition of the theatergoing audience. Although it may be superfluous to note, "dramatic literature" is in itself a paradoxical concept. Although there are a few exceptions to the rule,[1] plays were written primarily to be performed, and their subsequent publication was but a secondary endeavor. The study of Spanish Golden Age drama, already once-removed from the real object of investigation by virtue of the fact that our sole recourse is to the printed or, in many cases, the manuscript page, is the more difficult and frustrating because of the printing practices of the times and because of the special role played by the *autor de comedias*.[2] Not to be confused with the English term "author," the *autor* was the director or impresario of a theatrical company. He initially purchased the original manuscript version of a work from its playwright, deleted and modified passages prior to and during rehearsal, and frequently arranged directly for the publication of volumes which traditionally contained twelve plays. In an effort to guarantee the commercial success of these publishing ventures, plays of unknown or less well-known dramatists were attributed to literary giants whose names were more likely

21

to generate sales. Even for purely literary study, another printing procedure is responsible for great difficulties. It was common practice to correct errors as noticed during a press run. Thus, there is no assurance that any two copies of the same run are identical.[3]

Another term whose Golden Age connotation should be explained is *comedia*. In the most general sense, *comedia* means simply "play," but it came to serve really as an equivalent for "drama," and specifically for the three-act play of felicitous ending which evolved early in the literary career of Lope de Vega (1562–1635), creator of the modern Spanish theater.

Although Spanish literature of varying degrees of dramatic nature antedates the Golden Age by several hundred years,[4] it is interesting to note that something as commonplace to a twentieth-century theatergoer as a permanent theater building did not exist in Spain until well into the second half of the sixteenth century. There is speculation that Lope de Rueda (150..?–1565), playwright, *autor*, and actor, may have established the first Spanish theater in Valladolid,[5] but the earliest available documentation concerns the theaters of Madrid.

Curiously, the founding of the first permanent theaters received initial and continued support from a source usually alien to the theatrical world.[6] When Madrid became the capital of Spain in 1561, its entertainment facilities were undeveloped. A religious brotherhood, the *Cofradía de la Pasión y Sangre de Jesucristo*, which was founded in 1565 to administer a hospital for the poor, received authorization to sponsor the performance of plays in Madrid. The first rudimentary theaters were called *corrales*, and consisted simply of a yard at the center of a block of houses, at one end of which was erected a stage. Benches were installed and the windows of the surrounding houses were sold as box seats to the more affluent spectators. Female spectators were isolated in a rear gallery called the *cazuela* ("stew pan"), and the commoners stood in front of the raised stage. The first play presented under the auspices of the *Cofradía de la Pasión y Sangre de Jesucristo*, according to the earliest records we possess, was performed on May 5, 1568.[7] Subsequently this brotherhood rented the *Corral de la Pacheca* and, in 1574, another brotherhood opened the *Corral de Burguillos*, alsó in Madrid; the *Corral de la Cruz* was founded in the capital in 1579, as was the *Corral del Príncipe* in 1582.[8]

In Seville, among the earliest theaters was the famous *Corral del Coliseo*, completed in 1607, and renovated 1614–16 to make it, according to Sánchez Arjona, "superior, not only to the theaters of Seville, but even to the most celebrated ones of Madrid."[9] Plays were also performed in several other Spanish cities: in Valladolid's *Puerta de Santisteban*, in Valencia's *Corral de la Olivera* (1584), in Barcelona, and in Zaragoza.[10]

An ordinance of 1608[11] required that plays begin at two o'clock from 1 October to 1 April and at four o'clock in the summer. New ordinances of 1641[12] modified the hours slightly, specifying starting times of two, three, and four o'clock respectively for winter, spring, and summer. The purpose of these requirements was to assure that the audience would vacate the theater by nightfall. The theatrical year also observed several traditional dates and customs. The season lasted almost all year. It began on Easter Sunday and ran until the following Lenten season. During Lent, theatrical performances were not permitted. The *autores* used this period to contract members of their companies for the following season. Edicts of 1608 and 1615[13] required each *autor* to submit a list of members of his company[14] at Easter of each year.

From 1585 onwards, the *Corral del Príncipe* and the *Corral de la Cruz* were to be Madrid's only two public theaters.[15] Thus, throughout Moreto's span of dramatic activity, there were just two public theaters in operation in Madrid. In addition, however, there was the royal theater in the Alcázar and, after 1640, the famous *Coliseo* theater in the new palace of the Buen Retiro,[16] designed by the Italian architect Cosme Lotti. Although the latter two theaters normally commissioned special plays or contracted companies in advance, there is documentary evidence to prove that royal prerogative was occasionally expressed forcibly by the arrival of several of the king's officers in a *corral* just as the audience was assembling for a performance. Playbills were taken down, the spectators' admission fees were returned, and the actors and actresses were taken by coach to perform for the royal family in the Retiro or the Alcázar.[17]

Theatrical companies were controlled in a number of ways by

official legislation. Among the more interesting edicts was a
decree of 1587[18] which established the right of actresses to
appear on the Spanish stage (cf. England, where women were
not permitted to act until 1656).[19] The appearance of women
was subsequently prohibited by an order of the Council of
Castile in 1596,[20] but the prohibition was short-lived.

In 1603, the number of companies in Spain was limited to
eight.[21] A decree of the Council of Castile raised the number
to twelve in 1615,[22] a decision which was reaffirmed in the
Ordinances of Contreras in 1641.[23]

Throughout the history of the Spanish stage there raged a
controversy over the morality of the theater and conservative
theologians constantly sought its total abolition.[24] Largely through
their efforts, severe restrictions were placed on playwrights and
companies alike, and at times of national mourning the theaters
were closed completely.

Within the lifetime of Moreto, the death of Philip III, on 31
March 1621, caused the *corrales* to be closed until 28 July of the
same year.[25] They were again closed in 1644, following the death
of Queen Isabel, and reopened in the spring of 1645.[26] On 9
October 1646, they were closed again, to mourn the death of the
prince Baltasar. They were probably reopened in 1650,[27] first
in Seville.

A decree of 15 February 1651[28] permitted only historical plays
or the dramatization of saints' lives. Ruth Lee Kennedy has an
interesting theory related to this decree: "that those plays which
make this claim—and especially those which are so *novelescas*
in tone that the author feared that they would not pass the
censor—were almost all *printed* after 1651 (the public theatres
were closed completely a large part of the time between 1644
and 1650) and that in the case of many of these which are
known to be *written* before that time, the final lines at least
were altered to meet this new law of 1651 which includes the
phrase: 'In this Court historical plays have continued to
be tolerated.'"[29]

Jerónimo de Barrionuevo, a contemporary chronicler, includes
in his famous epistolary *Avisos*, which cover the period 1654–
1658, some very revealing remarks concerning the theater. Of
particular interest are several scattered references to the great

amounts of money expended on diversions of this sort at a time when the royal coffers were empty. Among the many pertinent items, we note in a letter of 23 January 1655 that preparations were under way for a play in the Retiro involving "stage machinery which will cost more than fifty thousand ducats; for here the only concern is to spend this poor life happily."[30] According to another of 27 February 1656, a special tax was assessed on oil to help defray the expenses of the Retiro theater.[31] On 19 June 1658 Barrionuevo reports the complaints of the country's soldiers to the effect that the theater takes in one thousand ducats daily, all of which apparently is spent on frivolity and celebrations, while for Spain's defenders there is nothing.[32] Similar uncomplimentary references abound throughout the *Avisos*, written with perspicacity during a period of political and social decadence which the monarchy tried to ignore.

Understanding of this period of Spanish theater is greatly enhanced when we visualize the *comedia* in the total context of its presentation. Far from being the sole attraction for the audience, the *comedia* was normally preceded by a *loa* (introit or introduction in verse) and, at the conclusion of the *comedia* there frequently followed a *mojiganga* or *fin de fiesta* (light, usually musical, one-act pieces). Between acts there were interspersed short one-act interludes called *entremeses*, usually comic and popular in nature, which were normally presented between acts I and II, and a *baile* or *jácara*, short dramatic pieces usually ending in a group dance, which came between acts II and III.[33] Much more than incidental compositions of scant interest to scholars, these *loas*, *entremeses*, *bailes*, etc., were written by most of the great dramatists. Moreto himself wrote several of these short pieces and, as an *entremesista*, is considered by many to be second in importance only to the great specialist in this genre, Luis Quiñones de Benavente (1589?–1651).[34]

The duration of a full theatrical performance varied from two to four hours. The average length of the *comedia* varied considerably from author to author. Romera-Navarro[35] cites an average length of 3,300 verses for Tirso de Molina (1584?–1648), among the great dramatists the writer of the lengthiest *comedias*, as compared with Moreto's average length of 2,750.

Critics of Spanish drama of this period often comment nega-
tively on the repetitive nature of the themes, plots, intrigues,
and dénouements, which frequently seem to recur with but
slight variation from play to play, and even from author to
author (a fact which obviously makes the study of doubtful
attributions even more difficult than one might expect it to
be). The "formula" followed by playwrights is better under-
stood when one considers the composition of a typical theatrical
company. The companies[36] typically had roles of First, Second,
and Third Lady, First, Second, and Third *Galán* (Gallant), a
witty servant, the *gracioso* (a role which increased in importance throughout the Golden Age, attaining its fullest exploitation in the theater of Moreto, and which frequently went
to the director of the company or to the best actor), a *barbas*
(old man), and the secondary figures.

Theater in Spain was considered to be a popular *divertisse-
ment* and a seventeenth-century theatrical performance was a
very democratic event. The lowest social element of the audience
consisted of the feared *mosqueteros* who, according to Pellicer,
"were named thus because of their uproar and their shouting,
with allusion to *los soldados de mosquete* (musketeers)."[37] These
groundlings stood in the patio, just in front of the stage, and
their power at times attained such heights that they were considered the most important arbiter of the success or failure
of a given play. Their importance is attested to by several contemporary literary passages, among which one of the most
famous is found in Lope de Vega's *Arte nuevo de hacer comedias*
(*New Art of Play Writing*), in which he justifies the non-
Aristotelian nature of his dramatic productions by affirming:
"Since it's the commoners who pay, one must speak foolishly to
them to give them pleasure."[38]

Another revealing passage dealing with the great power
wielded by the *mosqueteros* is found in the prologue to *El diablo
cojuelo* (*The Lame Devil*), the picaresque novel of Luis Vélez
de Guevara (1579–1644), who was also a well-known dramatist:

"Prologue to the *Mosqueteros* of the Madrid Stage"

Thanks be to God, my *mosqueteros* . . . arbiters of comic applause through custom and bad abuse, for once I will take up my

pen without the fear of your whistling, since this discourse on the *Diablo Cojuelo* was born . . . outside your jurisdiction for, because of your nature, it is even free from the risk of censure through being read, for almost none of you knows how to spell . . . you are the constables of fortune, most often praising that which doesn't even deserve to be heard, and you knock down that which deserves to be placed above the stars; but now I don't bother a bit about you. God help me with my prose, while others bob up and down on the surges of applause of you from whom may God deliver us through His infinite mercy.[39]

With this background on the stage and public for which Moreto wrote, let us now turn to his dramatic production itself.

CHAPTER 3

Moreto's Dramatic Production

THE succeeding chapters of this book will present brief analyses of Moreto's individual full-length *comedias*, his one-act plays, and his poems. Our concern in the present chapter is Moreto's dramaturgy in general, with emphasis on themes, techniques, and characteristics which are signficant either for their predominance or their noticeable absence.

I *Versification*

Verse was Moreto's medium for all of his artistic creations that have come down to us. Morley, in 1918, published the first serious study of Moreto's versification.[1] According to Morley, Moreto is comparable to Alarcón in the average length of his *comedias*, the longest being *Los jueces de Castilla* (*The Judges of Castile*), with a verse count of 3,154, and the shortest *Las travesuras de Pantoja* (*Pantoja's Pranks*), with a verse count of 2,068. The two most popular strophic forms are used by Moreto in the following percentages: *romance* (octosyllables in stanzas of indeterminate length having identical assonance in the even lines) is the predominant form, averaging close to 45%; the *redondilla* (quatrain of octosyllables, with rhyme abba), the predominant strophic form in the early plays of Lope de Vega (its popularity ultimately giving way to the *romance*), averages 15–35% in Moreto's plays.

Morley uses strophic data as objective criteria to resolve problems connected with doubtful attributions, a method which, in 1940, was to make such a magnificent contribution to the study of Lope de Vega's theater.[2] Moreto reveals to Morley two personal tricks of writing: (1) "he likes to introduce music, but seldom lets the words form more than a simple quatrain";[3] and (2) "these assonated songs usually do *not* fit into a *laisse* of

28

dialogue of the same assonance."[4] Morley affirms that there is much evidence to prove "that Moreto was not a finished versifier, despite his small output and his lifting of other men's plots. Frequent faulty rhymes indicate that he deserved the epithet of *paresseux* which Fitzmaurice-Kelly bestowed upon him."[5]

Aside from a claim by Pedro Henríquez Ureña in 1920 to the effect that Moreto's contributions to irregular versification are few,[6] and the supplement to Morley's figures and general corroboration of his conclusions provided by Ruth Lee Kennedy,[7] very little attention has been devoted to the poetic dimension of Moreto's theater.

II *Moreto's Language, Themes, and Attitudes*

It is interesting to note that Moreto's dramatic poetry is unencumbered by gongoristic tendencies. In several instances, notably in the dialogue between don Diego and the feigned countess in Act II of *El lindo Don Diego* (*Don Diego The Dandy*), he joyfully pokes fun at the excesses of this poetry which, years earlier, was the theme of a serious polemic. Writing, however, several years after the death of the movement's leader, Luis de Góngora (d. 1627), the satire, no longer a vibrant contemporary issue, has lost all touch of bitterness and attempts only to exploit the comic element. Lucile K. Delano[8] cites evidence that Moreto followed Lope's lead in using sonnets spoken by *graciosos* to parody this same strophic form and mock its gongoristic users and tendencies.

In several ways Moreto did not conform to contemporary literary conventions. The very direct, straightforward language he used was anomalous in the increasingly baroque days of the Calderonian cycle. Moreto's views on the famous code of honor were almost heretical, and he continually ridicules those who bend to the inflexible exigencies of this code rather than attempt solutions to their problems through the application of reason. Whereas his great contemporary, Calderón, was known for the frequent exploitation of jealousy in his *comedias*, the theme rarely appears in Moreto's theater.[9] As noted by Sturgis Leavitt, neither does the grotesque,[10] although it is employed by several contemporary dramatists.

Carlos Ortigoza uses the case of Moreto as the cornerstone of his objection to the theory that only love, jealousy, and honor motivate Golden Age protagonists.[11] He also, as had Ruth Lee Kennedy previously, detects the total absence of any patriotic impulse in Moreto's theater.[12] Disguised women, a stock device in seventeenth-century theater, are found infrequently in Moreto's plays.[13] Notable also for its absence in Moreto's dramaturgy is the element of tragedy. Even when closely following a source, as is the case with *El valiente justiciero* (*The Valiant Justice-Maker*), he transforms the tragic dénouement into a happy ending.

The nineteenth-century French critic Sismondi considered Moreto superior to Calderón on several counts: greater humor, plots which produced more amusing situations, and general verisimilitude, which Sismondi finds usually lacking in Spanish theater.[14] Ortigoza finds in Moreto the agile movement of Lope, the penetrating observation and moral intent of Alarcón, and the piquant, mischievous, and ironic tone of Tirso. These comparisons are adduced to show that Moreto has greater natural affinities with the cycle of Lope de Vega than with the Calderonian cycle with which he is traditionally identified.[15]

Ermanno Caldera has published a provocative volume on Moreto,[16] in which he develops a comparison between Moreto and Gracián. This comparison, along with others emphasized by Poyán Díaz[17] with Calderón and Descartes, all of whom pursue rational motivation rather than trust to their senses, marks Moreto as a true man of his epoch. Caldera opposes the generally accepted view of critics such as Fernández-Guerra, Gassier, Ruth Lee Kennedy, Hurtado and Palencia, and Pfandl that Moreto is one of the better Golden Age playwrights in terms of the psychological analysis of his characters. Caldera finds Moreto's characters to be unilateral, frequently lacking in psychological truth.[18] Ruth Lee Kennedy also compares Moreto to Alarcón and considers him "the precursor of modern Spanish comedy. From Moreto to Moratín [1760–1828] there is but a step—the step from poetry to prose."[19]

Running through the voluminous writing of Angel Valbuena Prat are several important observations and a generally favorable view of Moreto.[20] For Valbuena also, Moreto is the Alarcón of the second, or Calderonian, cycle of Golden Age theater. Rather than a purely moral sense, a purely aesthetic sense dominates in Moreto's plays. Valbuena Prat also detects "a tone of dance, an air of minuet, which announce the theater of Marivaux, the painting of Watteau, and the music of Mozart."[21]

Moreto's comic vein draws high praise even from the greatest detractors of other aspects of his dramaturgy. Schack lauds Moreto's comic talents every bit as enthusiastically as he condemns his religious plays.[22] His *graciosos*, whose role and importance are greatly expanded by Moreto, are considered to be the best of the epoch by García de la Huerta, who lauds their ability to "delight and cheer even the most saturnine and melancholic."[23] In her doctoral dissertation, Anna Marie Lottman studies Moreto's comic spirit and observes that, as Moreto used the genre, there were no rough incidents of brute force such as characterized early farce. She concludes, recalling traditional appraisals of Cervantes, that "Moreto's work is good comedy because he accepts the peculiarities of social conventions rather than constantly railing against them."[24] Viel-Castel declares that Moreto, although less rich in invention and imagination than Lope de Vega and Calderón, "habitually surpasses them in his comedies, or rather that he has created in Spain the true comedy, of which Lope had only a very vague idea, and of which Calderón didn't even seem to be aware, one which looks for its components not to Romanesque and extraordinary adventures, but to the dramatization of the foibles and the laughableness of humanity."[25]

III *The Question of Moreto's Originality*

The debated issue concerning Moreto's originality or plagiaristic tendencies has been a focal point of Moretian criticism for centuries. On one hand, first de Puibusque[26] and then Schaeffer[27] claimed that if so many Golden Age *comedias* had not been lost, it would be possible to find the source of every Moreto play. Frank Casa[28] is both the most recent and the most impassioned spokesman for Moreto's originality, but the issue is not reducible to a chronological evolution from charges of plagiarism to vindication of originality. Ruth Lee Kennedy at times seems all too inclined to write off Moreto's adaptations as plagiaristic, while nineteenth-century scholars such as de Puibusque,[29] Mesonero Romanos,[30] Gil y Zárate,[31] Ticknor,[32] and Viel-Castel[33] were quick to note the significant improvement wrought by Moreto when adapting a source play. Even Schack, after noting that Moreto lacked the inventiveness and imagination of Lope, Calderón, Tirso, and Alarcón, praises him for his rare ability to rework and perfect his sources; he refers to Moreto's reworkings as "mosaics made with ability and neatness."[34] Duncan Moir[35] and Charles Aubrun[36] are among the contemporary scholars for whom the alleged plagiarism of Moreto is no longer an issue; both simply praise the creative skill with which he recasts his source materials.

Several critics have contributed to a statement of the characteristics which constitute Moreto's dramatic "art" or "craftsmanship," but the best total presentations, in our opinion, are those of Ruth Lee Kennedy[37] and Frank Casa. From the work of the latter we have chosen to state several important conclusions:

(1)   Moreto did not simply rework earlier dramas in a mechanical manner; he studied the sources carefully and selected suitable elements. In so doing, he brought about significant modifications in the *comedia* which are due to his undeniable predilection for order.

(2)   The *comedia* of Moreto rejects unnecessary complications; that is, any elements which do not figure importantly in the plot.

(3)   The *graciosos* and events connected with them remain, but they are no longer irrelevant; they are integrated into the action so as to support or amplify the theme.

(4)   Most characteristic of Moreto is the long expository speech; it often appears in the first or second scene and narrates the background events that motivate the opening actions. This gives his first scenes a static quality that is not dispelled until he begins to develop the action.

(5)   The motivations of the characters are kept in check; the acts end at a logical break in the action; scenes intensify the overall effect by ending at crucial moments; the conclusions are derived from the action, never imposed.

(6)   Moreto's theater is both logical and rational. It is this inclination for the orderly, the planned, the relevant, the appropriate,

and the meaningful, that precludes the insertion of poetic flights.

(7) He chooses naturalness over effect, a realistic rather than a symbolic language.

(8) Finally, Moreto tends to choose subjects which deal with man and society rather than to explore the problems of the human condition.[38]

IV *Moreto's Canon*

If the study of Moreto's biography is beset with rumor, misinterpretation, and lack of information, the study of his literary production is complicated by a series of phenomena having to do with the difficulty inherent in establishing an accurate canon for dramatic works of an Age classified as Golden partly because of the burgeoning profusion of plays which it fostered.

Moreto's span of dramatic activity was somewhat reduced when Ruth Lee Kennedy, in 1936, excised three titles which had linked his name with the years 1635–1637.[39] *La luna africana* (*The African Moon*), written before 1643, in which Moreto was one of nine collaborators, is the earliest recorded instance of our author's dramatic efforts.[40] He is reputed by Fernández de Buendía[41] to have been in the process of writing *Santa Rosa del Perú* (*St. Rose of Peru*) when he died in 1669.

Although he saw the publication of individual plays in collections, including *San Franco de Sena* (*St. Franco of Sena*) in the first volume of the famous *Escogidas* (1652),[42] only one of the *Partes* of Moreto's plays was published in his lifetime. This was the *Primera parte*, published in Madrid by Diego Díaz de la Carrera in 1654.[43] A second edition of the *Primera parte*, identical to the first except for the title page and preliminary contents, appeared in 1677, published in Madrid by Andrés García de la Iglesia. A posthumous *Segunda parte* had two editions in 1676[44] and a posthumous *Tercera parte* appeared in 1681.[45] According to Cotarelo,[46] several other volumes which claim to be *Partes* of Moreto's *comedias* are apocryphal.

In some cases, a playwright himself prepared or supervised the preparation of the volumes of his plays, but most often their publication was undertaken by unscrupulous printers, who used actors' copies vitiated with all the deletions, additions, and modifications to which the play was subjected. Concerned primarily with the greatest profit possible, the printers also assigned to works of lesser-known playwrights the names of well-known dramatists, counting on their popularity to maximize sales. Moreto was famous enough to have had attributed to him in printed collections several plays which he did not write. A trustworthy canon is also difficult because of the seventeenth-century practice of collaboration in writing *comedias.* The most common procedure was the assignment of one act to each of three dramatists—but the most exaggerated known form of such collaboration is the play *La luna africana,* written, as we have already stated, by nine different authors. Of the several volumes of works attributed to Moreto, only the *Primera parte* (1654), as indicated above, was published in his lifetime. Thus, after using the twelve plays contained in that volume as the nucleus for his canon, empirical data are far less available for the remainder of the task. An early attempt at cataloguing Moreto's plays is the Medel list[47] of plays available for sale in the compiler's bookstore. Medel lists eighty-four works attributed to Moreto, of which several have subsequently been excised from his canon. Sixty years later, Vicente García de la Huerta, the eighteenth-century dramatic poet, published in his famous *Theatro hespañol* a catalogue of plays attributed to Moreto[48] which, he admits, represents essentially the Medel list, although corrected and expanded.

With the reawakening of interest in Spanish Golden Age drama which took place early in the nineteenth century, lists of titles proliferated;[49] but most represent only the most cursory acquaintance with the works themselves and contain many capricious attributions. In 1856, Fernández-Guerra published thirty-three *comedias*[50] attributed to Moreto alone or written in collaboration. In his introduction,[51] he lists as *comedias* of Moreto several more titles, many of which are spurious attributions. La Barrera, in 1890,[52] provides another catalogue of Moreto's dramatic works.

Although the aforementioned contributions to the establishment of Moreto's canon are of value, for our present knowledge on the subject we are almost exclusively indebted to Ruth Lee

Kennedy,[53] who has studied exhaustively all of Moreto's *comedias* and who has resolved most of the problems concerning doubtful attributions. In *The Dramatic Art of Moreto* she either excludes or casts serious doubt on some twenty-two attributions in addition to the fifteen previously excised by Fernández-Guerra[54] and Cotarelo.[55] Subsequent articles refine the list of works attributed to Moreto in her monumental study and evolve a canon which has yet to be modified. In 1935,[56] reversing two previous decisions, Miss Kennedy excludes *Antes morir que pecar* (*Die before Sinning*) and accepts the manuscript version of *El Eneas de Dios* (*The Aeneas of God*); she also claims for Moreto *El hijo obediente* (*The Obedient Son*) and *No puede mentir el cielo* (*Heaven Cannot Lie*), two plays excluded by Fernández-Guerra. In 1936,[57] Professor Kennedy concluded that *La milagrosa elección de San Pío V* (*The Miraculous Election of St. Pius V*) should definitely be removed from Moreto's theater and tentatively added to Montalbán's. Also in 1936, after refuting the Moretian attribution of six of the nine plays which she studies,[58] Miss Kennedy lists a total of sixteen titles which she would exclude from Moreto's theater and proposes a canon of thirty-three plays written by Moreto alone, nineteen collaborations, and six of doubtful authenticity. In studies of 1937[59] and 1939,[60] respectively, her 1936 decision on two plays is substantiated in separate articles. She adds to the list of collaborations *La renegada de Valladolid* (*The Renegade of Valladolid*), which she had not mentioned in *The Dramatic Art of Moreto,* and excludes *Sin honra no hay valentía* (*Without Honor There Is No Valor*). Again in 1939,[61] Miss Kennedy identified *El mejor esposo* (*The Best Husband*), long attributed to Moreto, as Guillén de Castro's *El mejor esposo, San José* (*The Best Husband, St. Joseph*). Two more studies deal with works classified in 1936 as doubtful attributions: in another 1939 article,[62] *La gala del nadar* (*The Charm of Swimming*) is categorically removed from Moreto's theater; in 1941,[63] she advances strong arguments in favor of Luis Vélez de Guevara's authorship of *Escarramán*, long attributed to Moreto.

The great importance of an accurate canon is obvious when we realize that most existing studies of particular aspects of Moreto's theater are based in part on spurious attributions.

V   *A Classification of Moreto's Theater*

Our study of Moreto's individual *comedias* is based on the canon established by Ruth Lee Kennedy[64] which is categorized as follows (plays written in collaboration are followed by an asterisk):

I.   RELIGIOUS THEATER

A.   *Hagiographic Works:*

1. *La adúltera penitente* (*The Penitent Adulteress*)*
2. *Caer para levantar* (*Falling in Order to Arise*)*
3. *Los más dichosos hermanos* (*The Most Fortunate Brothers*)
4. *El más ilustre francés, San Bernardo* (*The Most Illustrious Frenchman, St. Bernard*)
5. *San Franco de Sena* (*St. Franco of Sena*)
6. *Santa Rosa del Perú* (*St. Rose of Peru*)*
7. *La vida de San Alejo* (*The Life of St. Alejo*)
8. *La vida y muerte de San Cayetano* (*The Life and Death of St. Cayetano*)*

B.   *Episodes Taken from Holy Writ:*

1. *El bruto de Babilonia* (*The Brute of Babylonia*)*
2. *La cena del rey Baltasar* (*King Balthazar's Feast*)

C.   *Comedies Written in Honor of a Particular Shrine:*

1. *No hay reino como el de Dios* (*There Is No Kingdom Like God's*)*
2. *Nuestra Señora de la Aurora* (*Our Lady of the Dawn*)*
3. *Nuestra Señora del Pilar* (*Our Lady of the Pillar*)*

D.   *Miscellaneous:*

1. *La renegada de Valladolid* (*The Renegade from Valladolid*)*

II. SECULAR THEATER

A. *Plays of Plot:*

  a) Plays of Novelesque Interest:

    1. *Amor y obligación* (*Love and Obligation*)
    2. *El Eneas de Dios* (*The Aeneas of God*)
    3. *La fingida Arcadia* (*Arcadia Feigned*)*
    4. *Fingir y amar* (*To Feign and Love*)
    5. *Hasta el fin nadie es dichoso* (*Until the End, No One is Fortunate*)
    6. *El mejor par de los doce* (*The Best Peer of the Twelve*)*
    7. *No puede mentir el cielo* (*Heaven Cannot Lie*)
    8. *El príncipe perseguido* (*The Persecuted Prince*)*
    9. *Las travesuras de Pantoja* (*Pantoja's Pranks*)
    10. *Travesuras son valor* (*Pranks Show Valor*)*

  b) Plays of Intrigue:

    1. *El caballero* (*The Nobleman*)
    2. *La confusión de un jardín* (*The Confusion of a Garden*)*
    3. *El hijo obediente* (*The Obedient Son*)
    4. *El parecido en la corte* (*His Likeness at Court*)
    5. *Trampa adelante* (*On With the Trick*)

B. *Plays of Character and Idea:*

    1. *Antíoco y Seleuco* (*Antiocus and Seleucus*)
    2. *Cómo se vengan los nobles* (*How Nobles Avenge Themselves*)
    3. *El defensor de su agravio* (*The Defender of His Offense*)
    4. *De fuera vendrá quien de casa nos echará* (*We'll Be Evicted from Our Home by an Outsider*)
    5. *El desdén con el desdén* (*Disdain Conquered by Disdain*)
    6. *La fuerza de la ley* (*The Strength of the Law*)
    7. *La fuerza del natural* (*The Force of Nature*)*

8. *Hacer remedio el dolor* (*Making Grief a Remedy*)*
9. *Industrias contra finezas* (*Ingenuity vs. Goodness*)
10. *Los jueces de Castilla* (*The Magistrates of Castile*)
11. *El licenciado Vidriera* (*The Glass Licentiate*)
12. *El lindo don Diego* (*Don Diego the Dandy*)
13. *Lo que puede la aprehensión* (*What Apprehension Can Do*)
14. *La luna africana* (*The African Moon*)*
15. *El mejor amigo el rey* (*The Best Friend, the King*)
16. *La misma conciencia acusa* (*Conscience Itself Accuses*)
17. *No puede ser* (*It Can't Be*)
18. *Oponerse a las estrellas* (*Opposing the Stars*)*
19. *El poder de la amistad* (*The Power of Friendship*)
20. *Primero es la honra* (*Honor First*)
21. *El rey don Enrique el enfermo* (*King Henry the Sickly*)*
22. *El valiente justiciero* (*The Valiant Justice-Maker*)
23. *Yo por vos y vos por otro* (*I for You and You for Another*)

CHAPTER 4

Religious Theater

UNDER the general rubric of religious theater, we have five plays by Moreto alone and nine in which he collaborated. These plays are spaced throughout the period of Moreto's dramatic productivity. Although there is a numerical preponderance of them written late, a fact which may perhaps be explained by the playwright's religious involvements in Toledo after 1657, his best-known and most-praised play in this category, *San Franco de Sena* (*St. Franco of Sena*), was one of the first published (1652). Criticism is sharply divided as to the quality of Moreto's religious plays. Martínez de la Rosa, in 1838, laments the fact that Moreto "yielded to the fatal mania of his century, giving himself to the composition ... of lives of saints, in which he ranted just as all the authors did."[1] Fernández-Guerra's decision to include just two of Moreto's religious *comedias* among the thirty-three which he published in 1856[2] may perhaps represent another negative evaluation. Schack was another nineteenth-century detractor of Moreto's religious theater. In the twentieth century, clearly distinguishing between the two main branches of his dramaturgy, Professor Kennedy comments: "In developing the materials of his sources, Moreto has not given evidence of the taste that he ordinarily displayed in reworking secular plays. ... He has not used the poet's prerogative of selection, and as a result the unpoetic and the ludicrous are indiscriminately patched together into a wearisome chronicle."[3]

Having already postulated his failure in this genre, Miss Kennedy tries to explain as follows Moreto's shortcomings in religious theater: "His work shows clearly that he had not that appreciation of the mystical, that understanding of the sublime, nor that comprehension of the tragic depths of life which enabled his great contemporary [Calderón] to transform pictures of the commonplace into scenes of moving beauty and grandeur. One has only to read Calderón's *La cena de Baltasar* and compare it with Moreto's *La cena del rey Baltasar* to realize the chasm that separates the temperaments of the two men."[4]

As Miss Kennedy has pointed out,[5] the decree of 1644 which closed the theaters to all but historical and hagiographic plays until 1651 may have caused Moreto to write religious plays, assured of their acceptability. She sums up her feelings on this dimension of Moreto's dramaturgy as follows: "In his secular theatre Moreto was, as we shall see, ahead of his time. In the religious *comedia* he is entirely of his own day. Moreover, if put in comparison with other dramatists of his time, he cannot, in this genre, be said to rise above the level of mediocrity."[6]

Not all modern critics share Miss Kennedy's negative views on Moreto's talents as a writer of religious theater. Valbuena Prat has devoted extensive and most complimentary analyses to *San Franco de Sena,* judging it to represent "extraordinary modernity."[7] Casa concludes that Moreto, although he does not emphasize theological problems, deals masterfully with issues and emotions which are profoundly religious in nature.[8]

In reworking his religious sources, Moreto characteristically added or elaborated a love story, introduced a comic element and, as noted by Miss Kennedy, "did not fail to develop all hints of the supernatural, though he made little use of it in his secular theatre."[9]

The plays in this area, with the exception of *La renegada de Valladolid,* fall into the following categories established by Professor Kennedy: (1) hagiographic material, drawn for the most part from the *Flos sanctorum*; (2) episodes taken from Holy Writ, at times through the medium of an earlier play; (3) comedies written in honor of some particular shrine. *La renegada de Valladolid* does not correspond to any of these categories and will be discussed separately.

I *Hagiographic Works*

A. La adúltera penitente (The Penitent Adulteress)

First printed in *Parte IX* of the *Escogidas*[10] (Madrid: Gregorio Rodríguez, 1657), where it is attributed to Cáncer, Moreto, and Matos, this play concerns the life of St. Theodora of Alexandria and is the first of Moreto's dramatic works to be produced in the New World, having been performed in Lima in 1659.[11]

The beautiful and virtuous Teodora has acceded to her family's insistence that she marry the wealthy Natalio. Filipo, a prior suitor with whom she had been in love, undaunted by her marriage, persistently attempts to break down her resistance to his amorous advances. One of the more ineffectual devils of Golden Age Drama helps to set the stage for the satisfaction of Filipo's lust during an absence of Natalio.

The sinful deed done, the action and its setting have abruptly changed as Act II begins. Teodora, her facial beauty lost, and dressed as a man, is living in repentance in a monastery, where Morondo, the *gracioso,* is serving as *donado* (lay brother). Filipo has become a bandit in the surrounding mountains and the dishonored Natalio is seeking vengeance on his wife. The puerile devil, further to incite the irate husband, writes on all of the trees that Teodora is an adulteress. He also tries to coordinate events which will lead to the perdition of all of the principals, but the virtue of Teodora defeats him at every turn. Ejected from the monastery because of false witness borne against her, she saves Filipo's life and brings about his repentance and redemption. Teodora returns to the monastery, where songs from offstage proclaim her sanctity. She is readmitted and, following her death, is seen borne aloft in divine splendor.

The total lack of preparation for the events of the second act could, of course, be explained by the fact that the subject, easily accessible in editions of the *Flos Sanctorum,* was widely known and did not require dramatic cohesion. It could also suggest, however, the relatively uncoordinated work of two hands. Moreto does not seem to have intervened in the first act, which includes a very gongoristic passage on Satan's temptation of Teodora. Although parts of Morondo's role in the second act could be by Moreto, it is the third act which seems most typically his,[12] particularly in the language of the *gracioso* (who forms from his own name the spurious infinitive *merondear,* suggesting the verb *merodear*—"to scavenge"), and his references to the heat and sulphur odors emitted by the devil. Teodora recites six verses in *romance* which are but a slight modification of the fifth strophe of Jorge Manrique's famous *Coplas*.[13]

B. Caer para levantar (Falling in Order to Arise)

First printed in *Parte XVI* of the *Escogidas* (Madrid: Melchor Sánchez, 1662), this play is also included in the edition of Fernández-Guerra[14] and was published in French translation by Gassier.[15] Written by Moreto in collaboration with Matos and Cáncer, it is an adaptation of Mira de Amescua's masterpiece, *El esclavo del demonio*.[16] However, although there is much thematic parallelism between the two plays, we have tried to demonstrate elsewhere[17] that any accusation of plagiarism, taken in the twentieth-century sense, is ill-founded. Moreto and his collaborators have reduced the cast of characters, simplified and given greater cohesiveness to the action, limited the role of the supernatural and, in still other ways, created a new work representative of their epoch as contrasted with Mira's more primitive version.

The plot centers around St. Gil of Portugal, who fell from his saintly reputation to become a dissolute bandit, only to end his life in true repentance, which earns him eventual canonization. The action of *Caer para levantar* can be stated as follows: Don Vasco de Noroña has two daughters, the obedient Leonor and the disobedient Violante who, defiant of her father's wish that she marry don Sancho, announces her intention to marry don Diego de Meneses, assassin of her brother. As part of her plan to elope, she requests that don Diego arrange for music outside her window that night to serve as the signal for her to leave the house. Don Gil comes upon the waiting don Diego and, through the force of his sermonizing, dissuades the lover from carrying out his intention. When don Diego departs, don Gil succumbs to the temptation to substitute himself for Violante's lover. Successful in his deceit, don Gil departs with the deluded Violante as the first act ends. Six years have transpired when the action of the second act begins. Two peasants report the prevalent rumors that don Diego has abducted and perhaps even killed Violante. Don Gil, who is reported missing since the night of Violante's disappearance, is more revered than ever.

Don Vasco, en route to his country home with Leonor, is stopped by the disguised bandits Violante and Gil, who steal a box of jewels which had belonged to Violante. Gil is stricken by lustful desire for Leonor and enters into a traditional pact with the Devil, promising his soul for a chance to enjoy the favors of Leonor. Violante meets don Diego, who is now a hermit.

In Act III, Vasco, with a group of vigilantes, is in search of the bandits, thinking that don Diego is the culprit. The repentance of Violante, in progress since her meeting with don Diego, is now nearly complete. Violante tries to convince don Gil that repentance can assure pardon for him but, in a phrase reminiscent of the Comendador's final words to Don Juan in Tirso's *El burlador de Sevilla*, don Gil claims that *ya es tarde* ("it's too late").

As usual, when it is time to let don Gil have his way with Leonor, the Devil is unable to live up to his part of the bargain. Don Diego comes upon Gil just as he leaves a cave where he thinks he has been with Leonor. Don Diego pulls aside the veil of the figure to discover not Leonor, but a skeleton. Don Gil invokes the help of his Guardian Angel, whom he has still not renounced. The Angel and the arguments of Diego persuade the Devil to renounce his demand for Gil's soul. At this point the vigilantes arrive. They recognize don Diego and attempt to arrest him, but the repentant don Gil confesses all as Violante, who has died a penitent, is seen embracing a cross.

Although Mira's *El esclavo del demonio* is vastly superior to *Caer para levantar* in dramatic force and energy, it has been described by Ruth Lee Kennedy as "a formless, chaotic mass."[18] *Caer para levantar* does lack the epic dimensions of its source, but in terms of order, rationality, and verisimilitude, it represents quite an improvement.

C. Los más dichosos hermanos (The Most Fortunate Brothers)

The first dated edition is *Parte XIX* of the *Escogidas* (Madrid: Pablo de Val, 1662), where it is given the title *Los siete durmientes* (*The Seven Sleepers*), which has come down to us in the colloquial expression, *dormir más que los siete durmientes* ("to sleep all the time"; "to be a sleepyhead"). It is also included in Antonio de Zafra's 1681 *Tercera parte* of Moreto's *comedias*.

Penélope, sole heir to the throne of Macedonia, is a third-century Christian. Condemned to imprisonment in a tower by astrological indications that she will never accept all of the pagan gods, she is offered pardon by Caesar if she will marry Dionisio, one of the seven sons of the dictator, Valeriano. The considerate Dionisio restrains Penélope from audaciously proclaiming her Christianity and postpones the wedding to avert her martyrdom. When she extracts from the sleeping Caesar the admission that "Christ is the true God," she brings about the immediate conversion of Dionisio and his brothers, whom she sends to the mountains to be baptized by Timoteo. Eventually discovered and pursued by Caesar, they are sealed in a cave by their implacable persecutors.

As the third act begins, two peasants are picking away at the sealed cave. When one mentions the name of the Virgin, an opening appears and Dionisio and his brothers emerge. As they return to Ephesus for food, thinking that they have been asleep for just one night, they are bewildered to see crosses everywhere. An anthropomorphic devil tries to convince them that they will be discovered and slaughtered as Christians, but they proceed, meet more Christians, hear the word "Mass" for the first time, and enter a church in which the day of the martyr San Lorenzo—whom they think they saw killed just ten days ago—is being celebrated. Ironically, they see a victim brought forth to be killed, but he is a heretic. Discovery of a tablet dated 252 A.D. attests to the fact that the brothers have slept for two hundred years. This effects the conversion of the heretic and a magistrate dispatches an announcement of the miracle to the Pope as the play ends.

D. El más ilustre francés, San Bernardo (The Most Illustrious Frenchman, St. Bernard)

This work, which first appeared in *Parte XI* of the *Escogidas* (Madrid: Gregorio Rodríguez, 1659), is a hagiographic play in which Moreto includes, especially in the last two acts, several direct references to *Don Quijote*. The play portrays the many tests strewn in the path of Bernardo on his way to sainthood.

When he leaves his childhood sweetheart Matilde, she disbelieves the explanation of his intention to lead a religious life and suspects a female rival. When she is about to accuse him falsely in public of having stained her honor, she miraculously faints and is revived by Bernardo. She confesses her malicious plan and announces a decision to retire to a convent. The first act ends with the giving of Bernardo's sister Umbelina in marriage to Matilde's brother, the Duke. This prompts a witty rejoinder on the traditional ending of the *comedia* by the *gracioso* Colín: "The play has ended/since they will marry."

At the beginning of the second act, Bernardo is wearing the white habit of his Order, and Colín is a lay brother. The opening speech of Colín is heavily laden with reminiscences of Cervantes's immortal novel. He asks Bernardo if it wouldn't be better to go out and be a *Don Quijote a lo divino,* undoing wrongs from hill to hill rather than to be involved in religion, with no recompense to show for one's efforts. There follow direct references to Merlín, Gaiferos, and Quiteria; and, at the frightening sound of chains, Colín experiences the same intestinal problem that beset Sancho in the episode of the waterwheels.

After overcoming the temptation of sensuality presented by the Devil, who appears to him in the form of Matilde, Bernardo is summoned by Pope Innocent, who has convened the council in Pisa to combat a schism introduced in the Church. Bernardo resolves the schism. While on the return trip to France to continue to fight dissension, the Devil breaks the wheel of Bernardo's coach, prompting in Colín one of Moreto's typical plays on words: the accident involving the wheel has broken his nose, leaving him *romo* (flat nosed); would that he had not left *Roma,* he remarks, for such *romerías* (pilgrimages). However, his olfactory sense still functions well enough for him to detect the smell of sulphur in the air, a stock dramatic device to indicate the presence of the Devil. In a scene which would seem to present difficulties in staging, Bernardo catches his demonic adversary, ties his hands, and makes him serve as the broken part of the wheel. After an absence of five months, Bernardo returns with the Devil as his captive, feet securely chained.

Colín recommends the release of the Devil, remembering a proverb which says it is good to have friends, even in Hades.

Upon his release, the Devil sends a feast of bread and ham. Colín, with the food and his wineskin, eats and drinks voraciously until discovered by Bernardo, who shows his servant that the food is covered with a flaming serpent. He orders thirty lashes for Colín, reminiscent of those prescribed for Sancho, and the play ends on the glorious note of Bernardo's elevation to sainthood.

E. San Franco de Sena (St. Franco of Sena)

First published in *Parte I* of the *Escogidas* (Madrid: Domingo García y Morrás, 1652), the play also appears in the authentic *Primera Parte de comedias de D. Agvstín Moreto* (Madrid: Diego Díaz de la Carrera, 1654), and is included in Fernández-Guerra's edition.[19] It receives lavish praise from Valbuena Prat[20] and is also one of the five plays studied by Frank Casa[21] with specific reference to its artistic independence from its sources. Casa notes that it was probably written to celebrate the establishment of the cult of St. Franco in Spain in 1651.[22]

This play is another illustration of the adage that "the best sinners make the best saints." Franco, a reckless libertine, is presented fighting over Lucrecia, a woman he has just seen for the first time, and we learn that he has gambled away all of the wealth of his doting father, Mansto, who has sold his every possession to provide his son with money. The optimistic father, even in the face of his son's obvious depravity, prays that God will make him a saint. The orphaned Lucrecia is destined by her guardian brother to marry don Fabricio, the richest man in Italy, who also happens to be short, bald, and one-eyed. Lucrecia rebels against her brother's authority and plots with her lover Aurelio to elope with him that night. Coincidentally, Franco and Dato, searching for Lucrecia, come upon Aurelio. In an ensuing duel, Aurelio is killed and Lucrecia, mistaking Franco for her dead lover, leaves with him.

Lodged with Lucrecia in a castle, where he is honored by the governor for his military skills, Franco returns alone to Sena to bring back his crippled father. An illuminated cross appears on the door of Aurielo's home. When he tries to extinguish the light he is restrained by a mysterious hand.

Upon his arrival at his father's home, police officers are unsuccessfully trying to make Mansto testify against Franco. When a neighbor appears and bears witness against him, Franco kills them all and carries his father off. In leaving Sena, he passes again before the house of his victim, whose voice announces enigmatically an important event in the life of the future saint: "Franco, go and gamble; / for today, losing, you will win." Having deposited his father in the castle with Lucrecia, Franco goes to the gaming table. Desperate after having lost everything, Franco wagers his eyes, and loses again. The act ends with a long monologue by Franco on the theme of seeing for the first time after having lost his eyes. Reminiscent of the many *bandoleros*[23] of religious *comedias*, Federico and the abandoned Lucrecia each heads a group of bandits. A Guardian Angel reveals to Lucrecia that Franco has been a pilgrim and is now living in the same cavernous mountain in which her bandit forces are located, and to which Dato is to bring Mansto. When servant and father discover Franco, a miracle occurs and Mansto is no longer crippled. As Federico's band attacks, Lucrecia flees with the Guardian Angel, and finds Franco. Together they go to the Monastery of Carmen, where Franco receives the habit of Saint. Lucrecia dies and her body is borne aloft by angels as her brother is blinded by the resplendence of the heavens.

Dato announces a second part which, true to normal Golden Age practice, was evidently never written.

Schaeffer[24] first cited *El condenado por desconfiado* (*Condemned for Lack of Faith*)[25] and Lope de Vega's *La mal casada* (*The Poorly Married Wife*) as literary sources of *San Franco de Sena*, especially in the father-son relationship. Ruth Lee Kennedy cites the sources suggested by Schaeffer, but links this *comedia* much more directly to *Caer para levantar* (and therefore, indirectly, to Mira de Amescua's *El esclavo del demonio*).[26]

As Casa points out, *San Franco de Sena* has, on the one hand, been praised as the finest example of hagiographic theater while held by other critics to be the worst of Moreto's plays.[27] The latter judgment seems totally unjustified. The transformations and adaptations wrought by Moreto in the material of his hagiographic and dramatic sources lead us to agree with Casa's concluding statement: "While he does not deal with a complex theological problem, as does Tirso in *El condenado por desconfiado*, he treats with artistry and profound feeling the theme of contrition and forgiveness."[28]

F.   Santa Rosa del Perú (St. Rose of Peru)

Published first in *Parte XXXVI* of the *Escogidas* (Madrid: Joseph Fernández de Buendía, 1671), and again in the *Segunda parte* of Moreto's *comedias* in 1676, this may be Moreto's last literary effort. Fernández de Buendía, editor of the *Escogidas* edition, claims that the first two acts are the last composed by Moreto before his death in 1669, and that the third act was written by Pedro Francisco de Lanini y Sagredo.[29]

In advising his son Juan to marry a woman who is poor, chaste, and wellborn, don Gonzalo can think of no better match than Rosa, whose father, unbeknownst to her, has already consented to the union. Like many of Moreto's heroines, Rosa upbraids her father for having tried to arrange her marriage without considering her wishes. Just as the wedding is to be announced, she tells Juan that she cannot marry him because she is committed elsewhere. Taking advantage of the ambiguity of Rosa's excuse, the Devil momentarily appears masked. Juan takes him for his rival and rushes off in pursuit.

In the second act, Rosa has built a cell in her garden and is planning to take religious vows. Attempting to arouse jealousy in Juan, the Devil tells him that Rosa's lover visits her cell at will. While she sleeps, the Devil commissions the four vices of Vanity, Presumption, Self-love, and Lasciviousness to sing their temptations to her, but the saintly Rosa, while still sleeping, rejects their every proposal. The Devil then leads Juan in to attack her in her sleep. About to be ravished, Rosa invokes the name of Jesus. The vices disappear, a sword-wielding Angel descends to drive off the Devil, and Juan vows to spend the rest of his life bearing witness to Rosa's sainthood.

The work of a hand other than Moreto's is quite evident in the third act. A dice game between Rosa and the Christ-Child, which serves as an object lesson against gambling, and the miraculous appearance of chocolate for which Rosa has expressed a desire are but two of several scenes not typical of Moreto. The flamboyance and desultory nature of the principal action are also atypical.

The Devil overcomes the resolve expressed by Juan at the close of the second act and tries to have him kill Rosa's father. Hastened by her penitence and more than five thousand self-inflicted lashes, her saintly death thwarts Juan's attempt on her father's life. The defeated Devil sinks through the stage and Juan vows to enter the Dominican Order.

Miss Kennedy adduces a pointed reference to a Madrid tavern as further evidence of the absence of Moreto's hand in the third act.[30] In our opinion, the wit and wordplay of the *gracioso* Bodigo ("bread of fine flour used as an offering in church") rank him with some of Moreto's best comic figures. Most critics do not detect anticlerical lines in Moreto's full-length plays, but Bodigo claims that he is the descendant of a priest. He states that *bodigos* have virtues in the *masas* ("masses" or "dough"), and further plays with the literal meaning of his name and the word "crumb."

G.   La vida de San Alejo (The Life of St. Alejo)

There is no modern edition of this play, which was first printed in *Parte X* of the *Escogidas* (Madrid: Imprenta Real, 1658). We have references to two performances in 1657, by the company of Pedro de la Rosa, in January,[31] and by Osorio in Madrid on February 10.[32]

The Devil and a Guardian Angel compete for Alejo who, as the play begins, is about to marry Savina in Rome. Three times Alejo has heard in his sleep a voice urging that he consecrate his chastity to God but, upon the insistence of his father, he goes through with the marriage. Immediately following the ceremony, however, he accedes to the Angel's plea that he follow God. Moreto plays with levels of reality as the Devil conjures up false visions for Alejo, first one of Rome and then another of the wedding of Savina and a persistent but despised suitor, Duke Otón, nephew of the Emperor. Accompanied by his servant *gracioso* Pasquín, who attempts on many occasions to upstage his master and, in his absence, to attribute to himself

many of the saint's miracles, Alejo, after years of absence from
Rome, during which the Devil has announced his death, returns
on the day chosen by the nefarious Otón to abduct Savina. He
thwarts this plan but is physically beaten by Otón and his followers. Unable to rise, he is instructed by the Angel to write
out the story of his life. Alejo dies and his body is surrounded
by lights which reveal his sainthood. The dead saint rises and,
in the company of his Guardian Angel, delivers the story of his
life to Savina. Moreto announces a second part after informing
the audience that Alejo's wife will go to a convent.

Several verses of Garcilaso de la Vega are found intact or
partially recalled in the last two acts. Their inclusion seems
significant in the typical way in which Moreto, even in his
hagiographic works, skillfully places great emphasis on the
secular dimension of the lives of his protagonists. Alejo follows
the Guardian Angel, but at times falteringly, with a lingering
look at what he is leaving behind. Moreto's Alejo is convincingly human, a fact which makes his tribulations and final sainthood all the more impressive.

H.   Vida y muerte de San Cayetano (Life and Death of St.
     Cayetano)

Produced, according to Barrionuevo,[33] in 1655, this *comedia*
was first published in *Parte XXXVIII* of the *Escogidas* (Madrid:
Lucas Antonio de Bedmar, 1672). In its closing lines it is
attributed to six authors: Diamante, Villaviciosa, Avellaneda,
Matos, Ambrosio de Arce, and Moreto.

While on the road to sainthood, Cayetano has occasion to
stamp out heresy and resolve a secular love affair. In addition
to a few reported incidents involving the founding of his Order
based on humility and poverty, the main action involves the
sad plight of Laura, who gives herself to the heretical French
Lutheran Guillermo after his promise of marriage. When financial disaster hits her family, the false lover refuses to go through
with the marriage. The distraught father and daughter, with
their outspoken maid Celia, request the saintly Cayetano's intervention in Rome on Christmas Eve. In some dramatically
ingenuous scenes, Cayetano thwarts Guillermo's attempt to defile

a church's altar, sees the dagger of his would-be assassin disintegrate as Guillermo makes an attempt on his life in Naples, and partially effects the heretic's conversion by the "miracle" of having his prayers answered by peasants who bring food for the hungry members of his Order. Other miracles, such as the providing of bread for the hungry, calming stormy winds at sea, and mending a broken leg the night before it was to be amputated, are merely reported.

With his attainment of sainthood dramatically dependent upon his resolution of the secular intrigue, Cayetano offers his heart for Guillermo's salvation. In a dual dénouement, his death and sainthood coincide with the conventional marriage.

Miss Kennedy does not attempt to decide which sixth he wrote, but she does detect items in all three acts which are reminiscent of Moreto.[34]

II *Episodes Taken from Holy Writ*

A. El bruto de Babilonia (The Brute of Babylonia)

First printed in *Parte XXX* of the *Escogidas* (Madrid: Domingo García Morrás, 1668), where it is attributed to Matos, Moreto, and Cáncer, this play, as pointed out by Schaeffer,[35] is a reworking of Guillén de Castro's *Las maravillas de Babilonia (The Marvels of Babylonia)*.[36] As aptly put by Miss Kennedy, it "is the story of Daniel and Nebuchadnezzar in unhappy combination with that of Susanna and [Joakim],"[37] the latter story from an apocryphal addition to the Book of Daniel. Nebuchadnezzar's lustful designs on Susanna are grafted onto the biblical stories in an unconvincing way in this loosely constructed play. After using his kingly prerogative to take Susanna from Joakim, her lover and intended husband, Nebuchadnezzar announces that he will not force himself on her if she resists his advances because his reason is stronger than his desire. The elderly Hebrew magistrates Acab and Nacor, however, vengefully accuse Susanna of adultery with a slave when she repulses their advances. Daniel, who has already interpreted some of the king's dreams, spent six days unharmed with the lions, and witnessed the miracle of the furnace and the transformation of Nebuchadnezzar into a beast, resolves both plots through his wisdom and intercession with God. Discovering the magistrates' lies by interrogating them separately, he restores Susanna's honor and has her accusers punished.

Fernández-Guerra thought that the third act was Moreto's.[38] We strongly agree with Ruth Lee Kennedy[39] that the second, rather than the third act, is much more typical of Moreto's style. The *gracioso* Alcacer ("green barley") of the second act is a clear improvement over his churlish manifestation in the peceding act. His wit in the second act seems to be the work of Moreto, and it is interesting to note his use of the one French word found in our author's works, *Alón* (*Allons*).[40] Miss Kennedy also points out "that there is no instance in Moreto's theatre where the dramatist has borrowed so flagrantly from the original as has the author of Act III."[41]

B.   La cena del rey Baltasar (King Balthazar's Feast)

Mention in the *Entremés del doctor Carlino,* written between March, 1642, and June, 1648, enables Miss Kennedy to date this weak effort prior to the latter date.[42] The *suelta* which we have read in a bound collection in the Biblioteca Nacional[43] bears no date. According to Miss Kennedy, the first dated edition is *suelta* no. 58 (Barcelona: Pablo Nadal, 1796).[44]

The feast of Balthazar (Daniel: 5), during which his sacrilegious use and destruction of the goblets looted from the temple in Jerusalem evokes the mysterious hand which writes the words interpreted by Daniel to announce the imminent decline and division of Babylonia, is but a partial theme. Although it inspires the title of the play, the feast occupies just part of the third act and is not well integrated into the political and love intrigues which dominate the action.

The divine warning impresses Balthazar, but he intrepidly intends to go through with his plan to marry Fénix, Queen of Arabia, whom he has attempted to steal from her lover Ciro, King of Persia. Ciro, against whose life he has schemed, escapes with the aid of Daniel and returns to kill his rival and restore liberty to the Jews.

The two comic figures, Cansino, a captive Jew, and Bato, the weak-minded Persian lackey of Ciro, contribute some good humor which saves this unsuccessful blend of biblical story and secular intrigue from being a complete loss. Bato forms a nonsense verb *batear* from his own name and recalls Sancho Panza when he mangles terms of address, referring to Balthazar as *tu Gemestad* (for *tu Magestad*—"your Majesty") and *tu Insolencia* ("your Insolence").

Miss Kennedy is correct in recognizing the "chasm" which exists between this play and Calderón's *La cena de Baltasar*.[45]

III *Plays Written in Honor of a Particular Shrine*

A. No hay reino como el de Dios (There Is No Kingdom Like God's)

The copy which we have read of this trite play is *suelta* no. 5, published in Seville, but undated. In its concluding line it is attributed to Cáncer, Moreto, and Matos.

Don Luis Osorio, in a fit of jealous rage, has killed his own brother, whom he discovered with his faithful wife Leonor. While in flight following his crime, he is discovered during a battle by the Moor Zelim who notes don Luis's perfect physical resemblance to Hazén, leader of the invading forces, who has just been killed. Urged by Zelim to assume the role of Hazén, don Luis finds that his servant Mastuerzo ("Simpleton") and Leonor are both captives of the Moors. Although he tries to oblige Zelim by desisting from his impending marriage with Arminda, the Sultan's daughter, she will not free him from his contract. Even when he confesses his assumed identity and the fact that he is a Christian, Arminda insists that he marry her. More anxious to inherit the Kingdom of God than the one Arminda promises, don Luis, accompanied by his valiant wife, is impaled in martyrdom.

Although of slight interest in itself, this play is but one of several related variations on the theme studied by Ruth Lee Kennedy in *The Dramatic Art of Moreto*[46] and in a subsequent article.[47] The collaboration in which Moreto took part was based on *Los tres soles* (*The Three Suns*), attributed to Monroy, which in turn was derived from Lope de Vega's *Los mártires de Madrid* (*The Martyrs of Madrid*) and which, in its turn, spawned still more mediocre manifestations of the same theme.

B. Nuestra Señora de la Aurora (Our Lady of the Dawn)

Its first dated edition is in *Parte XXXIV* of the *Escogidas* (Madrid: Joseph Fernández de Buendía, 1670), and it was also included in the 1681 *Tercera parte* of Moreto's works. Although the latter volume attributes it to Moreto alone, the *Escogidas* version lists Cáncer as a collaborator. Fernández-Guerra, who believes that the play was written for festivities celebrated in honor of the Virgin of the Dawn from September 27 to October 4, 1648,[48] sees Moreto's hand in the last act and part of the first. Miss Kennedy points out that the heroine Madalena is sometimes referred to as the daughter of Juan Tarro and sometimes as his niece. She links Cáncer with the parts in which Madalena stands in the relationship of daughter and feels that only the last part of Act I and the first half of Act II should be attributed to Moreto.[49]

The attempts of the haughty *hidalgo* don Diego to win the favors of Madalena meet not only her staunch resistance, but even ignominious defeat at the hands of her rustic fiancé Manuel in the gentlemanly art of duelling. Reprimanded also by Juan Tarro in a manner reminiscent of Calderón's Pedro Crespo, don Diego desists from his amorous designs at the end of the second act, thus terminating the subplot with one act still remaining.

The town of Escamilla has elected Juan Tarro steward of its upcoming religious festivities. The town church's image of the Virgin, three hundred years old according to its papers, is badly in need of repair. A sculptor is commissioned to restore it, and orders it placed in the monastery's pond to soak loose the old varnish. While there, it miraculously saves the life of Manuel, who has fallen into the water while attempting to take refuge in the monastery after wounding the *hidalgo* don Diego. Forgotten when a new image is commissioned, the old one is taken by Brother Antonio and the *gracioso* to Madrid to find a new home for it. At dawn one day during their trip, while the image is perched on a boulder, it occurs to Brother Antonio to name it Our Lady of the Dawn.

When apprised of the renown enjoyed by the image, Juan Tarro and his whole family venture to Madrid to recover it for Escamilla. Unsuccessful in their recovery attempt, they finally agree that the image shall stay in Madrid and are witnesses to its last miracle of the play, the saving of the life of a boy who had given his own money to the Virgin, just before being run over by a coach.

C. Nuestra Señora del Pilar (Our Lady of the Pillar)

First published in *Parte V* of the *Escogidas* (Madrid: Pablo de Val, 1653), the play bears a heading identical to that of the *suelta* analyzed by Ruth Lee Kennedy:[50] "... the first act by don Sebastián de Villaviciosa, the second by don Juan de Matos, the third by don Agustín Moreto."

Around the founding of the church of Nuestra Señora del Pilar in Zaragoza, the collaborators have erected the scaffolding of a typical aristocratic love intrigue parodied by the servants.

Astiages, ruler of Africa, returns victorious from battle to pay homage to Queen Aurelia in Aragon. His pretensions seem to be for naught since Aurelia and her cousin Valerio share a reciprocal love. Foreshadowing the events of religious import, Aurelia, in her account of a dream, reports that a man on horseback erected a huge pillar before her and announced that he had come to construct the temple of another queen. A rather artificial Devil reveals that he plans to kill Valerio, who has more Christian tendencies than the rest of the cast. In implementation of this plan, Marcio and Hermógenes, the court astrologer, close the first act with the news that the gods have ordered the sacrifice of Valerio to Neptune in the Ebro.

Act II opens with a scene reminiscent of Segismundo's first monologue as Aurelia listens to the lamentations of the imprisoned Valerio. After he has been led away to die, a letter is brought from the Emperor Tiberius, announcing that a certain James is headed toward Aragon, preaching Christianity. Tiberius reports having trouble with a similar fellow named Peter in Italy. St. James arrives with an image of the Virgin, who instructs him to mount it on a pillar which he will find next to the Ebro. After doing this, and beginning the construction of a church to house the image, St. James hears the cries of the drowning Valerio, saves him, and prepares him for baptism. As the second act ends, Aurelia recognizes St. James's voice as the voice of the man in her dream. Astiages realizes that this is the man of whom Tiberius wrote, and begins seriously to attempt his persecution.

The last act is the story of the battle inevitably won by St. James and Christianity. Aurelia, who drifts aimlessly during most of the final two acts, is converted to Christianity when she learns that St. James has saved Valerio's life. The victory is decided as St. Michael intervenes and an equestrian St. James is lowered from the skies by stage machinery to decimate the pagan forces. The last disbelievers are converted as a majestic vision of St. James, resplendent upon an altar, causes the Devil to confess his deceits.

IV *Miscellaneous*

A.   La renegada de Valladolid (The Renegade from Valladolid)

In *Parte I* of the *Escogidas* (Madrid: Domingo García Morrás, 1652), the play is ascribed to Belmonte Bermúdez. Although Professor Kennedy does not mention this play at all in *The Dramatic Art of Moreto,* she assembles scholarly comment on it in a subsequent article[51] in which she reports having found a manuscript version of this *comedia* which she has dated February, 1637, from the internal evidence of a contemporary allusion. She also corroborates the conclusions reached by Juliá Martínez[52] that Moreto probably wrote Act II of the original version in collaboration with Belmonte, to whom Act I can safely be assigned, and Martínez. Alonso Cortés makes brief reference to the *comedia's* historical background.[53] The 1652 printing represents for Miss Kennedy a considerable revision of the manuscript version by a second-rate writer. The printing in the *Biblioteca de Autores Españoles,*[54] attributed to Belmonte, is based on the *Escogidas* version.

Destined by the will of her father and brother, Melchor, to the life of a nun, the rebellious Isabel runs off with her lover, the Captain don Lope. In Africa, along with their servants Beatriz and Naranjo and the Spanish troops, they are taken captive by Moorish forces under the command of Ceilán who, unaware of the relationship of the couple, becomes enamored of Isabel and seeks her hand in marriage. Through a series of insincere repudiations of her Christianity in which she indulges for practical reasons, Isabel encourages the suit of her captor.

Meanwhile, Melchor, in order to assuage the grief of his ailing father over Isabel's behavior, has become ordained as a priest in Rome. On the return trip, he is coincidentally shipwrecked off the Algerian coast and joins the rest of the captive Christians. Melchor is favored by Isabel after she accidentally spears him while hunting. Brother and sister, unrecognizable to each other because of the changes wrought by time, finally discover each other's identity when they unburden themselves of the anguish of their respective pasts. Inspired to immediate repentance by this scene, Isabel plans and successfully implements that very night the escape by boat of all the Christians, leaving a distraught Ceilán on the beach the eve of their intended wedding.

CHAPTER 5

Secular Theater–Plays of Plot

THE plays in this category are not, as a class, comparable in quality to Moreto's best efforts, which will be examined in our next chapter. It is generally agreed that Moreto's plays of plot, subdivided into *comedias* of novelesque interest and of intrigue,[1] should be assigned to a youthful period. They tend to exhibit serious weaknesses, such as episodic plots and inconsistent and unconvincing characterizations, which do not appear in the work of Moreto at his best.

Of the scant critical attention which has been devoted to this category of Moreto's *comedias*, much has been harsh. Ruth Lee Kennedy expresses the following judgment: "Everywhere it is evident that Moreto lacked that lyrical magic which enables the romanticist to spin a gossamer web of poetry from the unreal and the improbable."[2] Although her general comments on the plays of intrigue are rather negative, Miss Kennedy does make an exception for *Trampa adelante* and *El parecido en la corte*, which "among their kind, are the best that the Spanish stage of the seventeenth century can offer."[3]

I Plays of Novelesque Interest

A. Amor y obligación (Love and Obligation)

First printed in *Parte XII* of the *Escogidas* (Madrid: Andrés García de la Iglesia, 1658), this is one of many plays of novelesque interest whose setting Moreto has placed outside of Spain.

Filipo, Duke of Athens, and Lidoro, having heard of the imperialistic designs of the Scythians, have come to defend Astrea and her father, the Prince of Bosporus. Monologues by each reveal that both are in love with Astrea.

Typical of Moreto's passion for clear, initial exposition of

58

significant past events, the *gracioso* Zancajo delivers a monologue which informs us that, in their desire to control Bosporus, the Scythians had captured its prince, his wife, who died in captivity, and his son and daughter. The male heir was killed and a vain attempt was made to force Astrea to marry a Scythian. The prince and his daughter were freed for a heavy price: a tribute of one hundred maidens every five years, from which Astrea is not granted exemption. When they hear that the prince has tried to marry his daughter, the Scythians object and send a captain named Tebandro to extract the tribute, which is to include Astrea.

Dejected because his own people will not fight against Scythia, the prince is elated to welcome Filipo and Lidoro. In a clever and typical parody of the action of the nobles, the *gracioso* Zancajo and Filipo's servant Tostón proclaim in the ceremonious language of their masters that they will both defend and vie for the hand of Astrea's maid Nise. The three parody the poetry competitions of nobles by reciting three sonnets, including one by Tostón in which all verses rhyme in -*z* and Nise's, in which all rhyme in -*x*. Nise is supposed to select and reward the winner. Unable to decide, she announces that she will alternate lovers every day and declares that the first twenty-four hours go to Tostón.

Meanwhile, justifying their servants' parody, Lidoro and Filipo leave the choice between them to Astrea, with her cousin Fénix going to the loser.

After capturing Filipo and learning of his rivalry with Lidoro for Astrea's hand, Tebandro promises to remove Lidoro from the competition and to leave Astrea to Filipo after the anticipated Scythian victory. The tables are turned however, as Lidoro's victory is proclaimed, just as Astrea begins to reveal her preference for Filipo. In typical Moretian scenes, Astrea debates the right of people, the kingdom, or her father to force her to act contrary to the dictates of her will, but she finally subdues passion with reason and is willing to marry the victorious Lidoro. At this point, however, Tebandro, having been released by Lidoro to negotiate with the Scythians for the return of prisoners in exchange for guarantees against invasion, reveals that Lidoro is really the prince's son, whom he was ordered to kill. Compassion caused him to disobey his orders and to raise the child. Since Lidoro cannot marry his sister, the marriages pair Lidoro with Fénix and Filipo with Astrea. Zancajo wins Nise's hand.

B. El Eneas de Dios (The Aeneas of God)

In *The Dramatic Art of Moreto*, Ruth Lee Kennedy[4] asumed that the first known printing of this play, that of *Parte XV* of the *Escogidas* (Madrid: Melchor Sánchez, 1661), contained the same version as the seventeenth-century manuscript of the Biblioteca Nacional[5] which she, at that time, had not been able to examine. In his review of *The Dramatic Art of Moreto*, in which Miss Kennedy called into question the authenticity of the play, W. L. Fichter declares that the "manuscript version . . . invalidates her argument at every point."[6] He agrees that the published play must be rejected as Moreto's, but both he and Miss Kennedy, in a subsequent article,[7] claim the manuscript version for Moreto's canon.

The action common to both plays, as first pointed out by Schaeffer,[8] has as its source a play by Lope which bears the title *El caballero del sacramento* (*The Knight of the Sacrament*). Isabela, daughter of the Count of Barcelona, has three pretenders: the King of France, whose suit is pressed by the admiral, and two cousins, the King of Sicily and don Luis de Moncada, with the latter of whom she is in love. For political reasons, the count pledges his daughter's hand to the King of Sicily. In desperation, Luis and Isabela plan to escape together on the eve of her appointed departure for Sicily. Moments before their meeting, cries ring out that the Church of Santa Olalla is burning. Don Luis responds heroically to supplications from a priest that someone rescue the Holy Sacrament. Successful in this enterprise, don Luis returns to find that his servant Ramón has unwittingly taken down a sign left for Isabela. She, attributing Luis's absence to cowardice, departs the following morning for Sicily.

Disguised as pilgrims, Luis and Ramón follow Isabela. A *memorial* prepared by Luis for Isabela falls into the hands of the king, who condemns Luis and Ramón to be burned at the stake. Isabela frees them when everyone's attention is diverted by the mishap of the king's falling into the water. They return to Barcelona where, upon arrival, Luis replaces his dying cousin don Gastón in battle against the invading French, and successfully turns the tide and captures the admiral. Luis's heroics go unrewarded, however, as the Count of Barcelona, outraged by news of his disruptive acts in Sicily, imprisons him. The cruel and vengeful King of Sicily then attacks, bringing along the distraught Isabela, whom he has never married, and whom he is punishing by starvation. Freed by the empathetic admiral, Luis defeats the Sicilian forces and marries Isabela, while the admiral is rewarded with the hand of Rosaura.

The role of the admiral and the subplot of the French pretender have been eliminated in the printed version. It is not often that Moreto further complicates the plots of his sources, and this structural difference would indicate that the printed text derives from the manuscript.

C. La fingida Arcadia (Arcadia Feigned)

First published, according to Fernández-Guerra,[9] in *Parte XXV* of the *Escogidas* (Madrid: Domingo García Morrás, 1666), where it is attributed to "A Wit," Moreto, and Calderón, it was also published in 1676, in Moreto's *Segunda parte*, and in volume XIV of the *Biblioteca de Autores Españoles*, in which Hartzenbusch assigns it to Calderón.[10] Several contradictory theories on Moreto's part in the collaboration are reviewed by Miss Kennedy,[11] who is inclined to designate the third act. Cotarelo conjectured that the *Arcadia* presented before Philip IV in 1664 was Moreto's treatment of this popular theme.[12]

Porcia, daughter of the deceased King of Cyprus, under the guardianship of her uncle Filiberto until she marries, has become addicted to pastoral novels. Under the harsh scrutiny of Filiberto, who obviously does not want to lose the regency, all of her many suitors desist, with the sole exception of Enrique, son of the King of Naples. Unbeknown to Filiberto, however, his favorite, Federico, also loves Porcia and, when commissioned by the ambitious regent to kill her by delivering a letter written with "a poison so malign" that it will kill its reader, he reveals the plot to Porcia, who feigns madness. Federico retains the

unused letter for later use, and the members of her court humor
Porcia in her apparent folly to simulate an Arcadia in which
all will lead a bucolic existence with appropriate pastoral
pseudonyms.

Enrique ("Anfriso") and Federico ("Olympo") are joined
by Carlos ("Salicio"), Prince of Sicily, as a third competitor for
Porcia ("Belisarda"). Filiberto ("Cardenio") and his daughter
Casandra ("Anarda") round out the pastoral cast. In the midst
of the languid pastimes of the feigned Arcadia, Federico informs
Porcia of Filiberto's attempt to have Parliament declare her
incapable of ruling. While signing pleas for the help of neigh-
boring kings, Porcia and Federico are discovered by Filiberto,
who demands to see what they have written. Federico mingles
the poisoned letter with the others. Filiberto's death is slow
enough to allow a complete confession. Federico's unswerving
loyalty is awarded Porcia's hand and Enrique and Casandra
are united.

Schaeffer claims that Moreto's is a reworking of a play by
Tirso of the same name.[13] Ruth Lee Kennedy finds little debt,
if any, to Tirso and, while noting similarities with Lope's treatments of this popular theme, especially the use of the same
pastoral names, declines to impugn the originality of Moreto
and his collaborators.[14] In addition to the obvious parallel of
Porcia and Don Quijote as examples of extreme over-dosages of
popular escape literature, the *gracioso* Cascabel ("tinkle bell"),
seems clearly to refer to the Knight of La Mancha in the second
act: "He who is a knight-errant and a shepherd at the same
time represents both poles on which rests the sphere of brain-
lessness."

D. Fingir y amar (To Feign and Love)

First published in *Parte XV* of the *Escogidas* (Madrid: Melchor Sánchez, 1661), this novelesque effort is not available in
a modern edition. Cotarelo[15] and Pérez Pastor[16] believe that
the play was composed prior to 1659.

The succession to the throne of Albania and competition for
the hand of Flérida, niece of the deceased ruler, provide the
framework for one of Moreto's more complicated plots. Prior

to his marriage, the Prince of Albania fathered an illegitimate
son named Segismundo, whose upbringing was left to Arsenio,
elderly uncle of Flérida. Unsuccessful in twenty years of marriage in producing a legitimate male heir, the dying prince
declared Segismundo heir in his will and specified that he
should marry Flérida, preferred legal heir as daughter of the
ruler's brother. Another provision of the testament called for
the marriage of Fisberto and Celaura, offspring of sisters of his.
Fisberto, who fell in love with Flérida the day she arrived in
Croya, defies the will and, armed with popular support, con-
tends that he will marry Flérida out of interest only in her
and not in the succession. His lust for power soon shows through
his insincerity, however, and the Senate, anxious to follow the
prince's wishes, calls upon Segismundo to leave his rustic
mountain home and aid in defeating the arrogant pretender.

His royal blood assures quick assimilation to courtly activity,
and Segismundo dispatches Arsenio to seek military help from
the King of Hungary. Until Arsenio returns with the necessary
help at the end of the third act, the crafty Segismundo, imple-
menting the scheme suggested by the title, feigns love for
Celaura and total disinterest in Flérida. The deception works
on Fisberto until Flérida mistakes him for Segismundo in a
garden scene. By that time, however, the Hungarians have
arrived. They defeat Fisberto's forces and the weddings
prescribed in the prince's will are carried out.

E. Hasta el fin, nadie es dichoso (Until the End, No One Is
    Fortunate)

This is one of the twelve *comedias* published in 1654 in the
Primera parte of Moreto's works. It is the only *comedia* from
this volume not included in the Fernández-Guerra edition.
Both Schaeffer[17] and Ruth Lee Kennedy[18] are harsh in evalu-
ating this play, which found its inspiration in Guillén de
Castro's *Los enemigos hermanos* (*The Enemy Brothers*).[19]

Set in Aragon, the action revolves around the envious, hateful,
and competitive relationship of two brothers, Sancho and
García, sons of the Count of Urgel, and cousins of the king.
Sancho has met and fallen in love with Rosaura (Ruth Lee

Kennedy mistakenly calls her Rosana),[20] daughter of an admiral,
Ramón de Cardona. García claims that he also loves Rosaura,
and provokes an argument which leads to a duel. The king
plans to have Sancho marry his sister, the Infanta, but Sancho
reveals his preference for Rosaura.

Don Gastón, uncle of the brothers, who has always favored
García, presents in the second act a letter signed by the deceased countess, whose signature her husband recognizes, in
which she states that Sancho is not her son. In years past, while
fighting against the Moors, the count had suffered an injury
which made it doubtful that he would live and be able to
father an heir. Wanting to be sure of succession, the countess
had the admiral, Rosaura's father, who now has been missing
for years, bring her a baby boy whom he reputedly obtained,
just born, from a gardener. That baby was Sancho. However,
the count did return safely and fathered García. This revelation
causes Sancho's fortune to decline to the point that the cynical
Gastón employs him as his gardener, so that he can have the
same coarse occupation as his father.

The vindictive García continues to torment Sancho. In a
fight with garden tools, García cuts his own hand. Sancho flees
and, by coincidence, hides in the count's room, appointed meeting place for García and don Gastón, who intends to deliver
a letter from the admiral which was long ago entrusted to him
to be given to the count. Gastón has opened and read it, and
its contents cause him to want to put it in the hands of García
but, in the dark room, he delivers it instead to Sancho. The
tables are turned as Sancho discovers that the queen had been
the count's lover before the court made him marry Gastón's
sister. The queen retired to a convent, where she died giving
birth to the count's son. She confided her secret only in the
admiral, just at the time that the countess was looking for a
male infant. Sancho was, of course, that infant. Now, more than
restored to his former rank, Sancho happily marries Rosaura
and García is betrothed to the Infanta.

F. El mejor par de los doce (The Best Peer of the Twelve)

The first dated edition of this collaboration with Matos
appeared in *Parte XXXIX* of the *Escogidas* (Madrid: Josef Fer-

nández de Buendía, 1673). Schaeffer was the first to point out
that the play's action is derived from Lope's *Las pobrezas de
Reinaldos* (*Reinaldos's Poverty*).[21] Interestingly, approximately
one page beyond the middle of the second act, we read, in a
speech by the *gracioso* Coquín, *y aquí lo ha dejado Matos, /
entre Moreto otro poco* ("here Matos has left off, / let Moreto
come in for another such stint"). The versification, characterizations, and style in general do not incline us to dispute the
assigned entry of Moreto's pen.

Reduced to its simplest terms, the play dramatizes the unjust
exile of Reinaldos by Charlemagne, the continual vilification
of this paragon of knightly virtues by the treacherous Galalón
and his cowardly brother Florante, and Reinaldos's final reinstate-
ment as "the best peer of the twelve" through his acts of un-
wavering courage and loyalty.

Having incurred the Emperor's wrath by slapping the presumptuous Galalón in his presence, Reinaldos sees his place
as one of the twelve peers given to Florante. During the Moorish
siege of Paris, he discovers his pusillanimous replacement attempting to hide the royal standard and avoid combat. Seizing
the royal colors and, with the standard on high and his face
covered, Reinaldos is mistaken for Florante as he defeats and
captures the King of Fez. Spurning the Moor's offers of power
and riches, Reinaldos accepts only the King's ring and asks that
his captive appear before Charlemagne to promise peace and
that he allow his daughter to marry her beloved Celindo instead
of the Prince of Tunis.

Impressed with the virtue of their captor, the King of Fez
and his daughter Arminda save him from an unjust death
sentence by exposing the deceit of Florante. Commenting on a
comparison of the *comedia* with its source, Miss Kennedy
remarks that the "gain in technique can not compensate for
the loss of spirit."[22]

G. No puede mentir el cielo (Heaven Cannot Lie)

Mentioned in *The Dramatic Art of Moreto* only in a footnote
in which we are told that Cotarelo has excluded it from
Moreto's canon,[23] subsequent examination of the eighteenth-

century manuscript[24] of *No puede mentir el cielo* led Miss Kennedy to reclaim the play for Moreto.[25] She also postulated that the play is a recasting of Lope de Vega's *Dios hace reyes* (*God Makes Kings*).

In a long, typically Moretian expository monologue, Clorinda, daughter of Conrado, German Emperor, condenses some two decades of relevant happenings. Already furious with Count Leopoldo for having denied him his vote in the election for Emperor, Conrado was warned by a voice that Leopoldo's newly born son would succeed him to the throne. To belie this prediction, Conrado commissioned Rodulfo (not Rugero, as stated by Miss Kennedy) to kill the infant. To guarantee his own succession, Conrado is planning to marry his daughter to Astolfo, who is despised disdainfully by Clorinda, but loved by her cousin Fenicia. Clorinda's heart belongs to Enrique, son of Duke Ricardo, and currently a favorite of the Emperor.

Driven by insecurity spawned by the threatening prediction, Conrado has persecuted Leopoldo and even commissions his death to Enrique, who, restrained by an unexplained affection for the oppressed victim of the Emperor, spares his life and substitutes the corpse of an old man whose face has been disfigured. A note in which the dying Ricardo informs Conrado that Enrique is not his son, but a child he found in the mountains, convinces the insecure Emperor that the prediction has not yet been belied. He sends Enrique to Astolfo with a letter ordering the bearer's immediate death. The letter is intercepted and modified by Rudolfo to an order that Astolfo, upon receipt, marry Enrique to Clorinda. When confronted with the marriage as a *fait accompli,* Conrado stoically resigns himself to the fact that "heaven cannot lie"; he accepts his son-in-law, restores Leopoldo to his favor, and marries Astolfo to Fenicia.

H. El príncipe perseguido (The Persecuted Prince)

La Barrera[26] first noted the existence in the library of the Duke of Osuna of an autograph manuscript of this collaboration in which Belmonte wrote the first act, Moreto the second, and Martínez the third. Now in the Biblioteca Nacional, the manuscript[27] carries a *censura* dated December 21, 1650 at the end of the second act. This act and *El poder de la amistad* are the only dramatic writings of Moreto which are known in autograph. Fernández-Guerra[28] cites 1653 as the year of the first printing, but Miss Kennedy cites an earlier edition of the same volume in which the play is included, dated 1651.[29]

The collaborators' source was Lope de Vega's *El gran duque de Moscovia y emperador perseguido* (*The Grand Duke of Russia and Persecuted Emperor*), but the recasting has drastically eliminated subplots and given greater cohesiveness to the action.

The testament of the Emperor of Russia bypasses his seemingly demented son, Juan Basilio, and declares his precocious ten-year-old grandson Demetrio heir to the throne, under the regency of his cousin, Jacobo Mauricio. Two proposed marriages will weld relations with Poland. Its prince, Ladislao, is to marry Jacobo's daughter Elena, and Ladislao's sister Margarita is betrothed to Demetrio.

The projected course of events is disrupted by the ambition of the treacherous regent, who commissions the boy's tutor, Filipo, to murder Demetrio. Allowed by Filipo to escape, Demetrio, already an unconvincing prodigy of royal virtues at ten, has matured in a decade of hiding which has transpired between the first two acts. Demetrio's flight sees him disguised as a priest in the Monastery of San Francisco, in which his ancestors are buried, and as a gardener of the now King Ladislao. Ultimately, with the latter as his ally, in advance of the troops that will restore his rule, he bravely returns to see his father, whose apparent idiocy has been transfigured into wisdom by the harsh treatment and imprisonment which he has suffered at the hands of Jacobo.

Son and father separately seek vengeance and justice in Jacobo's death. The redeemed Juan Basilio is first to find the usurper. He kills him with a deft stroke of his sword, is proclaimed Emperor by the popular consent which follows the fealty sworn by his magnanimous son and, after a hiatus of ten years, the projected marriages take place.

I. Las travesuras de Pantoja (Pantoja's Pranks)

First printed in *Parte XIX* of the *Escogidas* (Madrid: Pablo de Val, 1662), this humorous cape-and-sword play is also in-

cluded in the Fernández-Guerra edition.[30] It was adapted by
Zorrilla as *La mejor razón la espada* (*The Best Reason Is the
Sword*),[31] and a scene in the third act was taken from the
comedia to serve independently as the *Entremés de la burla de
Pantoja y el doctor*,[32] a scene singled out by Ruth Lee Kennedy
as the only one worth salvaging from Moreto's novelesque plays.[33]

The magistrate Lope intends to marry his daughter Juana to
don Diego de Gamboa, but Juana, one of the more rebellious
of Moreto's heroines, is in love with the rough-and-ready don
Pedro Pantoja, not wealthy although of noble blood. The impetuous Pantoja is constrained by the rational counsel of his
servant Guijarro from resorting to drastic action until he has
at least made a formal request for Juana's hand. In a scene
awkward because of his rival's presence, Pantoja's suit is denied
by don Lope. Insulting words ensue, and Pantoja and don Diego
exit duelling. Invited to her window at night, Pantoja is suggesting to Juana that they elope, when don Diego appears with
Arjona. A fight erupts, and Arjona is killed.

In Act II, Pantoja and Guijarro escape arrest for the killing
by hiding in a cellar. First disguised as a peddler and then as
a student, Guijarro carries messages between his master and
Juana, who has decided to defy her father and run away
with Pantoja.

The day that don Diego is to sign the official papers for his
marriage to Juana, Guijarro, disguised and under the pseudonym
of don Antolín Garapiña, comes to don Lope for legal consultation. Piling double-talk upon double-talk, Guijarro distracts and
confuses don Lope while Pantoja stealthily enters and then leaves
the house with Juana. The lovers are later found hiding in a
house adjoining the home of the Duke of Arcos, to whom don
Lope is beholden for several favors. When he hears of Pantoja's
valiant exploits, the Duke asks Juana's father to permit her
marriage to the man she loves. In a consolation match, don
Diego will marry doña Angela, Juana's cousin. Guijarro, in spite
of his vow, reminiscent of Calderonian servants, to remain
single,[34] will parallel the happy matrimonial fate of his master
by marrying Leonor.

Although there are several good comic scenes, the *comedia*
is not well organized and contains many elements not well inte-

grated into the action. The fact that a promised second part was apparently not written is not very disappointing.

J. Travesuras son valor (Pranks Show Valor)

There exist two plays of this title. The first, published in *Parte VIII* of the *Escogidas* (Madrid: Andrés García de la Iglesia, 1657), and attributed to "a wit," is loosely episodic, has a tragic ending, and is probably not a product of Moreto's pen. We have read a more tightly structured recasting of this play, with a happy ending, attributed to Moreto, which exists in a 1747 *suelta*, No. 264. According to Ruth Lee Kennedy,[35] this is apparently a reprint of a similarly numbered *suelta* of 1729.

Set in Flanders, the action revolves around the impetuous don Sancho el Malo, son of don Sancho el Bueno, aged and distinguished officer of the Duke of Alba's forces. In carrying off his beloved doña Elvira to save her from a marriage arranged by her avaricious father, the younger Sancho incurs the duke's wrath. Protected by a former lover, the Flemish doña Laura, and finally pardoned by the duke on the condition that he will thereafter draw his sword only on the enemy, don Sancho el Malo, true only to the *letter* of his promise, kills by crushing in his arms the Flemish captain Brondux for having accused him of lying. For this he is imprisoned. Abetted by a father torn between obedience to the duke and to his paternal instincts, Sancho escapes. Upon hearing of his father's imprisonment for disloyalty, however, he returns and brazenly kills a lieutenant and several of his father's captors. Although inwardly sympathetic to Sancho's obdurate adherence to the honor code, the duke turns deaf ears to entreaties of still another pardon addressed to him by don Sancho el Bueno, by doña Elvira, and by doña Laura. When the happy news arrives that a prince has been born in Spain, however, this gives the jubilant duke just the excuse he needed to pardon the rambunctious Sancho and reward him with doña Elvira's hand.

Although Miss Kennedy's versification analysis indicates but a small debt to the source play,[36] the fact that the heaviest borrowing occurs near the end of Act II, precisely the scene in which Sancho strangles Captain Brondux, prompts the following hypothesis: "Inasmuch as the instances in Moreto's secular theatre where a character meets a violent death on the stage are rare, if they exist at all, the retention of this repulsive scene suggests a collaborating hand."[37]

Bordering on caricature in their unswerving allegiance to an inflexible code, the overdrawn characterizations of the two Sanchos and the contrived happy ending are another illustration of Moreto's light-hearted treatment of a theme to which he never could lend Calderonian seriousness.

II *Plays of Intrigue*

A. El Caballero (The Nobleman)

Fernández-Guerra, who includes this play in his edition,[38] claims that the *Parte XIX* of the *Escogidas* (Madrid: Pablo de Val, 1662), was the first printing.[39] Miss Kennedy had accepted the *comedia* as Moreto's in *The Dramatic Art of Moreto*,[40] but subsequently has cast doubt on his authorship.[41]

Don Félix de Toledo has returned to Madrid from Flanders because of the death of his brother. Originally obliged to leave Madrid after killing an adversary in a duel, he had also left behind his beloved doña Ana Enríquez. Choosing to remain incognito until certain that there are no lingering complications over the death for which he is responsible, he arrives to find Ana regaled by music arranged by don Diego de Ribera, whose sister Luisa is courted by Ana's brother, don Lope. Don Félix persistently refuses to reveal his name to anyone, even his father, and identifies himself simply as *El Caballero*. Because Ana's maid, the avaricious and scheming Inés, has deceived don Diego into thinking that her mistress is favorably disposed to his wooing, don Félix suffers violently from jealousy. Although it has been kept a secret from the couple, the marriage of Ana and Félix has been arranged by her brother and his father. As the crowd gathers for the dénouement, Félix overhears Inés' confession to don Diego and his jealousy is dispelled. Lope and Luisa are united, as are Félix and Ana. Seemingly not in the least distraught by his ill fortune, don Diego announces that he is better off than all, because he will remain a bachelor.

With *Trampa adelante* and *El parecido en la corte*, this play rounds out Moreto's contribution to the cape-and-sword sub-genre. It is smoothly organized and filled with sparkling dialogue, enlivened humorously by the contributions of the *gracioso* Manzano ("apple tree") who also disassociates himself from the traditional cowardly servant by a demonstration of real valor in the first act. We detect a note of fine irony in the portrayal of don Félix's extreme sense of honor. Manzano, who makes a witty reference to the title of Lope's *El caballero de Olmedo*, openly satirizes several points of honor in the first scene, and, throughout the play, one feels that Moreto joins his *gracioso* in lightheartedly deriding the conformity of the noble victims of an irrational code.

B. La confusión de un jardín (The Confusion of a Garden)

The first dated edition was that of Moreto's *Tercera parte* (Madrid: Antonio de Zafra, 1681) and Fernández-Guerra included it in his edition,[42] noting the presence of a collaborating hand in Acts II and III, perhaps that of Figueroa.[43] Based upon versification and the virtual disappearance of the witty *gracioso* after the first act, Ruth Lee Kennedy concludes that the play is a collaborative effort, but she is not willing to limit Moreto's part to Act I.[44] Hurtado and Palencia[45] first pointed out that the play is derived from Castillo Solórzano's novel, *La confusión de una noche*.

Doña Beatriz, elder daughter of don Jerónimo, has, through the offices of her saucy maid Jusepa, provided don Luis de Toledo, a persistent suitor for two years, with a key to her garden where, that night, she has asked him to make official declaration of his intentions.

Don Diego de Silva, former suitor of Beatriz, on the night of his return to Madrid after an absence of three years during which he is thought to have died, is mistaken for someone else and forced into a duel, in which he wounds an adversary. As he flees from the authorities, he comes upon don Jerónimo, who offers the protection of his garden and home. After Luis's entry, there ensues a truly Calderonian intrigue founded upon mistaken identities, disguised voices, and improbable situations. Jusepa mistakenly leads don Diego to her mistress and Jerónimo returns to the garden and offers his room to don Luis. Upon learning that Diego is very much alive, Beatriz renounces any affection she may have had for don Luis and aspires to dissipate the jealousy provoked in her former lover, who realizes that he has accidentally stumbled upon her rendezvous with another man. The father, aware of the fact that his honor is threatened by one of the two men, plans vengeance when the identity of his offender becomes clear. All is resolved by the discovery that Luis and Diego are brothers. Luis, disillusioned by a confession of her true sentiments which Beatriz delivered to him thinking him to be Diego, "magnanimously" drops out of the competition for the leading lady and settles for her younger sister Leonor, by whom he has been ardently loved all along.

C. El hijo obediente (The Obedient Son)

In *The Dramatic Art of Moreto* this play was listed only once,[46] as an attribution classed as doubtful by Fernández-Guerra,[47] which Miss Kennedy at that time thought was probably Beneito's. Subsequently, following an examination of the unpublished manuscript version[48] of the play in the Biblioteca Municipal of Madrid, she reclaimed the work for Moreto.[49]

The action revolves around the contrasting personalities of the two sons of Juan II of Aragon. Carlos, the firstborn, from Juan's former marriage to doña Blanca, granddaughter of the King of Navarre, is envious and ambitious to the point that he wages war against his father and even plots against his life in order to attain possession of Navarre. His half-brother Fernando, from Juan's second marriage, is a model of generosity, valor, and loyalty. Ironically, he is at times disobedient to his father, as shown by his decision not to follow the king's orders to imprison Carlos's wife Brianda. By switching two documents, Fernando also causes Carlos to reveal to the king his own conspiracy against his father's life. Carlos finally is thrown from a horse and killed. The virtues of "the obedient son" win for him the thrones of Castile and Aragon.

Miss Kennedy notes that this play is a revision of Lope's *El piadoso aragonés* (*The Pious Aragonese*).[50] As she also remarks,

Act II contains reference to two personages who recall Carlos's rivals for the hand of Diana in Moreto's masterpiece, *El desdén con el desdén*: the Count of Fox and the Prince of Bearne.

D. El parecido en la corte (His Likeness at Court)

Critics long accepted the views expressed by Fernández-Guerra[51] and Schaeffer,[52] who supposed *El parecido en la corte* to be Moreto's recasting of one of his earlier works, titled *El parecido,* even though the five manuscript versions which exist in the Biblioteca Nacional, although bearing the short title, were all of the work considered to be the *refundición.* In 1936, Ruth Lee Kennedy argued convincingly another interpretation, according to which Moreto wrote only the version preserved in the five manuscripts, which was not printed until it appeared in eighteenth-century *sueltas,*[53] subsequently to be included in Fernández-Guerra's edition.[54] The seventeenth-century printings of *El parecido,*[55] she maintains—adducing an example of the textual mention of a character which has been eliminated—represent a later version of Moreto's original, cut and revised by the editors of the *Parte* volumes in which they appeared. Juana de José Prades, in her 1965 edition of *El parecido en la corte,*[56] takes credit for having arrived independently at the same conclusions that Miss Kennedy published twenty-nine years earlier.

Don Fernando de Ribera, a young Sevillian noble, has wasted his inheritance while neglecting his duties as guardian of his sister, doña Ana, until he finds her in the arms of her lover, don Lope de Luján, whom he wounds without learning his identity. Believing himself dishonored, Fernando departs for Madrid where, by chance, he is taken by don Pedro de Luján for his son Lope, who has been away in the Indies for fourteen years. Physically indistinguishable from his sister's lover, Fernando's inability to converse on family matters is explained away by the quick-witted Tacón, who claims that his master is suffering from amnesia. Fernando and Lope's sister Inés gradually fall in love, much to the bewilderment of the latter. By further coincidence, Ana, having come to Madrid to search for don Lope, whom she has not seen since the night he was wounded, obtains employment as Inés' maid, using the assumed name of Lucía.

Don Pedro's arrangements to marry his daughter to a certain don Diego are impeded at every step by Fernando, playing the role of brother. When the real don Lope returns home, his father treats him as an imposter and bends every effort to cure his supposed son of his amnesia. Finally, after a true cape-and-sword third act in which each principal attempts to redress the dishonor wrought to him by his likeness, Fernando and Lope unite in the home of don Félix, clear up their misunderstandings, and the play ends with three marriages, each of the *parecidos* being awarded the hand of his beloved, and the servants Tacón and Leonor following the lead of their masters.

One of a long list of works dealing with Plautus's *Menaechmi* theme, the play has certain analogies with Tirso de Molina's *El castigo del pensequé* (*The Punishment for Inadvertence*) which were first pointed out by Fernández-Guerra.[57]

E.   Trampa adelante (On with the Trick)

Published first in 1654 in Moreto's *Primera parte*, this *comedia* was also included in the edition of Fernández-Guerra.[58]

The play's humor is based much more on stage movement and contrived coincidence than on the combination of wit, characterization, idea, and verisimilitude achieved by Moreto at his best. Nevertheless, it is a rollickingly funny piece which must have been a delight to see presented.

The love of doña Leonor and don Juan de Lara is tested by jealousy after he has been seen defending a lady in a coach, with whom he has subsequently exchanged notes. Telling the truth, don Juan explains that it was a chance occurrence, that he didn't even see the lady, and that, in his note, he refused an invitation to call upon her. Ana, the wealthy lady in question who, coincidentally, is Leonor's next-door neighbor, aware of don Juan's extreme poverty, uses liberality with her brother's wealth to enlist the aid of his servant Millán in her attempt to win his master's love. The witty *gracioso*, without consulting his master, attempts thereafter to extract money from Ana by misleading her into thinking that Juan corresponds to her love.

The intrigue is complicated by the fact that each of the female leads is loved by the brother of the other. Don García de Toledo, Leonor's brother, closes the first act by announcing his projected wedding with Ana, and Leonor's with Ana's brother, don Diego de Vargas.

There follow cape-and-sword scenes, cases of mistaken identity, false notes, and unconsummated duels, all revolving around the presence of Ana and Leonor in the house of don Juan, now well dressed and financially comfortable through the successful enterprise of Millán. Discovery of the women in a man's house makes each brother feel honor-bound to marry his sister to Juan. Disaster is averted as Millán confesses his guilt in the intrigues of which Leonor and Juan are totally ignorant. The lovers unite in marriage and García wins Ana's hand, leaving the ridiculous Diego to lament his misfortune in love, as well as the loss of his money which he has indirectly and unknowingly bestowed upon his rival. The play has enjoyed success on the Spanish stage for three centuries, and one cannot disagree with Miss Kennedy's judgment that comedies such as *Trampa adelante* and *El parecido en la corte* rate among the best of their kind in Spanish Golden Age theater.[59]

CHAPTER 6

Secular Theater–Plays of Character and Idea

M ORETO appears to have attained maturity as a dramatic author by the date of the publication of the *Primera parte* of his plays in 1654, for in this volume there appeared several of his finest works, including his masterpiece, *El desdén con el desdén.*

The plays examined in this chapter clearly represent Moreto's best, and include in their number titles which figure among the outstanding dramatic productions of all of Spanish Golden Age literature. It seems appropriate to introduce the plays in this category with the perceptive phrases of Ruth Lee Kennedy, to whose monumental work Moretian scholarship is so deeply indebted:

It is, however, on those comedies classed as plays of character and idea that Moreto's fame must finally rest. In these, as in his plays of intrigue, there are interesting situations skilfully directed to a satisfactory climax and dialogue that is, as a rule, delightfully natural. But one finds more. Moreto has shown consummate art in introducing his characters, in analysing their motives, and in presenting them before us as human beings who are consistent in thought and deed. Characterization, action, and idea go hand in hand to form a play of symmetry and beauty.[1]

I Antíoco y Seleuco (Antiocus and Seleucus)

First published in the *Primera parte* of Moreto's *comedias*, in 1654, it is also included in the Fernández-Guerra edition[2] and is one of the five plays analyzed by Casa.[3] The play's subtitle, *A mejor padre, mejor hijo* (*A Better Son to a Better Father*), is found frequently as the principal title of the *comedia*.

In a plot that parallels some general lines of the Phaedra theme, Antíoco has been sent to meet Estratónica, daughter of Demetrio the Great, who is to become Seleuco's fourth wife. Destined to marry against his will his cousin Astrea, Antíoco has already fallen in love with an unknown woman whose picture a servant has found and given to him. Antíoco meets the future queen's party at night, unburdens his grief to Estratónica and, at her request, offers to show her the picture of his beloved. Servants bring torches and both realize that it is a picture of Estratónica.

When the escorted party arrives at the palace, Antíoco is extremely distraught and ill. Seleuco charges the doctor, Erasistrato, with his cure and intends to delay his own marriage until his son is better. Erasistrato determines first through his patient's choice of music that the indisposition stems from love; through Antíoco's reaction when in the presence of Estratónica, he discovers the precise source of the problem. The king, after hearing that the general problem is unrequited love, ironically expresses amazement that there could exist a woman who would be unattainable for Antíoco, and claims that he will make his son happy. When the doctor reveals the whole truth to him, the king, in despair, ends the second act by lamenting that either Antíoco or Seleuco must die.

Dramatic irony runs high in the third act, peaking in the jibe of the *gracioso* Luquete that Antíoco should marry his father's intended bride. Seleuco reveals to Estratónica, who has been suffering from melancholy, that he knows their secret and plans to marry her to his son. She dissimulates the joy that this news produces. When Seleuco makes the same revelation and announcement to his son, Antíoco lies and says that he loves Astrea. The happy Seleuco, taken in by his son's deception, decrees that the four shall marry immediately. Left alone, Antíoco prays that his reason will prevail, but with little success. When the wedding party arrives, Erasistrato informs the king that his son has nearly expired from the heroic attempt to surpass his father's magnanimity. Not to be outdone, Seleuco marries Astrea, gives Antíoco to Estratónica, and all ends happily.

The sources of this play from classical times to Moreto's epoch are studied in detail by Ruth Lee Kennedy[4] and Frank

Casa.[5] They disagree only on the debt of Moreto to Lope de
Vega's *El castigo sin venganza* (*Punishment without Vengeance*).
Casa objects to Miss Kennedy's reference to *Antíoco y Seleuco*
as a recasting of Lope's play, but does admit that *"El castigo
sin venganza* (1636) is the single most influential source for
Moreto's work."[6] In Lope's play, Casandra and Federico both
pay for adultery with their lives as the duke dispenses justice in
a tragic dénouement. As pointed out by Casa, "the importance
of Lope's play to Moreto as source material declines after the
first act."[7] In order to avoid the need for a tragic ending and
at the same time to avoid offending Christian sensibilities, Moreto
does not present Estratónica as the wife of Seleuco, but as his
betrothed. This permits the development of the theme of paternal
and filial generosity. Miss Kennedy laments Moreto's ending,
stating that "the situation is basically tragic and calls for a
tragic outcome."[8] On this point we tend to agree with Casa,
who lauds Moreto's development of "a powerful story of man's
conquest over himself . . . the struggle between love and duty
in Antíoco and Estratónica."[9]

Carlos Ortigoza[10] has maintained that Moreto's destruction
of the honor motive which undergirded the source play should be
seen as an escape from the prison established by Lope. He sees
the elimination of the honor conflict, in itself an act of heresy
in the Golden Age, as a daring attempt by Moreto to chart new
courses in the development of dramatic action based on
other motives.

II   Cómo se vengan los nobles
(How Nobles Avenge Themselves)

Published for the first time in *Parte XXIX* of the *Escogidas*
(Madrid: Josef Fernández de Buendía, 1668), it is considered
by Ruth Lee Kennedy to be one of Moreto's late works and,
as originally pointed out by its editor, Fernández-Guerra,[11] the
plot was borrowed from Lope's *El testimonio vengado* (*The
Avenged Testimony*).

One of the many Golden Age treatments of the theme of
inherent nobility, the plot revolves around the fortunes of
Ramiro, firstborn although illegitimate son of King Sancho of

Navarre. In order to avoid any attempts on Ramiro's life by the queen and their three sons, the king has had Ramiro brought up far from court. Attention is first called to Ramiro by his gallant bearing when elected "King" for Easter celebrations in the Navarrese city of Eibar. It is here that the venerable Fortún, father of the king, with the queen eavesdropping, reveals to don Sancho that the impressive young man is his son. The queen immediately begins to plot. When her three sons are unable to kill Ramiro, she hires Ordoño and Nuño to do the job.

A seemingly trite item is to have significant importance in the development of the plot. When he departs to do battle against the Moors, don Sancho decides not to take with him his favorite Andalusian steed. He leaves it with Pedro Sesé, with strict instructions that *no one*, not even his own sons, is to be permitted to ride it. While Nuño and Ordoño are failing to drown Ramiro in the River Ebro, García, third of the king's legitimate sons, asks to ride the horse. Pedro Sesé denies the request and, when the queen backs his decision, García conceives and then spreads the vengeful rumor that his mother and Sesé have committed adultery.

According to law, the accused have thirty days to be vindicated in an open battle against the three accusers: García, who claims to have been an eyewitness, and his two brothers who believe his story. On the way to imprisonment in the castle, the disillusioned queen meets Ramiro. She reveals to him the secret of his identity and confesses the attempts on his life which she ordered. Magnanimously, Ramiro forgives all and, disguised, appears to fight his three brothers in defense of his stepmother. In the first attack, García is defeated. His confession includes even the trite motive which set his perfidious mind to action. The grateful monarchs want to name Ramiro heir to Castile, Navarre, and Aragon. He magnanimously refuses such generosity and accepts only Aragon, leaving the rest for his legitimate half-brothers.

Buscón, who is a disappointing *gracioso* when compared with Moreto's best creations in this area, informs us in his last speech: "This has all been accomplished without a wedding, a novelty for the *comedia*."

III   El defensor de su agravio (The Defender of his Offense)

First printed in *Parte XXXV* of the *Escogidas* (Madrid: Lucas Antonio de Bedmar, 1671), and included in the Fernández-Guerra edition,[12] this *comedia* is a well-written and structurally balanced variant of the traditional Golden Age love intrigue.

The married Duke of Athens has fallen in love with Nisea, who also happens to be the object of the affections of the duke's favorite, Alejandro, and the scheming Lidoro. The *gracioso* Comino, Alejandro's lackey, wittily establishes the contrast between the lofty, amorous interests of his master and his own pragmatic and overwhelming concern with food. He also, from the start, plays a commanding part in the dialogue and engages in some of the word play for which Moreto is famous, toying with Nisea's name as if the verb *ser* were one of its components: *Ni-sea, ni-es,* and *ni-será.*

Hoping to throw public opinion and his suspicious wife off the scent, the duke, oblivious to Alejandro's amorous involvement, orders him to declare himself Nisea's suitor. In a complicated garden scene in which all of the principals are present, Nisea rejects Lidoro, who has been led to believe by her maid Irene that he is the favored suitor. The duchess appears just in time to prevent Alejandro from inflicting physical harm on Lidoro. She reprimands the latter's boldness as the duke emerges from hiding. Alejandro generously defends Lidoro, who, chafing at the duchess' rebuke, and contrasting his ignoble character to Alejandro's, swears vengeance on the two.

Early in the second act, an anonymous message, delivered and explicated by Lidoro, suggests to the duke that Alejandro is transgressing with the duchess. Alejandro, hurt by the duke's sudden show of anger toward him, determines to return to his native Crete with Nisea. When he attempts to enlist the aid of the duchess, however, the duke overhears and misinterprets their conversation. The duke jails both of the accused. Athenian law holds severe punishment for the duchess, charged with adultery, unless Lidoro withdraws his accusation.

Nisea, thinking that the duke is simply anxious to remove all obstacles to win her hand in marriage, reveals that she is already Alejandro's and accuses the spurned Lidoro of vengeful treachery. Typically of Moreto's protagonists, reason initiates in the duke a renunciation of his designs on Nisea and a desire for reconciliation with the duchess. Anxious for conclusive proof, however, he appears disguised first to his imprisoned wife and then to his favorite. To each he offers liberty for the purpose of permitting consummation of the love they are alleged to share. The rejection of his offer by Aurora and Alejandro and their unequivocal demonstration of integrity and loyalty remove his last doubts. He himself satisfies the Athenian law by challenging and mortally wounding their false accuser. Before dying, Lidoro confesses his guilt to pave the way for a royal reconciliation and the marriage of Alejandro and Nisea.

D. De fuera vendrá quien de casa nos echará (We'll Be Evicted from our Home by an Outsider)

One of the twelve titles included in Moreto's *Primera parte*, 1654, the play's thematic similarities with Lope's *De cuando acá nos vino* (*When Did it Hit Us?*) were first noted by Fernández-Guerra in his edition.[13]

Two soldiers have just returned from Flanders, both poverty-stricken because of their minor vices. Captain Lisardo squanders his money on women, and Lieutenant Aguirre at the card table. They arrive in Madrid with a letter of introduction from Captain Luis Maldonado to his rich widowed sister, Cecilia. While re-united at the steps of San Felipe on the Calle Mayor with their only three local friends, Cecilia coincidentally comes to the same spot with her beautiful niece Francisca. The thesis of the play, the danger of overprotective policies in fulfilling a guardian-ship, is caricatured by the amorous aspirations of the aunt, who swears that her niece will not marry before she does. When it becomes clear that this is Captain Maldonado's sister, the two soldiers revise his letter to request that doña Cecilia lodge them in her home. Drawn to each other from their first meeting, Lisardo and Francisca are able to be together frequently thanks to the convenient living arrangement. Discovered together by Cecilia from time to time, Lisardo is able ingeniously to explain his presence to the satisfaction of the aunt, once going as far as to assert that it is really Cecilia whom he loves and claiming to have come to seek the intercession of her niece on his behalf. Two of the three "friends" of the initial reunion in Madrid, the philandering don Martín de Herrera and the Licentiate Celedón, have also become enamored of Francisca and actually request her hand formally in writing.

At this point, Captain Maldonado returns by surprise to Madrid. He learns all, including the fact that Cecilia has given two thousand ducats to Lisardo. Maldonado also discovers that Martín and the Licentiate have been found hiding in his house, and, at the peak of his furor, the vicar sends an order that Francisca must be freed from her aunt's control to marry Lisardo. Maldonado insists that one of the two men caught hiding restore his honor by marrying Cecilia, and the timorous Licentiate is selected. The play ends as the not-too-scrupulous Lisardo announces that he has just spent the two thousand ducats to buy jewels for his wife.

The play is extremely funny and we cannot disagree with Ruth Lee Kennedy's judgment that there is "no play where Moreto has reworked a comedy to greater advantage than this."[14]

IV   El desdén con el desdén (Disdain Conquered by Disdain)

This play was published first in the *Primera parte* of Moreto's plays in 1654. In addition to its appearance in the editions of Fernández-Guerra,[15] Alonso Cortés,[16] and the excellent recent edition of Francisco Rico,[17] it has been published frequently in anthologies and in noncritical editions. In spite of his neoclassic proclivities, Luzán registers praise for the play in 1737.[18] Eugenio de Ochoa in 1838 stated unequivocally that it is "without contradiction the best *comedia* which our language possesses."[19] Adolphe de Puibusque, almost as enthusiastic, judged in 1843 that "*El desdén con el desdén* is among the four best plays of the Castilian repertoire."[20] Critics from the beginning have lauded the psychological depth of the play and its dramatic structure, and Bruce Wardropper cites it as a demonstration that "Moreto is the first Spanish dramatist to achieve a fully disciplined art."[21]

Its fame is also attested by the fact that it has served as the inspiration for a number of adaptations and translations.

Roger Bauer[22] analyzes three: Molière's *La Princesse d'Élide* (1664),[23] Carlo Gozzi's *La Principessa filosofa, o sia il contro-veleno* (1772),[24] and Joseph Schreyvogel's *Donna Diana* (1816).[25] George Hyde also wrote *Love's Victory* or *The School for Pride*, first performed at the Theatre Royal, Covent Garden, on Wednesday, November 16, 1825, admittedly founded on Moreto's play.[26] The *British Museum Catalogue* lists several less well-known translations and Turkevich[27] notes a 1946 Russian translation.

Carlos, Count of Urgel, has come to Barcelona with his servant Polilla ("moth"). He finds himself in the company of Gastón, Count of Fox, and the Prince of Bearne, both of whom are attempting to win the hand of Diana, daughter of the Count of Barcelona. Diana, like her mythological namesake, the goddess of the hunt, opposed to marriage, is disdainful of her pretenders' efforts. Carlos, who upon arrival was not particularly attracted to Diana, finds that her very disdain kindles in him a fiery passion. With his servant, he conceives a strategy of fighting fire with fire, or disdain with disdain. He agrees to participate in a series of games and competitions with the other rivals, but tells them he is doing so only for diversion and not for their purpose, which is to impress Diana and to overcome her firm opposition to marriage. Since Carlos is the first man of her acquaintance who does not openly avow a desire to marry her, Diana becomes interested in him. When his feigned disdain matches hers, she vows to make him fall in love with her and then punish him with even greater disdain. Since he really is smitten, Carlos on several occasions is almost unable to maintain his feigned disdain, but on these occasions he is staunchly supported and brought through the crisis by Polilla who, under the assumed name of Caniquí ("cotton cloth"), has entered Diana's service to work with great success as an infiltrator behind the enemy lines. After a series of exasperating experiences in which she realizes not only that she is not conquering Carlos's disdain, but rather that her own is eroding, Diana confesses that she has been conquered and offers her hand to the man who has defeated "disdain with disdain."

Moreto's felicitous choice of theme, fused with structural perfection, produced in *El desdén con el desdén* a true masterpiece. The psychological dimensions of love, vanity, disdain, and ambition are carefully woven into a plot which, although it highlights the momentary weaknesses in resolve of the protagonist, also illustrates step by logical step his inexorable progress toward victory, if he will only follow the sage counsel of Polilla. This servant, one of Moreto's greatest comic creations, plays a truly dominant role, speaking, according to the calculations of Dedrick,[28] 28.3 percent of the play's lines.

Although the play has been accorded high praise in all the manuals, it is surprising, as Frank Casa notes, that there is a "near-complete absence of serious studies on his [Moreto's] two most famous works, *El desdén con el desdén* and *El lindo don Diego*."[29] There is the meticulous and important work of Mabel Harlan in which twenty *comedias* which have been proposed as sources for *El desdén con el desdén* are studied,[30] but the essence of this work is primarily historical rather than critical or interpretive.

V   La fuerza de la ley (The Strength of the Law)

Published first in Moreto's *Primera parte* in 1654, and included in the Fernández-Guerra edition,[31] this play, according to Schaeffer,[32] was inspired by a now lost source. Cotarelo tells us that the play was to be presented by Sebastián de Prado in 1651.[33]

Set in Antioch, the action deals with the uncompromising compliance of King Seleuco to the harsh laws which he boasts of having promulgated when he founded the city. As the play opens, Seleuco assesses upon Celio, the captain of his guard, the penalty for adultery—removal of both eyes.

The king's son and daughter, Demetrio and Nise, love respectively their cousins Aurora and Alejandro. When Demetrio refuses a match with Fénix, Queen of Egypt, which has been arranged by his father, Seleuco impulsively retracts his permission for the marriage of Nise to Alejandro and forces the latter to marry Aurora. Devoid of reason and spurred on by uncontrollable desire for his lost love, Demetrio first awakens jealousy in Alejandro by visiting Aurora in his absence. Abetted by the intervention of the malefic servant Irene, he finally succeeds in bending the will of Aurora, but the two are apprehended by

Alejandro. He kills his wife to wash the stain from his honor, and abjectly offers his own life to his prince. Seleuco imposes the penalty for adultery on his son but, when urged to forgiveness by the grandees, by Nise, and even by the offended Alejandro, he settles on a compromise more befitting his law-abiding nature. The law must be obeyed: it demands two eyes and two will be given—one by Demetrio, to represent punishment, and one by Seleuco himself, representing mercy.

Although the reduction of the historical penalty of two eyes would be typical of a modification made independently by Moreto, Schaeffer has found lines in Lope's *El marqués de Mantua* (*The Marquis of Mantua*) which indicate that a similarly revised version may very likely have been available to Moreto.[34] Ridicule directed at Gongorism by the *gracioso* Gregüesco ("wide breeches"), seems too contemporary for it to reflect Moreto's own views and could very well have been appropriated from a source play.[35]

The second of Moreto's plays to deal with the same royal family of Antioch, this play elicited interesting views, recorded by Ruth Lee Kennedy: "Professor Anibal points out to me that *La fuerza de la ley* is complementary to *Antíoco y Seleuco* and could well be called *A mal padre, peor hijo.*"[36] Miss Kennedy noted in *The Dramatic Art of Moreto*[37] that Aurora is the *only* feminine character in Moreto's theater who is faithless, even in intention, to her husband. In a later article, she adduces significant new findings: "I have, since making this observation, been fortunate enough to see the very rare 1654 edition of Moreto's plays (the only volume put out under his aegis), and in collating it with the *B. A. E.* edition, I discovered that the invitation which brings Demetrio to Aurora's side was in the *princeps* written by Irene, the faithless serving maid, not by Aurora herself."[38]

VI La fuerza del natural (The Force of Nature)

First printed in *Parte XV* of the *Escogidas* (Madrid: Melchor Sánchez, 1661), where the play's final lines attribute it to Cáncer and Moreto, it was also included in the Fernández-Guerra edition.[39] Plot similarities caused Mesonero Romanos to charge that the *comedia* is an imitation of Leyva's *Cuando no se aguarda y príncipe tonto* (*When One Doesn't Wait and the Dumb Prince*).[40] Knowledge of the chronology of the latter's work, however, leads Ruth Lee Kennedy to attribute the imitation to Leyva rather than to Cáncer and Moreto.[41]

Carlos and the impossibly dull and stupid Julio are brought up in Ferrara as sons of the rustic Roberto. Although Carlos constantly aspires to higher things than one would expect, given his birth and upbringing, it is Julio whom Roberto reveals to be the natural son of the duke. Upon the death of his jealous wife, the duke decides to take Julio, his only male heir, to the court, where he is sure all of his deficiencies will be remedied. In a series of scenes which contrast Julio with Carlos, the thesis that environmental conditions can improve the former are belied. Carlos shows great aptitude for every skill lacking in Julio and a strong mutual love awakens between Carlos and Aurora, the duke's niece and heir, and Julio's intended bride. To avoid an impossible marriage to Julio, Aurora offers to renounce her nobility. Roberto, however, reveals that his wife confessed to him with her dying breath that, hoping to give him a better lot in life, she had switched her own son with the duke's. Knowing that Carlos is his son, the duke marries him to Aurora, Alejandro to Aurora's cousin Camila, and Julio to his rustic paramour Gila, with a dowry of two thousand ducats.

The play formulates interesting queries on the relative importance of birth as opposed to environment and personal merit. Carlos, believing himself to be of humble origin, asks hopefully in the first act if good things must be guaranteed at birth or whether they can be earned. Scattered throughout the play are saddening indications that although nature may have erred with respect to Carlos and Julio, it almost always prevails. Sad though this theory makes Carlos feel throughout virtually the entire play, its application in the light of his true identity explodes the myth he cherished in the first act, and is responsible ultimately for his happiness.

VII   Hacer remedio el dolor (Making Grief a Remedy)

First published in *Parte XI* of the *Escogidas* (Madrid: Gregorio Rodríguez, 1659), where it is attributed to Moreto and

Cáncer, this comedy, probably written in or before 1649,[42] has been called by Ruth Lee Kennedy *El desdén con el desdén* in embryo and, with Moreto's masterpiece and *El poder de la amistad*, the initial work of a "trilogy of disdain."[43]

Considerably more complicated, and encumbered with a subplot, the theme revolves around the irrational appeal exerted by disdain in the beloved. In contrast with *El desdén con el desdén*, however, it is the heroine, Casandra, who successfully counteracts disdain with disdain.

After six years of stimulating Carlos's suit in Milan with disdain, she loses him when she finally declares her love. His ardor for Casandra now cold, Carlos ventures to Naples to compete with other gallants for the hand of Aurora, who organizes competitions similar to those of *El desdén con el desdén*. While questioning the irrationality of his nature, Carlos admits that he is fleeing "from another love, of a woman who freezes me only by loving me a great deal; for to me, to be loved a lot is like snow."[44]

Driven herself by the cold disdain of her erstwhile passionate lover, Casandra pursues Carlos to Naples and, disguised and using the pseudonym Rosaura, secures a position in Aurora's household. At the conclusion of the first act, it dawns on Casandra that disdain is the key to the restoration of Carlos's love. The coyness of the mysterious Rosaura captivates Carlos. His passion is rekindled and fanned to a flame by continual ploys and manifestations of feigned disdain until he abjectly falls at Casandra's feet and is rewon by the woman who knew how to "make grief a remedy."

VIII   Industrias contra finezas (Ingenuity vs. Goodness)

First printed in the *Segunda parte* of Moreto's *comedias* in 1676, this play was also included in Fernández-Guerra's edition.[45] Schaeffer postulates a lost Lopean source for the play.[46] Carole Christian has studied the play in relation to Moreto's earlier play, *El mejor amigo el rey* (*The Best Friend, the King*) and to Tirso's *Palabras y plumas* (*Words and Feathers*).[47] The action takes place in Presbourg, capital of Hungary until 1784.

The aging Hungarian king is expected to leave the crown to

one of his nieces, Dantea or Lisarda. Both Roberto, the Prince of Transylvania, and Count Palatino play up to Dantea, but, secretly, the count and Lisarda plot her death. Shortly before she is told by the seneschal that her uncle has declared her his successor, Dantea has heard rumors of a plot to poison her. As a ploy to protect her life and to discover the identity of her would-be assassins, she has the seneschal announce publicly that the king has decided in favor of her sister, knowing that, when it ultimately arrives, the written declaration will reverse the false announcement. The promulgation of the latter causes people to show their true colors: Lisarda becomes arrogant and both Roberto and the count declare that they really always loved her and not Dantea. Fernando, a poor noble, convinces Dantea of his love, regardless of the succession to the throne.

Reckless in her security, Lisarda rejects the count as no longer necessary. Intent upon vengeance, he tells Dantea of the plot to kill her, placing all of the blame on Lisarda. The dramatic irony heightens as both Roberto and the count, while eavesdropping, discover the stratagem of Dantea's false announcement of Lisarda's succession to the throne. Roberto again plays up to Dantea, while the count and Lisarda make another pact. She will be his if he obtains the crown for her. The count reports that the seneschal has drowned in the river. Dantea panics, swears that she is the appointed heir, and confesses her trick, but no one believes her. Lisarda has Dantea arrested and plans to kill her. Roberto, having learned of Lisarda's plans to marry the count, again rallies to Dantea. The old seneschal, washed by the current to the bank of the river and safety, marches with Roberto, Fernando, and Dantea to the court, where Dantea receives the crown, magnanimously pardons her sister, shocks Roberto by revealing her knowledge of how self-interest motivated his every friendly gesture, and rewards the loyal and sincere Fernando with her hand.

IX   Los jueces de Castilla (The Magistrates of Castile)

One of the twelve *comedias* included in Moreto's *Primera parte,* this play was also published in the Fernández-Guerra edition.[48] According to Cotarelo, it was performed by Diego de

Osorio before the end of the theatrical year of 1650.[49] The only known play of Moreto's written in *fabla* (imitation of archaic speech), this *comedia*'s lengthy cast of characters, its blend of history, legend, and intrigue, and its almost independent scenes of comic relief certainly lend weight to the theory of a Lopean source advanced by Schaeffer.[50]

Prince Ramiro, after feuding with his older brother Alfonso, is driven from Leon by their father, King Ordoño. He takes refuge in Castile, whose counts, Nuño Fernández and Almondar Blanco, along with the latter's son, Diego, are treacherously killed by Ordoño. Ruy Peláez, whom the counts had left in charge of Castile, plots to kill the heiress, Countess Geloira, and be elected count and sole ruler. In a succession of cape-and-sword scenes involving disguises, mistaken identities, unfounded and petulant jealousy, Ramiro is selected to be the assassin of Geloira, becomes instead her protector, father of her son, key witness in the trial of the traitor Ruy Peláez, and, upon the magnanimous abdication of his brother, who has succeeded Ordoño to the Leonese throne, unites Leon and Castile.

The title is based on the wise decisions of the historico-legendary judges of ninth-century Castile, Nuño Rasura and Laín Calvo, who also was the Cid's grandfather. Originally squires who accompanied the two counts to their execution in Leon, these two exemplars of loyalty return to Castile with their sad tidings, audaciously thwart Ruy Peláez's usurpation of the Castilian throne, and are elected magistrates. They sublimate their passionate inclinations to vengeance into objectivity and fairness.

The *gracioso*, Sancho, engages in wordplay typical of Moreto's servants, specifically recalls his Cervantine namesake in one instance, and is quite humorous. The use of *fabla* by Golden Age dramatists was apparently tempting to most, but their record of success is not impressive. Such is the case with respect to *Los jueces de Castilla*.

Lope de Vega cited a play, now lost, of identical title in his second *Peregrino* list. Basing his conclusions on elements seemingly atypical of Moreto, Menéndez Pelayo considers *Los jueces de Castilla* such a servile reworking of Lope's lost play that he publishes it in its place.[51] Versification statistics adduced by Ruth

Lee Kennedy,[52] and subsequently corroborated by Pedro Henríquez Ureña,[53] along with a comic element not well integrated
into the main plot, lend weight to the theory that Moreto relied
heavily on a now lost source.

X El licenciado Vidriera (The Glass Licentiate)

First published in *Parte V* of the *Escogidas* (Madrid: Pablo
de Val, 1653), and included in the Fernández-Guerra edition,[54]
this play, inspired by Cervantes's exemplary novel of the same
title, is also one of the five *comedias* studied by Casa.[55]

Carlos, born poor but of noble blood in Urbino, enjoys a
mutual love with Laura, and has won the conditional promise of
her hand from her father, Pompeyo, if he can but acquire wealth.
In Bologna, Carlos becomes a successful academician. When
three pretenders vie for control of Urbino, Carlos returns to
demonstrate the duke's legal right to rule rather than Casandra
or Federico. In a conciliatory move, the duke has publicly announced his aspiration to marry Casandra. She, although neither
one has seen the other, despises the duke and joins with Federico
in waging war against him.

Carlos ingenuously requests the intervention of his old friend
Lisardo on behalf of his love for Laura. The audience alone
learns that Lisardo has also sought Laura's hand in marriage,
only to be rejected.

Having demonstrated his talents in "letters," Carlos also ful-
fills the ideal of his epoch in "arms" by single-handedly capturing first Casandra and then Federico. The act ends as Casandra
sees her competitor and would-be suitor the duke for the first
time, and realizes that he is not as bad as she had supposed.

In a second act somewhat weaker in dialogue, the wily
Lisardo, who had been asked by the duke to care for the
wounded Carlos, leaves his rival in a wretched inn where he
is nearly starved and given poor medical treatment. In tatters,
Carlos tries to secure the aid of several important figures while
Lisardo takes credit for Casandra's capture and does his best to
obtain the hand of Laura who, although she still loves Carlos,
has acceded in filial obedience to her father's desire that she
plan to marry Lisardo. Carlos, after discovering the falseness of

Lisardo's friendship and realizing that virtue is not rewarded (the real theme of the play), announces to his servant Gerundio, just before the end of the second act, that he is made of glass.

During his feigned insanity, Carlos receives the attention of all in the form of gifts, invitations, favors, etc. This, in essence, is the point of his moral plaint: Virtue has won nothing for him, while his "madness" has made him a celebrity. Not knowing that Laura still really loves him, Carlos includes her with the duke and Lisardo among those from whom he vengefully seeks retribution. Just as Laura is about to follow her filial obedience into marriage, Carlos appears, sane and well dressed, to level accusations against his offenders. He receives Laura's hand, the duke will marry Casandra, and the villainous Lisardo gets his well-deserved *calabazas* ("the gate").

The moral issue planted by Carlos in his feigned madness (i.e., that the world has a false set of values) is, of course, the same as the one found in the parallel situation of Tomás Rodaja in Cervantes' exemplary novel. However, whereas the madness of Tomás Rodaja is real, that of Moreto's hero is feigned. In each case, however, the protagonist's condition bestows upon him a freedom to criticize which would have been denied to him if sane. Although Moreto's complaints about the ingratitude of society are more somber than the lighthearted indictments of Cervantes, his unflagging faith in the power of reason causes him to end his play on a happy note, while the disillusioned Licenciado Rueda of the novel leaves the court to die as a soldier in Flanders.

XI El lindo don Diego (Don Diego the Dandy)

Published first in *Parte XVIII* of the *Escogidas* (Madrid: Gregorio Rodríguez, 1662), this masterpiece is included in the Fernández-Guerra collection[56] and is available in several modern editions.[57]

Moreto is clearly indebted to Guillén de Castro's *El Narciso en su opinión* (*Narcissus to Himself*), first published in 1625.[58] Moreto's adaptation, however, represents gigantic improvement over its humorous but loosely-structured source. Frank Casa[59] ably studies the systematic transformation wrought by Moreto

to give dramatic cohesiveness to this play which, close behind
El desdén con el desdén, enjoys an undisputed place of honor
very near the pinnacle occupied by the greatest plays of the
Spanish Golden Age.[60]

The play is essentially a comic exposé of the conceited and
fastidious dandy, a type well known in Moreto's contemporary
society. The very title of the play was a well-known contemporary designation applied to such men.[61]

Don Tello refuses an invitation to accompany his friend don
Juan to Granada because of the expected arrival of two nephews
from Burgos. Unbeknown to don Tello, don Juan is the lover
of doña Inés, one of his two daughters. Thus, he shocks his
friend by announcing that the two nephews, don Diego and don
Mendo, are coming to marry respectively Inés and her sister,
Leonor. Don Juan initially feels betrayed by Inés, but it soon
becomes clear that the sisters know nothing of the plans that
their father has made. The *gracioso*, Mosquito, has been on
a reconnaissance mission and returns with a long, hilarious
report on his initial observation of don Diego. With example
after example of his extreme fastidiousness, Mosquito recounts
that after don Diego consumed nine hours in dressing, he com-
plained about having been rushed.

In contrast to his cousin Diego, Mendo is in every way a
gentleman and Leonor is pleased with the match proposed for
her. Inés, however, although firmly committed to filial obedience,
finds the prospect of marriage to the ridiculous don Diego un-
thinkable. An initial strategy hit upon by the two girls is to try
to make a bad impression on their two imported fiancés. Since
Leonor's objections to Mendo no longer exist, she attempts to
aid Inés. In marvelous comic scenes, however, the narcissistic
don Diego interprets absolutely everything said to him, from
veiled to diaphanous insults, as testimony of love and affection. He is certain that Inés and Leonor are jealous of each
other because each loves him more passionately than the other.
Don Diego's invincible egotism defeats the first stratagem but
becomes the target for the project suggested by Mosquito to help
Inés. Thanks to Mosquito's intervention, doña Inés has taken back
into her service a maid named Beatriz who had been dismissed
by don Tello. Mosquito's plan is to have Beatriz impersonate a

cousin of don Juan, who is a countess and currently out of town. Willing to forego marriage with his cousin to climb the social ladder with a countess, don Diego agrees to a secret meeting with the woman of nobility who will be his new conquest. In one of the funniest scenes in Golden Age drama, Beatriz, decked out in the countess's finery, teases don Diego with language satirizing the excesses of Gongorism. Although the obscurity of most of the passages can be penetrated by an average reader, the allusions and jumbled word order completely escape don Diego, who again interprets open and deliberate insults as adulation of his person and acceptance of his suit.

Twice following this scene, don Diego accidentally discovers Mosquito embracing the "countess" and both times the quick-witted Beatriz dispels his anxiety by saying that she has heard that he is to marry Inés that evening and that she has come disguised as a servant to verify the report. After the second such encounter, there is just enough time for her to hide before Tello, Juan, Mendo, Inés, and Leonor arrive for the final scene. When don Diego states that he cannot marry his cousin because his heart is committed elsewhere, Leonor and Mendo are joined and don Juan is given the hand of his beloved Inés. Tello, joyfully expansive after marrying his two daughters, grants Inés' request to readmit Beatriz to the household. Mosquito announces that he and Beatriz plan to marry, and when he invites her to come out of her hiding place, don Diego's claim that she is his countess is greeted with laughter as the curtain falls.

El lindo don Diego, throughout the years, has been traditionally considered an example of the *comedia de figurón*, a type of play in which a farce is developed from a rather grotesque caricature of the protagonist. Edwin Place[62] has argued that the play is comedy, not farce, and, on that basis, questions the accuracy of its traditional classification.

XII Lo que puede la aprehensión (What Apprehension Can Do)

One of the twelve *comedias* published in Moreto's *Primera parte* in 1654, it is also included in the Fernández-Guerra edition.[63] Three source *comedias* have been identified: Lope's *Mirad a quien alabáis* (*Be Careful Whom You Praise*), Tirso's *La celosa de sí misma* (*Jealous of Herself*), and Calderón's *La desdicha de la voz* (*The Voice's Misfortune*). Moreto, in his turn, is the admitted source of Thomas Corneille's *Le Charme de la voix* (*The Voice's Charm*).[64]

Built upon an essentially simple structure, the plot is complicated by cases of mistaken and feigned identity and by extensive use of dramatic irony.

The typical long, early expository monologue of Fenisa, daughter of Federico Esforcia, brother of the deceased Duke of Milan, outlines the necessary background information. The young Duke of Milan has fallen in love with the voice of his cousin without having seen its possessor. Her father has kept the duke from seeing Fenisa because he has already arranged for him to marry the Duchess of Parma, who is on the way to Milan. Charged with meeting her and escorting her the remainder of the journey, Federico's son Carlos falls in love with the duchess at their first meeting. Emboldened by the duke's avowals that he will not go through with the arranged marriage, Carlos cannot repress a declaration of his own affection for the duchess. Offended by the duke's obvious disinterest, the duchess decides to make Carlos Duke of Parma to avenge the duke's rebuff. Piqued by his scorn, however, she first plans to see him for herself. Following an artificial scene in which Fenisa is confronted by the duke and claims to be his cousin's servant, the duchess is able to pose as Fenisa and not as her servant, as she had originally planned. Fenisa, playing the role of a maid, panics when the duke seems to transfer his interest to the visible charms of the duchess, but his enraptured and confused reaction to her off-stage singing while he is in the presence of her supposed rival reassures her. In a rapid and bland dénouement, the duchess enters in regal splendor to announce her marriage to Carlos. Fenisa quickly identifies herself to the befuddled duke, and all ends in happiness, seemingly genuine in all but the duchess, whose vanity has suffered some rather severe assaults.

XIII   La luna africana (The African Moon)

A seventeenth-century manuscript in the Biblioteca Nacional not only attributes this work in its final passage to nine collaborators, but its copyist also indicates in the text where the contribution of each ends.[65] The fairly equal parts correspond to the only scene changes in the play and are attributed as follows: Act I—Belmonte, Luis Vélez, Juan Vélez; Act II—Alfaro, Moreto, Martínez; and Act III—Sigler de Huerta, Cáncer and Rosete. If this is in fact the work of these nine collaborators, it was written before 1643, the date of Alfaro's death, and therefore represents one of Moreto's earliest dramatic efforts.[66] The play appeared under the title *La mejor luna africana*, and was attributed to "three wits" in at least two eighteenth-century *sueltas*.[67]

Ending with a gallant defense of honor in open combat similar to that of *Cómo se vengan los nobles*, the plot pits the calumny of the envious and treacherous Gomel against the upright and valiant Hazén, both military leaders of El Rey Chico in Granada during the last stages of the Reconquest. Hazén, sterling exemplar of the noble Abencerrages, captures Leonor, a beautiful Christian, with whom he falls in love. Assigned to the service of the Sultana, Leonor, under the assumed name of Esperanza, is spied upon by Gomel and the king as she keeps an evening rendezvous at her window with Hazén. An interruption by her mistress is the basis for Gomel's charge that the Sultana is guilty of adultery with Hazén. The latter escapes imprisonment, but the innocent Sultana is granted thirty days to have three defenders champion her cause against her accusers. Don Juan Chacón, a formidable Christian warrior, cousin of Leonor, friend of Hazén, and past emissary to Granada, answers the Sultana's plea to come to her defense. Juan, Hazén, and Rodrigo Téllez Girón, the Maestre of the Order of Calatrava, all disguised as Turks, defeat Gomel and his two companions to vindicate the honor of the Sultana. Hazén announces his conversion to Christianity, which removes the last obstacle to his imminent marriage with Leonor.

Moreto's part contains a good comic scene in which the *gracioso*, Cosme, attempts to convince a Moorish guard to admit him to the palace, a lamentation by the Sultana of her sad plight, and an indirect threat by Hazén intended for Gomel.

Schaeffer is kinder in his judgment of the play[68] than is Ruth Lee Kennedy, for whom only "the portrayal of the character of blunt Don Juan Chacón ... could hope to save it from an otherwise merited oblivion."[69]

96 AGUSTÍN MORETO

XIV El mejor amigo, el rey (The Best Friend, the King)

First published in the *Primera parte* of Moreto's *comedias* in 1654, this play's source, as noted by Fernández-Guerra, is Tirso's *Cautela contra cautela* (*Cunning vs. Cunning*).[70] Opinions based on a comparative study differ, however. For Fernández-Guerra, Moreto's debt is slight, while Ruth Lee Kennedy notes that forty-one of Moreto's fifty-six scenes have their partial or complete equivalents in Tirso's.[71] Although she agrees with Schaeffer[72] that Moreto's *comedia* is inferior in diction to its source, she does not agree that *Cautela contra cautela* is superior in plot development. In character portrayal, she affirms, Moreto has shown a distinct gain over the earlier play.

The theme of this play is the test of true friendship. Count Enrique, favorite of the King of Sicily, wants to verify the sincerity of the love proffered to him by Porcia and Laura, who in turn are loved respectively by Carlos and Filipo.

Alejandro, covetous of Enrique's post as favorite, plans to obtain it as a reward for aiding Naples in its impending attack on Sicily. Suspecting Alejandro's treachery, but anxious for incontrovertible proof, the king removes Enrique from his post and gives it to Alejandro.

Virtually all of the second act consists of a series of tests which pair off Enrique's friends, women, and servants as either loyal (Carlos, Laura, Macarrón) or disloyal (Filipo, Porcia, Lelio). Alejandro produces three falsified documents in which Enrique is accused of treason. The weight of the false testimony finally causes the king to suspect Enrique's loyalty, but Laura arrives in time to initiate a series of clarifications which result in Enrique's total vindication. Filipo kills Alejandro at the king's behest and is then killed himself. Carlos receives Porcia's hand, and Enrique marries Laura.

XV La misma conciencia acusa (Conscience Itself Accuses)

One of the twelve plays which appeared in Moreto's *Primera parte* in 1654, it is also included in the edition of Fernández-Guerra.[73] As Schaeffer has indicated,[74] its plot is taken from Lope's *Despertar a quien duerme* (*Waken the Sleeper*).

The Duke of Parma has usurped the throne from Carlos,

natural son of his cousin César, the former duke. The duke's guilty conscience should be eased when he sees, while on a hunting trip, the genuine pleasure which Carlos derives from the simple rustic life. The constant accusation by his conscience which is suggested by the title, however, drives the duke to obtain more proof of his security. In a situation not devoid of parallelism with the case of Segismundo in Calderón's *La vida es sueño* (*Life Is a Dream*), Carlos is brought to court to see if any latent envy can be detected in his attitude. None is evident, but the insecure duke decides to imprison Carlos just to be on the safe side. As he is led away, Carlos and the duke's daughter Margarita realize that they are in love.

Aroused from his passivity by this combination of indignation and an awakening love, Carlos seeks help from his cousin, the Duke of Milan. The Duke of Parma learns of Carlos's plea for help and orders his favorite, Enrique, to poison him and send his body to the Duke of Milan. Enrique, with compassion born of his interest in the victim's sister, plans only to give Carlos a sleeping potion. The *gracioso*, Tirso, eats the drugged meal intended for Carlos and, while Margarita helps Carlos to escape, is substituted for him in the box destined to be sent to the Duke of Milan.

After the comic scene of the discovery of Tirso, The Duke of Milan takes Parma. In an extremely short and weak dénouement, Carlos is betrothed to Margarita and proclaimed the new Duke of Parma.

XVI No puede ser (It Can't Be)

First published in *Parte XIV* of the *Escogidas* (Madrid: Domingo García y Morrás, 1660), frequently in *sueltas*, and in the Fernández-Guerra edition,[75] this play, derived from Lope de Vega's *El mayor imposible* (*The Greatest Impossibility*), has long been applauded by critics and by theater audiences as one of Moreto's best.

In the Academy of doña Ana, her suitor don Pedro Pacheco and don Félix de Toledo debate the issue which is the play's theme, the possibility of guarding a woman's reputation against her will. Don Pedro maintains the affirmative and wagers that he will be able to defend his beautiful sister Inés against the sun itself. Doña Ana, anxious to see her fiancé cured of his hyperprotective attitudes before she becomes his bride, proposes to don Félix that he court Inés and win the bet. Leaning heavily on the aid of his witty servant, the *gracioso* Tarugo, don Félix first arranges an exchange of pictures which awakens love on both sides.

Tarugo's stratagems engineer don Félix's admittance to the garden to meet Inés, her escape from the house, and the final revelation to don Pedro in the house of doña Ana that Félix and Inés have married, in spite of the confinement which her brother has enforced. In dignified surprise, Pedro recants his position in the debate and receives Ana's hand.

The influence exerted by *No puede ser* was immediate. In 1668, a five-act prose adaptation in English, written by Thomas St. Serfe, and entitled *Tarugo's Wiles: or, The Coffee House,* was published in London.[76] Its title page reveals that it had been performed at the theater of the Duke of York. A line in the unpaginated prologue, spoken by the Poet's Man, "My Master was lucky then at his first setting out to cruise the Coast of Spain," admits a Spanish influence, but there is no specific reference to Moreto or to the title of a source. Another line humorously alludes to the repetition of stock themes: "The Plot is like all others of the time; viz, a new toot out of an old horn." Although the names of all characters but Tarugo have been changed, the plot is virtually identical to Moreto's. Certain modifications have been effected to adapt the play to conventions acceptable to an English audience. Tarugo is not a servant, but rather the cousin of don Horatio, counterpart of don Félix in Moreto's play, and virtually the entire third act, which is set in the Coffee House, is devoted to short scenes which pass in review contemporary British types and issues.

In 1685, the English dramatist John Crowne published *Sir Courtly Nice,*[77] another five-act play in prose, with verse prologue, finis, and epilogue, based upon Moreto's *No puede ser,* a copy of which King Charles is reputed to have put in Crowne's hands. Substituting a feud between the families of Farewell and Belguard for the motif of the wager, Crowne's most drastic modification is the transformation of ˙don Diego, Moreto's insignificant potential rival of don Félix, into Sir Courtly Nice, one of the most memorable of Restoration fops, whose role may have been inspired by Moreto's *El lindo don Diego.* In her critical edition of *Sir Courtly Nice,* Charlotte Bradford Hughes aptly compares the play with its source: "The total effect of the character and plot alterations in Crowne is to contribute farcical and satirical effects at the expense of the wit of the Spanish original."[78] She further adds: "There could be no greater contrast to the high-comedy dialogue and the dignified moral plane of Moreto's play."[79]

The first play to come to the stage after the death of Charles II, *Sir Courtly Nice* opened at the Theatre Royal, Drury Lane, on May 4, 1685. It subsequently enjoyed great popular success and was both translated and adapted in German.

XVII Oponerse a las estrellas (Opposing the Stars)

First published in *Parte V* of the *Escogidas* (Madrid: Pablo de Val, 1653), where it is attributed to Matos, Martínez, and Moreto, the play's structure indicates to Fernández-Guerra that the collaborators did not always divide their work by acts, as he detects Moreto's hand at places in all three.[80]

The King of Athens has offered the hand of his daughter Fénix to the most victorious of the princes who are fighting for him in the battle against Ptolemy, King of Egypt. Alejandro, second son of the King of Thrace, is clearly the winner over Filipo and Lidoro, his competitors from Crete and Thebes, but the astrologer king, just prior to the end of the battle, has read in the stars that a Thracian prince will succeed him. Indignant, he does not award Fénix to Alejandro and announces further competition before a decision will be made.

Extremely disturbed by the adulation showered upon Alejandro by the populace and fearful of his potential alliance with Ptolemy, the insecure king arranges in the third act to have Alejandro killed. Our hero escapes, however, and returns as a disguised adventurous prince to challenge the princes of Crete and Thebes to fight for the hand of Fénix. While attempting to discover the identity of the mystery prince, the king's life is nearly lost as his horse goes berserk. He is saved by the dis-

guised Alejandro. When, the following day, he learns that
Alejandro is both the victor and his savior, the king concludes
that "opposing the stars" is wrong, and summarily gives Fénix
to Alejandro.

We tend to agree with Ruth Lee Kennedy that, if one must
assign acts to the collaborators, the second should be attributed
to Moreto.[81] The *gracioso* Merlín's impersonation of a foreign
prince, as Miss Kennedy points out, is Moretian in flavor, and
the atmosphere of much of the second act is reminiscent of the
competitive exercises of *El desdén con el desdén*.

XVIII El poder de la amistad (The Power of Friendship)

This is the only play of Moreto's which exists in a complete
autograph manuscript. Dated April 29, 1652,[82] it was first printed
in Moreto's *Primera parte* (1654), subsequently in the Fernández-Guerra edition,[83] and edited in 1968 by Dedrick.[84]

This *comedia* represents sufficient thematic parallel with *El
desdén con el desdén* to justify the contention that it could have
served as a source for Moreto's masterpiece.[85] In the disdainful
Princess Margarita, courted by the protagonist and two members of royalty, who is expected to select one of the three for
her husband on the basis of several competitions in which they
engage, one can see a situational, albeit pale, reflection of
Diana. The ultimate victory of the protagonist is partially
achieved by attacking the vanity of the haughty Margarita, but
the theme of the play, indicated by its title, is the power
wielded by friendship in bringing about a happy conclusion.

Alejandro, sent as an emissary of peace to Crete by the Scythian senate, has fallen in love with Margarita but, in spite of the
fact that he has saved her life from the attack of a wild boar,
he is rewarded with nothing but her scorn. He proposes to the
King of Crete that his marriage to Margarita would pave the
way for peace between their two nations, but is informed that
local practice requires princesses to select their own husbands.
Already in competition for Margarita's hand are the Prince of
Thebes and the Duke of Athens, each of whom counts heavily
on his great wealth and power. Alejandro, to the amusement
of all, claims that his friendship with Tebandro and Luciano

constitutes his greatest asset. In a handy division of labor, the scholar Luciano plans to help conquer Margarita while Captain Tebandro wages war against her father. Intelligence is thus used against the daughter and force against her father—*armas* and *letras* in tandem.

News that Tebandro has broken the truce impels both of Alejandro's competitors to depart for battle, leaving proxies to carry on for them in the competition for Margarita's hand.

Luciano wounds Margarita's vanity by telling her that Alejandro really loves her cousin Matilde and is just going along with the competitions as a courtesy to her father. There is also a garden scene reminiscent of a similar one in *El desdén con el desdén* in which the *gracioso* Moclín, recalling Polilla, keeps his master from succumbing to the temptation to look at his beloved.

At word of the approach of the victorious Tebandro, the king himself leaves for battle, threatening to behead Alejandro if Crete is victorious. When a report of Tebandro's defeat reaches the court, Margarita makes one more attempt to be haughty and domineering but when it is revealed that the first news was false and that her father has lost, she offers a full and open avowal of the love which has been growing in her for Alejandro. In addition to the marriage of the principals, Luciano will marry Matilde, and Moclín the maid Irene. The power of friendship has truly prevailed.

XIX   Primero es la honra (Honor First)

Published first in *Parte XVII* of the *Escogidas* (Madrid: Melchor Sánchez, 1662), and also in Fernández-Guerra's edition,[86] this *comedia* is founded upon the Appius Claudius-Virginia story. Schaeffer, unwilling to admit any originality on Moreto's part, claims, on the basis of internal evidence, that Moreto's play has a lost source and draws a parallel with Lope's *La ley ejecutada* (*The Law Enacted*) with which, though their themes are different, it manifests a similarity in plot structure characteristic of Lope rather than of Moreto.[87]

Set in Palermo, the action revolves around the machinations employed by the married King of Sicily to force his attentions upon Porcia, who shares strong mutual love with her cousin, Federico. The king's actions are no secret to anyone but Porcia's father, the admiral, who ingenuously requests royal permission for his daughter to marry Federico. The king grants the request but, doing his biblical counterpart King David one better, sends both Federico and the admiral to Messina to quell a rebellion.

The victorious warriors return too quickly and find the king attempting to dishonor Porcia. In secret conversation, the king claims that he would have married Porcia had the admiral not arranged for him another marriage. The only solution seen by the admiral to this honor dilemma is to kill his daughter. His attempt is unsuccessful, and Porcia is secretly restored to health by the queen.

The ensuing depression of the king is not relieved by the absence of Porcia. He has imprisoned the admiral. The king and Porcia simultaneously visit a distraught Federico, unheeded in his request that his servant Torrezno kill him to end a life which is but misery without Porcia. Recalling Garcilaso's famous sonnet, "Oh dulces prendas por mi mal halladas,"[88] he falls asleep. The king sees with him a picture of Porcia and, enraged, is about to kill Federico when Porcia shouts and awakens her lover. The king interprets her voice as a warning from heaven and instantaneously repents. In a crescendo of honor-motivated magnanimity, the queen offers to retire to a convent to permit the king to marry Porcia. The latter swears that she would kill herself before allowing that to happen. Not one to be outdone by his wife's magnanimity, the contrite king awards Porcia's hand to Federico, a marriage paralleled by the union of the servants of each.

XX   El rey don Enrique el Enfermo (King Henry the Sickly)

In *The Dramatic Art of Moreto*,[89] Ruth Lee Kennedy accepted Paz y Melia's[90] assertion that the Biblioteca Nacional manuscript version[91] of this play was identical to a printed version which appeared in *Parte IX* of the *Escogidas* (Madrid: Gregorio Rodríguez, 1657). When she subsequently was able to examine the manuscript, however, she discovered that the two versions are entirely different.[92] The printed version, which she postulates to have been written at an earlier date, although not printed until after the manuscript version had been presented on the stage, is announced in the table of contents and on its title page as the work of *seis ingenios* ("six wits"), who go unnamed, although the claim is made in its final lines that it was written by *un Toledano* (a resident of Toledo). The manuscript carries precise indication of the exact portion which should be attributed to each of the six collaborators, who are named in order of their contribution: Zabaleta, Martínez de Meneses, Rosete, Villaviciosa, Cáncer, and Moreto. According to Miss Kennedy, the three major dramatic episodes common to both versions derive, in the manuscript, from Lope de Vega's *Los novios de Hornachuelos* (*The Sweethearts from Hornachuelos*).[93] Whereas the action of the loosely-woven printed play centers around the historical figures Enrique III (1379–1406) and his cousin Enrique of Aragon, Marquis of Villena, well-known Spanish author whose study of alchemy and occult sciences earned for him the reputation of a sorcerer, the manuscript, according to Miss Kennedy, centers its interest on the political struggle between Enrique III, weakened by fevers, and the rich nobles who attempt to rob him of his patrimony. The insolent don Mendo, who has dishonored doña Elvira under a promise of marriage which he never intended to keep, is ultimately beheaded and simultaneously married to Leonor as Enrique manifests his regal power.

The fact that Moreto's contribution is the final sixth of the play leads Miss Kennedy to remark: "The conviction that the ending of *El rey don Enrique el Enfermo* is very near the original is strengthened by the fact that this is the only play in Moreto's whole secular theatre which has a tragic end."[94]

XXI El valiente justiciero (The Valiant Justice-maker)

Subtitled *El rico-hombre de Alcalá* (*The Grandee from Alcalá*) and printed first in *Parte IX* of the *Escogidas* (Madrid: Gregorio Rodríguez, 1657), then in the Fernández-Guerra collection,[95] in a 1966 variorum edition,[96] and in a 1971 edition of Frank Casa,[97] this *comedia* is generally cited as the most flagrant example of Moreto's plagiarism,[98] although it is acclaimed by some critics as a skillful adaptation.[99] The source play is *El rey Don Pedro en Madrid y el infazón de Illescas* (*King Pedro in Madrid and the Grandee of Illescas*), inconclusively attributed both to Lope de Vega and Tirso de Molina. Miss Kennedy points out that in the third act, "at least twelve out of the eighteen scenes of Moreto are in content virtually identical"[100] with those of the source play. Casa sees the source play essentially as a struggle involving a king who felt compelled to prove his worth as a man against an individual adversary. In his opinion, regardless of the evident parallels, Moreto has reoriented the theme to a political struggle between the monarchy and rebellious feudal nobles.[101]

Prior to the play's action, the villain don Tello has dishonored Leonor under a promise of marriage. He then has the audacity to have his men abduct María, intended bride of Rodrigo, just before their wedding ceremony is to take place. Rodrigo and Leonor seek King Pedro, from whom their hope of retribution raises the question of which of the two frequently used sobriquets of the famous King Pedro I of Castile (1350–1369, b. 1334), "the Cruel" or "the Just," was the more applicable.

At this point, Moreto introduces a subplot involving Enrique de Trastamara, Pedro's historical half-brother and eventual assassin, who is seen fleeing from the king. When Pedro's horse gives out, Leonor and Rodrigo aid him. Having heard their accounts of Tello's behavior, but without revealing his identity, Pedro instructs them to go to Madrid and promises that he will arrange for them to talk with the king. Using the pseudonym Aguilera de la Montaña, Pedro visits Tello and is witness to his extreme arrogance and disrespect for the king. Deciding to take no immediate action, Pedro ends the act by soliloquizing that he will take care of Tello in such a manner that those for whom he is "the Cruel," will, in the future, hold him to be "the Just."

Act II is set in court, where Pedro is giving audience. Rodrigo, Leonor, and Tello arrive in order, all realizing for the first time that the man they had met earlier was the king. Pedro humiliates Tello, first by ignoring his presence, then by obliging the troubled antagonist to return a glove which he has intentionally dropped, and finally by smashing his head against a post. Pedro orders Tello to give his hand in marriage to Leonor as he had promised but adds that, whether he chooses to obey or not, he will be beheaded the following day.

In the third act, the action is less well organized and another subplot is introduced. After rejecting requests by María and Leonor that Tello be pardoned, Pedro carries out a scheme designed to prove his superiority to this upstart grandee. He arranges for Tello to escape and then, disguised, defeats him in a duel. After revealing his identity, he allows Tello to flee. At this point Pedro is confronted by the ghost of a priest whom he has killed. The apparition drops the king's dagger and announces it as the instrument by which Enrique will kill him. Emphasizing the ominous symbol, Enrique arrives, picks up the fallen dagger, and returns it to the king. Tello has been apprehended. Pedro orders the death sentence carried out, but Enrique intercedes, and pardon is granted. Tello will marry Leonor and María will be united with Rodrigo.

Typical of Moreto's adaptations, his gains are in the area of structure, which is improved at the expense of lyricism and poetic flights. It is hard to account for the fact that Moreto has retained both of the subplots found in the source play. He does reduce the appearances of the ghost from three to one but, as Miss Kennedy points out, the two subplots "though interrelated, have little connection with the main thread of the story."[102]

In spite of the degree of dependence on its source, however, *El valiente justiciero,* in the opinion of Casa, "develops in the same manner as in the original, but with so many changes in the attitudes and motivations of the characters that a completely new conception of the theme evolves. In refashioning Pedro from a disturbed man to a confident monarch, Moreto has abandoned the theme of the personal struggle between two violent individuals, and presents a play based on challenge to royal authority."[103] There is a nineteenth-century *refundición* of this play by Dionisio Solís.[104]

XXII Yo por vos y vos por otro (I for You and You for Another)

Published in the Fernández-Guerra edition,[105] it was first printed in the *Segunda parte* of Moreto's *comedias* in 1676. Both Mabel Harlan[106] and Fernández-Guerra[107] note an analogy with *El desdén con el desdén* which Miss Kennedy considers so slight as not to be of concern.[108] As we have noted elsewhere, although not central to the action, the theme of defeating disdain with disdain is obvious in *Yo por vos y vos por otro*, and several expressions definitely recall Moreto's masterpiece.[109]

While in America, don Iñigo de Mendoza and don Enrique de Ribera were close friends of don Gómez de Cabrera who, after becoming a widower, returned to Madrid to arrange the marriages of his two daughters, Margarita and Isabel. Don Gómez, hoping to pair Iñigo with Margarita and Enrique with Isabel, sent pictures of his daughters which pleased the men. When their pictures were sent in return, they were accidentally switched and the girls fell in love with the wrong men. The action is composed of several comic scenes in which the young gallants, following the advice of the witty lackey, Motril, attempt to change the minds of the girls. In the first act Motril paints false verbal pictures of each man to the girl who loves him, emphasizing negative traits which he knows are repulsive to each girl. Margarita and Isabel see through this and remain firm in their choices.

From the beginning of the second act, Motril suggests the substitution of deeds for words. Enrique pretends to be the jealous lover of Margarita, and Iñigo to be the overbearing and possessive suitor of Isabel. It is here that lines recalling *El desdén con el desdén* abound, including such obvious examples as *el picado con el desdén quiere más* ("someone stung by disdain loves even more") and *el desdén a amor irrita* ("disdain stirs up love"). The girls finally discover, through the eavesdropping of their maid Inés, that each man is feigning traits to discourage a love to which he is not inclined to correspond. Caught in their act, Iñigo and Enrique declare that they will give in and marry according to the girls' wishes. However, speaking magnanimously for her sister, Margarita settles the matter by saying that they will marry according to the men's preferences. Paralleling the marriages of their masters, the servants Marcelo and Motril are paired with Juana and Inés.

This delightful, fast-moving comedy was recast in 1826 by don José Fernández-Guerra, father of Moreto's editor, under the title *Ir contra el viento* (*Going Against the Wind*).[110]

CHAPTER 7

Teatro Menor *(One-Act Plays)*

AS is so frequently the case, general, widespread knowledge of Spanish Golden Age theater is limited to the relatively few plays which have been at one time or another "consecrated" by editors and critics, and subsequently published and republished. It is probably correct to assume that the name of Lope de Vega evokes little more than *Peribáñez* and *Fuenteovejuna* to thousands of dilettante *aficionados*; that Calderón represents *La vida es sueño* (*Life Is a Dream*), and perhaps *El alcalde de Zalamea* (*The Mayor of Zalamea*), etc. In the case of Moreto, the two titles which "signify" Moreto to thousands of students of Spanish literature are *El desdén con el desdén* and *El lindo don Diego*. It seems obvious that nothing approaching full appreciation of Spanish Golden Age authors can be accomplished until the texts of more works of these authors are made available to a wide reading public.

This is particularly true with regard to Moreto's *teatro menor*, comprised of thirty-eight short pieces, of which, excepting those edited in two unpublished dissertations,[1] only sixteen are available in editions published or reprinted later than 1691, of which eight did not appear before the recent date of 1965. That these short pieces represent facets of Moreto not usually revealed in his full-length plays would seem even more to underscore the need for their availability.

In the witty roles assigned to his *graciosos* in the full-length plays, we see a glimmer of the joy with which Moreto must have conceived, structured, portrayed, and integrated comic situations in a frequently noncomic context. It is only very infrequently, as in the case of the caricature of the dandy in *El lindo don Diego*, that this humorous, satiric thrust is predominant. The hilariously satiric *costumbrista* dimension of Moreto becomes jubilant, unrestrained, and the dominant feature of the delightful and perceptive *entremeses, bailes,* and *loas* which he created.

Catalogues of titles with limited descriptive and bibliographic comment were published by Fernández-Guerra,[2] La Barrera,[3] and Cotarelo,[4] but, with the exception of eighteenth- and nineteenth-century *sueltas,* and the nineteenth-century printing of his sole *auto,*[5] the appearance of modern editions of Moreto's short pieces possibly did not begin until 1932, when Robert J. Carner published the *Entremés del vestuario.*[6] It was eight years later that he edited thirty-one of Moreto's short pieces for the Harvard doctoral dissertation mentioned above. Rafael Balbín has edited four titles, including *El vestuario,* of whose prior publication he was unaware;[7] Sainz de Robles published two in 1943;[8] another appeared in 1944 in a collection edited by E. Juliá Martínez;[9] Felicidad Buendía published two more in 1965;[10] two pieces which first appeared in the rarest of the seventeenth-century collections became available in 1969;[11] Hannah Bergman's 1970 anthology[12] contains two more; and another two were published the following year by Francisco Rico.[13] Balbín has promised a more complete study of Moreto's *teatro menor,*[14] but as these lines are written, it has yet to appear.

Since no comprehensive treatment of Moreto's entire dramatic production has appeared in a single volume, it is necessary to realize that judgments such as the following, by Ruth Lee Kennedy, are based on the study of only his full-length plays: "Moreto's theatre, as a picture of customs, is on the whole disappointing. It is an idealized world, one filled with courteous gentlemen and charming women who move about in a milieu of semi-intellectualism. Of the corruption of the court, its love of ease, its ostentation, its crafty selfishness, its flagrant dissipation, there is only an indirect reflection. . . . Only rarely does stark reality penetrate the elegant atmosphere of his drawing-room."[15] Even the most cursory glance at his short pieces will reveal that, in this genre, Moreto is a master in the portrayal of the customs and of the nonidealized lower strata of society which are notable for their absence from his full-length plays.

The thematic distribution of his short plays is most indicative of Moreto's predilection for lively, lighthearted satire inspired by his contemporary society. Typically, a stereotype, a profession, or a custom is either satirized, or simply dramatized with few if any satiric or didactic overtones. As a matter of fact, the satire of Moreto is so joyous that one often doubts that he intended a moral lesson.

For convenience, we will discuss Moreto's short pieces under the following headings: Religious Works, Parodies of Traditional Ballads, Vehicles for Juan Rana, Burlesque Pieces, and Works of Circumstance Presented as Part of Royal Celebrations. A separate chapter will be devoted to plays dealing with several areas of social satire and various nonsatiric portrayals of society.

I *Religious Works*

A. Auto de la gran casa de Austria y Divina Margarita (Auto of the Great House of Austria and the Divine Margarita)

First published in *Navidad y Corpus Christi* (Madrid, 1664), the *auto* also appears in Eduardo González Pedroso's collection in the *Biblioteca de Autores Españoles*.[16] John Reynolds[17] has shown Moreto's *auto* to be an adaptation of Mira de Amescua's *La fe de Hungría (The Faith of Hungary)*.

The work, in short, anachronistically explicates unsuccessful attempts of the avowed English reformer Wycliffe (1320?-1384) to dissuade Ladislao and his queen Margarita from their Catholic faith. Spurred on by the Devil, Wycliffe then steals a monstrance and an image of the Virgin from the church and takes them to a hermitage, where the two villains plan their desecration. The monstrance is left to burn in the hermitage while the image of the Virgin is thrown into the river. Both are saved miraculously by Margarita and Ladislao, and Wycliffe is converted. Jaime Mariscal de Gante praises the *auto* as poetry while rejecting its theology because of its portrayal of "brutal and horrendous ... sacrilege."[18]

What is of particular interest, as noted by González Pedroso,[19] is Moreto's rejection of the formula of allegorical figures found in the Calderonian *auto*. He limits himself to dramatic use of the Devil and to no more than incidental use of the Three Kings. This secularization is not common to the *autos* of the period and, if it had succeeded in replacing its antecedent form, it might have drawn the genre back closer to profane drama. Instead, the *autos* continued to range farther and farther from reality and, in so doing, set in motion their eventual demise.

As in the case of his *comedias*, Moreto here also demonstrates his great skill in the creation of comic figures. The singing Sacristan, who first sees the thieves and then appears later for comic relief during the recovery of the monstrance and the image of the Virgin, provides a delightful scene while cleaning the church. In his mangled pronunciation of words, he reminds us of Sancho Panza; in his initial detection of the Devil by the smell of sulphur, and in his attempt to exorcize him by using the infernal language of the *culteranistas*, he gives genuine humor to this atypical *auto*. It is regrettable that we do not have more examples of Moreto's work in this genre.[20]

B.   Loa sacramental para la fiesta del Corpus, representada en Valencia (Sacramental Prologue for the Celebration of Corpus Christi in Valencia)

Although Sánchez Arjona[21] reports that Moreto wrote *loas* and *sainetes* for the celebration of Corpus in Seville in 1656, of the four extant *loas* of Moreto, this is the only *loa sacramental*. The one known printing of this *loa* is found in *Vergel de entremeses* (Zaragoza, 1675). Although written for a religious celebration, it is a gloss of Góngora's secular ballad, "El español de Orán" ("The Spaniard of Oran"), in which allegorical figures provide an account of the world from its creation to the crucifixion of Christ. Written to introduce an *auto* which is announced at its conclusion, the *loa* contains an interesting definition of allegory and a comic scene in which the allegorical figure "Ignorance" charmingly mispronounces words in a manner reminiscent of Sancho Panza, but it contains little to invalidate Cotarelo's claim[22] that this work contributes nothing to Moreto's fame.

II   *Parodies of Traditional Ballads*

Rafael Balbín edited two of Moreto's previously unpublished *bailes* in 1942.[23] In a preliminary study, he elaborates his reasons for calling these two works, and another similar in nature, *bailes paródicos* ("parodic dances"). Balbín finds in these three works the development of two parallel elements:

1. An historical or tragic anecdote, or series of events, deeply and traditionally known by the author's public, and therefore only briefly dramatized.

2. The same anecdote carried to its full development by the same dramatic figures and in parallel form, but which, although it leads to the same dramatic dénouement, evolves with the following alterations:

a) A notable change of epoch.

b) An evident change of setting.

c) Atmosphere transposed to a low social level.

d) Scenic exaggeration.

e) A degrading of the motives of the protagonists.

f) Truncation of the psychic processes of the characters.

g) Conversion of the tragic sense of the anecdote to a comic sense.

The three pieces in question are all among Moreto's shortest plays, ranging in length from 144 to 180 verses. They are all frequently interspersed with music and are characterized by a rich literary and parodic development.

A. Baile del Conde Claros (Dance of Count Claros)

The *baile* parodies the ballad accounts[24] of the love of Count Claros for the Princess Claraniña in Paris during the reign of Charlemagne. This aspect is lightly treated by Moreto, who develops his parodic parallel in the following ways (compare with Balbín's categories):

a) Through allusions to the seventeenth-century popular dance, the *Juan Redondo*, to the siege of Santa Fe, and to well-known verses of Góngora.

b) Through mention of Zamora, Sierra Nevada, Yepes, and Ocaña.

c) Through the use of slang expressions in the speeches of the Princess and Charlemagne, and cynical reference to the celebrated *jaque* ("bully") Añasco el de Talavera.

d, e) Through conversion into abject fear of the "respectful dread" that Count Claros felt for the King.

    f)   Through elimination of the long passages in which the King consults the grandees of the court and those in which the *degollación* ("throat-cutting") is ordered and described. Here the decisions of the King are brusque and mechanical.

    g)   The tragic death of Claraniña, which follows the execution of Count Claros in the ballads, is converted into a *baile* in which even the deceased count resuscitates to take part.

B. Baile de Lucrecia y Tarquino (Dance of Lucretia and Tarquin)

This *baile*, which, like the *Baile del Conde Claros*, existed only in manuscript until published by Balbín, was also transcribed by Raymond MacCurdy in 1963.[25] Its source is the rape of Lucretia by Tarquin and her subsequent suicide, for which Moreto followed fairly closely *romance* 519 of the Durán collection.

In a true parody of the legendary pursuit and rape, Tarquino intends to use force to bring Lucrecia to his will, but a *dueña* intervenes and suggests that he pay for the favors he seeks. He offers her the niggardly sum of half a *real*, and she begins to doubt that her resistance will withstand the king's "liberality." Just as Lucrecia affirms that she has decided to be honorable and resist, the king steals a kiss on the hand. Distraught with shame, and buckling under her dishonor, she stabs herself with Tarquino's fallen dagger. In response to a musician's question as to whether they should call a priest for the dead woman, Lucrecia suggests a *baile* instead, as the customary way to end *fiestas*.

Her husband Colatino comes on the scene and, upon learning that the king is to blame for his wife's death, swears vengeance. Just then, an old man appears and exhorts the populace to vengeance. Led by Colatino, the insurgents kill Tarquino; when he says that he is already in the other world, Colatino urges him to marry Lucrecia there (to repair the honor which has been stained). Parodying the *comedia* formula, the two dead characters join hands in symbolic marriage as the *baile* ends.

Balbín, in his analysis, calls attention to examples of all of the areas outlined in his description of Moreto's parodic formula: reference to contemporary coins, songs, dances, social customs, etc. Substantive changes include the substitution of a furtive kiss for the historical rape, a change which diminishes justification for the indignant anger of Colatino and the abrupt decision of Lucrecia to stab herself to death. Moreto, by transforming the tragic demise of Lucrecia and the tumultuous punishment of Tarquino into a preposterous marriage in death, offers, in his desire to achieve harmony, a substitute formula for the typical Golden Age practice of resolving affronts of honor through vengeance.

C. Baile entremesado del rey don Rodrigo y la Cava (Interlude-like Dance of King Rodrigo and La Cava)

This is one of the shortest of Moreto's pieces, consisting of only 144 verses. It first appeared in *Autos sacramentales con cuatro comedias nuevas* (Madrid: María de Quiñones, 1655). The object of Moreto's parody is the legendary rape of Florinda, known as La Cava, daughter of Count Julian, governor of Ceuta, by Rodrigo, last Gothic king of Spain (709–711). According to the legend, the irate father, to avenge this affront to his honor, aided the Moors in their initial conquest of Spain.

As in *Lucrecia y Tarquino,* the "violation" is represented symbolically by nothing more than a kiss on the hand, taken by force. Many lines from ballads are incorporated into this piece, but the disparate elements of the parody are less well integrated than is the case in the other two works which comprise this group. The wittiest part is one section of a dialogue between Rodrigo and La Cava in which she chides him for his action by asking what future books and histories will say about his horrid act. He suggests they will probably justify him by imagining that it happened on a sultry St. John's Eve.

III *Vehicles for Juan Rana*

Several authors wrote short works exclusively as vehicles for the greatest comic actor of the time, Cosme Pérez,[26] a well-known *gracioso* in the company of Juan Bautista as early as

1617. He appeared on the stage as late as 1665 and died in Madrid in 1673. He became so identified with the stage name of Juan Rana that it is used in some legal documents. According to a single portrait which hangs in the Real Academia Española de la Lengua,[27] he was quite fat and excessively short. Contemporary comment attests to the fact that by merely appearing on the stage, without even speaking, he moved the audience to laughter and applause.[28] Cotarelo has catalogued more than forty *entremeses* written exclusively for Juan Rana.[29]

A.   Entremés del retrato vivo (Interlude of the Live Portrait)

First published in *Rasgos del ocio* (Madrid: Joseph Fernández de Buendía, 1661), this delightful *entremés* is available in the anthology published by Hannah Bergman in 1970.[30]

Juana reports to her friend the great success of a trick which she has played on her husband, Juan Rana. She has, with the help of a painter, made him think that he is a portrait of himself. The ingenuous spouse has accordingly remained in his frame all day without making a sound. With Juan in this ridiculous state, Juana now plans to receive visits from the very people who have motivated his jealousy. Juan Rana submits to having himself dusted, shaken, and moved about; he sees a courtier regale Juana with a fancy hair ribbon, he trembles as a *valiente* feigns sword thrusts at "his portrait" and, when the ravenous husband begs to be fed, the painter stifles the pleas for food by painting Juan's mouth a little smaller. After the retouching, he orders the painting placed in the sun to dry.

The slapstick builds to a crescendo as Juana suggests that all present point out the portrait's imperfections and how to correct them. While dancing around the picture, everyone contributes his critique and corresponding remedy: because the nose is not long enough, it is pulled; the open mouth is pinched to make it close, etc. Each remedy is punctuated by a cry of "¡Ay!" which emanates from "the portrait." Thus is jealousy punished in this farcical but witty and entertaining *entremés*.

Cotarelo[31] feels that the work was first staged in 1660, but reference in it to an Italian stage engineer named Vaggio del Bianco, who died in 1657, leads Hannah Bergman[32] to assign the middle of that year as a *terminus ad quem*.

B. Entremés del ayo (Interlude of the Tutor)

First published in *Autos sacramentales y al nacimiento de Christo* (Madrid: Antonio Francisco de Zafra, 1675), this piece could also be cross-referenced in our last category, since it was performed at court as part of a birthday celebration for Philip IV. Its contents, however, are clearly the typical vehicle for Juan Rana, who presents himself for an announced position as tutor. Morales, his employer, appears to be but slightly more intelligent than Juan Rana, and their repartee, although farcically funny, does not attain a very high intellectual level.

Fencing and dancing teachers are sent away by Juan Rana, who does not want others to do what he can do himself. The dancing master finally challenges Juan Rana to show how much he knows about dancing. Caught up in the mood, all ends in a flurry of dances as Juan Rana says he will make the dancing master's group perform the dances of Valencia and Catalonia, as well as the *Tarantela* and the *Guineo*.

C. La loa de Juan Rana (Juan Rana's Prologue)

First published in *Rasgos del ocio*, segunda parte (Madrid, 1664), this *loa* was performed, according to Cotarelo,[33] before the King and Queen on December 22, 1662, and was frequently reprinted. Though it does not appear in Balbín's list of the works comprising Moreto's *teatro menor*, it is one of two works by Moreto published by Hannah Bergman in 1970. Basing her conclusion on the fact that the actors who are mentioned as participating in the *loa* were all together only for a short time, she suggests the probable dates of 1662–1663.[34]

Juan Rana serves as a comic pretext to present the principal actors in the *comedia* to which the *loa* is prefatory. The device used is based on the fact that Juan Rana, in *entremeses* written by Moreto and by other dramatists, is always gullible in the extreme. The actor Orozco, requesting that Juan Rana perform a *loa* in which he will play six different roles, claims that he will be able to place him in front of a mirror in which he will see himself as someone else.

As the unbelievably naïve Juan Rana steps in front of the false "mirror," which in reality is just a frame, he successively "sees himself" as Escamilla, Olmedo, Godoy, María de Quiñones, and María de Prado.[35] The astonished Juan Rana draws each successive manifestation of his "reflection" from the frame, and thus presents to the audience the other principal actors.

D. Entremés de los muertos vivos (Interlude of the Living Dead)

Found in *Flor de entremeses, bailes y loas* (Zaragoza: Diego Dormer, 1676), this is cited by Balbín[36] as one of the nine pieces falsely attributed to Moreto, an assertion which he plans to prove in a forthcoming publication. The work is not included in Cotarelo's list, nor is it mentioned in Carner's dissertation. It may very well not be Moreto's; if it is, it certainly is not one of his best *entremeses*. Juan Pérez wants to marry Isabel, but her brother, Juan Rana, will not give his permission. After a mock sword fight, the ever-gullible Juan Rana is persuaded of his own death. Isabel covers him with a sheet and begs alms for his burial. An old man, who has nothing else to offer, gives bread and wine, but when musicians come to offer a snappy tune, Juan Rana pops up and dances to its strains. After saying that he is metaphorically "dying" to speak to Isabel, Juan Pérez lies down and plays dead. While Juan Rana is dancing, the old man, seeing that he was tricked into contributing for an unnecessary burial, leaves to dress as a devil and exact vengeance. Upon his return, both Juans are lying on the ground as if dead. They both rise and the pedestrian farce ends as all flee in mutual fear of one another.

IV *Burlesque Pieces*

Some of Moreto's *entremeses* appear simply, or at least predominantly, to be burlesque pieces in which human foibles and accidental or contrived circumstances are portrayed for their comic value, with no apparent pretension of more weight.

A. Entremés de la reliquia (Interlude of the Relic)

First appearing in *Theatro poético* (Zaragoza: Juan de Ybar, 1658), this *entremés* was subsequently published at least three times in the seventeenth century and was reworked, according to Cotarelo,[37] by Malo de Molina.

The *gracioso* Gilote complains of being beaten by his wife Aldonza. A neighbor offers to pass on to him a relic which he has received from a cleric and which worked well when he faced a similar problem early in his marriage. It turns out that the relic is a stick, and the slapstick humor on which the *entremés* is based consists of instructions for its bearer first to lift his right foot, then his arm, and then to administer it in a striking motion. After trying the "relic" out on his neighbor, Gilote then uses it on his wife when she refuses to obey his order to speak more softly.

Worlds apart from the nobles of Moreto's full-length plays, the characters in such short pieces as this are intensely earthy. Aldonza was pregnant when she married Gilote. When asked if he was not aware of that circumstance, he replies: "No sir, for pregnancies are like winter clouds; we see where they empty but not where they swell."

B.   Entremés de los órganos y el reloj (Interlude of the Organs and the Clock)

Published first in *Rasgos del ocio* (Madrid, 1664), the intrigue is related to three pressing needs of a small town:

1. The barber has died and must be replaced.
2. The sacristan, who has resigned, must also be replaced.
3. The church needs both an organ and a clock, but no one can decide which to buy first.

The lovers of the mayor's nieces, Luisa and Tomasa, arrive in town posing as organ maker and barber respectively, followed by Teresa and Quiteria, whom they have jilted. To avenge their jealousy, Teresa and Quiteria disguise themselves as students and each obtains a position as sacristan. In a thoroughly slapstick scene, after attempting to deceive the mayor with an organ painted on a screen, the four women and two men are caught arguing by the mayor. In an inversion of the Mambrino's helmet episode of *Don Quijote*, the barber protects himself from the hammer blows of his former lover by boasting as he dons his basin: "My basin will serve me as a helmet." Pushing farce to its limit, the spectacle of the girl with a hammer pounding on the barber's head is stated to resemble a clock, the other item needed by the church. Luisa and Tomasa declare their intentions of marrying their lovers, and the sacristans, their vengeance satiated, are satisfied to have bruised the heads of their deceivers.

C. Entremés de la Perendeca (Interlude of Perendeca)

Fernández-Guerra claims to have possessed the autograph manuscript of this piece,[38] which was first published in *Tardes apacibles* (Madrid: Andrés García de la Iglesia, 1663). La Perendeca, played by Jusepa Manzana, has, against her husband's wishes, invited friends home during his absence. Three times he returns home before the guests can leave, the last time with a dinner guest, and each time the hostess has her guests pose as objects as diverse as a boiler, a chimney, and the dining room table. The visual humor of this piece may have been great, especially the scenes in which the husband pokes Frutos, who is playing a chimney, with a roasting spit and the latter blows ashes all over his tormentor, and the dinner scene in which the "table" reaches up, pilfers, and consumes food and drink before the host and his guest are able to partake.

The work, obviously much paler on paper than it would have been on stage, contains several references to the subtitle of Tirso's Don Juan play, *El convidado de piedra* (*The Guest of Stone*).

D. Entremés de la campanilla (Interlude of the Little Bell)

Seemingly inspired by Quevedo's *La hora de todos* (*Everyone's Time*), as noted by Cotarelo,[39] the earliest editions of this play are found in *Floresta de entremeses* (Madrid: Antonio de Zafra, 1691) and the undated Dormer edition of *Entremeses varios*. It is simply the story of a magic bell which, when sounded, causes all but the striker and the holder of a special ribbon to be frozen instantly, the spell to last until the end of the world unless broken by the music of a guitar, harp, or castanets.

Manuela criticizes her husband Escamilla for having spent

all of his money (forty *reales*) to buy a bell which resembles nothing but a common cowbell. Escamilla reveals that it belonged to an astrologer and offers to demonstrate its special properties. Four pairs of passersby are victims of the bell: a fastidious gentleman and his tailor, a gallant and his money-hungry lady, two *valientes* who have just completed the verbal preliminaries to a duel which never materializes, and two young ladies about to picnic. Just before being frozen in her tracks, however, one of these ladies prepares for the dénouement by announcing that don Roque is on the way with harp and guitar music.

After arresting the motion of the fourth couple, Escamilla carelessly leaves the bell and goes for their food. Manuela then sounds the bell, freezing its owner, and begins to feast, but the musicians arrive and all are released from the spell.

E. Entremés de los sacristanes burlados (Interlude of the Deceived Sacristans)

Found first in *Primera parte del Parnaso nuevo y amenidades del gusto* (Madrid: Andrés García de la Iglesia, 1670), this play contains some of the more ludicrous slapstick to be found in Moreto's theater. The father of Isabel and Luisa objects violently to his daughters' relationships with two sacristans whom he considers *pícaros*. While the father is out, the two sacristans come to visit. Both are social climbers and their use of Latin is designed simply to impress the girls. The sacristans insult each other and decide to have a recitation contest, to be judged by Isabel and Luisa. The ensuing deadlock provokes a physical scuffle, interrupted by the arrival of the father and a neighbor. Caught red-handed, the girls make the sacristans bring a brazier and pose as bellows. The supercredulous father leaves to instruct the blacksmith to come and pick up the bellows. Prior to his return, the girls have placed one sacristan on top of the other and pass them off as a bench. When it wavers, the father and neighbor tie its parts together to make it steady, and then "the bench" is beaten by the four remaining characters. Amidst this rambunctious ending, the neighbor advises the father to let his daughters marry the men of their choice.

F. Entremés de la burla de Pantoja y el doctor (Interlude of
    Pantoja's Trick and the Doctor)

Published as Moreto's in *Autos sacramentales y al nacimiento
de Christo* (Madrid, 1675), it is, according to La Barrera,[40]
attributed in a 1664 edition to Quiñones de Benavente. A discussion of the work is included here because of a definite
relationship to a very authentically Moretian source. This *entremés* is essentially a scene but slightly modified from the
full-length play *Las travesuras de Pantoja* (*Pantoja's Pranks*).[41]
Pantoja, in love with doña Juana, daughter of the overly protective barrister don Lope, has his problem solved by his crafty
servant Guijarro ("Pebble"), who goes before don Lope with
a feigned case involving intricate, ridiculous, and utterly con-
fusing genealogies. When the barrister is totally befuddled,
Guijarro stands in front of him to block his view as Pantoja
steals from the room with Juana. When her father discovers her
absence, the two return, announce they are already married,
and—to music—Lope blesses their union and issues the moral
warning so often sounded throughout Moreto's theater: "He
who guards his daughters in this manner deserves to have them
stolen from him in this manner."

V *Works of Circumstance Presented as Part of
Royal Celebrations*

Few, if any, of the distinguished playwrights were exempt
from the obligation to compose works to celebrate or commemorate events of importance to royalty.

A. Entremés del alcalde de Alcorcón (Interlude of the Mayor
    of Alcorcón)

Published in *Tardes apacibles de gustoso entretenimiento*
(Madrid, 1663), this piece is part of the elaborate celebration
of the birth of Prince Próspero on November 28, 1657.[42] Although
Juan Rana has a lead role, the play emphasizes the Prince's
birth rather than the typical exploitation of the humorousness
of its protagonist. The towns of Alcorcón, Mósteles, and Leganés
have all elected Juan Rana mayor. He haltingly and comically

delivers congratulatory lines to the proud royal parents, presents a catechism to the Infanta Teresa, and hails the birth of the long-awaited heir to the throne.

B. Entremés de las fiestas de palacio (Interlude for the Palace Celebrations)

Also published in *Tardes apacibles* (Madrid, 1663), this is yet another jubilant celebration of the birth of the Prince. According to Cotarelo[43] the play was performed for the Queen on December 6, 1658 as she went to Mass. The mayor asks what his bailiff plans to do about fireworks for the celebration. The burlesque answer is that even houses will be burned to create a real celebration. All sorts of festivities in Madrid are announced as the capital revels in its jubilation.

C. Loa para los años del Emperador de Alemania (Introit for the Birthday of the German Emperor)

In a slightly different subgenre, this *loa*, first published in *Rasgos del ocio* (Madrid, 1661), was written to celebrate the visit to Madrid of Emperor Ferdinand III of the Holy Roman Empire. Ferdinand, born in 1608, was married to the Infanta María Ana, daughter of Philip III and sister of Philip IV. Crowned King of Hungary in 1625, of Bohemia in 1627, and of the Roman Empire in 1631, his three crowns are the chief topic of the play. Luisa Romero, one of the four famous actresses who recite the *loa*, plays the allegorical role of Spain. Francisca Verdugo, Gerónima de Olmedo, and Mariana Romero all bring flowers symbolizing the virtues of Ferdinand. They weave their flowers into a wreath and present it to Philip IV. Cotarelo states that the *loa* was performed on July 13, 1655.[44]

CHAPTER 8

Teatro Menor *(cont.)*

COTARELO[1] praises the quantity, variety, and quality of the *costumbrista* vein of Moreto's *teatro menor* and ranks him ahead of all contemporary practitioners of the genre excepting only Cervantes and Quiñones de Benavente. The short pieces treated in this chapter are abundant proof of Moreto's capacity to observe and dramatize levels of society far distant from the dignified drawing room and palace scenarios which almost completely monopolize his full-length plays. Following satires of the *valentón*, women of easy virtue, social climbers, picaresque backgrounds, and the honor code, we will close our treatment of Moreto's *teatro menor* with a group of plays which vividly bring to life the theater of Moreto's day.

I The *Valentón*

One of Moreto's favorite objects of satire is the false, fraudulent *valiente*, or, in its augmentative form, the *valentón* ("hired ruffian"), a decadent and parasitic type ridiculed in several *entremeses*. Neither Cervantes nor Molière, according to Cotarelo,[2] surpasses Moreto in the conception and elaboration of his satirically comic situations involving the bully and other characters who lent themselves so readily to mockery.

A. Entremés del cortacaras (Interlude of the Face Slasher)

First published in *Primera parte del Parnaso nuevo y amenidades del gusto* (Madrid: Andrés García de la Iglesia, 1670), this *entremés* dramatizes the amorous success of Lorenzo who, told by Juana not to love her until he becomes a brave fellow, enrolls as a student of Master Rodrigo. During the training period, Master Rodrigo receives a commission to slash the face of a certain young woman. He decides to send his apprentice to help him gain some practical experience. Lorenzo, in the town plaza, discovers that the girl, whom he finds surrounded by four *valientes*, is none other than his beloved Juana. He boldly approaches Juana and measures the area of her face which is to be his target (he is supposed to cut specifically from the nose to the ear!). When asked by Juana's four escorts what he is doing, he effects the speech of a real tough. Upon hearing that he has come to cut up Juana, her escorts reveal their cowardice and flee.

It is obvious from several of his lines that Lorenzo represents the *gracioso*, as in the instructions to the servant who accompanies him: "Hold her tightly so that I won't err in my stroke, because I could cut too low . . . and that would cost more money." Moreto's use of such a comic figure to put false bullies to shame heightens the opprobrium heaped on this inglorious prototype.

B.   Entremés de los galanes (Interlude of the Gallants)

Cotarelo[3] claims that there is an autograph manuscript of this *entremés* in the Biblioteca Nacional; it was first printed in *Tardes apacibles* (Madrid: Andrés García de la Iglesia, 1663). Lorenzo, the *gracioso*, is apprised by his uncle that his wife regularly receives visits from three lovers. The uncle goes off to fetch a *valiente* whom he has hired to kill the offenders of his nephew's honor. The braggart arrives, exudes toughness in his every utterance, and roughs up both Lorenzo and his uncle to warm to his task. Then, when the gallants arrive and enter one by one, the braggart finds excuses not to hurt them—the first is too short and the second is sickly looking and thin and weak. As the third gallant arrives, the exasperated Lorenzo wants to kill him himself, but the *valiente* prevents him from taking matters in his own hands since Lorenzo does not have the proper experience. When Lorenzo and his uncle try to enter, the *valiente* takes to heart his commission to guard the door, and beats both of them. As the wife and her three lovers leave the house, Lorenzo verbally lashes out at her and at the false *valiente*, and then all sing and dance as the play ends.

C. Entremés de los cinco galanes (Interlude of the Five
    Gallants)

First published in *Flor de entremeses, bailes y loas* (Zaragoza:
Diego Dormer, 1676), this is another of the nine pieces which
Balbín claims to have been falsely attributed to Moreto. It is
an obvious reworking of Moreto's *Entremés de los galanes*. Added
touches are the old man's (referred to as Lorenzo's father!) own
infatuation with Lorenzo's wife, and the fact that both the father
and the hired *valiente* follow the first three lovers into the house.
The role of the *valiente* is not at all central here; he is not even
present as the first three lovers arrive. Since they all know
Lorenzo, each in turn befuddles him and talks him into guarding
the door. As the second is admitted, the first sticks his head
out to ask if Lorenzo cannot be a better guard, and so on.

The old man and the hired bully then arrive. When told that
three gallants have already entered, the *valiente* goes in after
them and the old man follows. To give the action a charming
end, Lorenzo decides to follow the five lovers into the house.
Expressing disappointment in the disloyalty of his friends, he
begs the audience to serve as rear guard for him.

D. Entremés para la noche de San Juan (Interlude for St.
    John's Eve)

This work was published first in *Parnaso nuevo* (Madrid,
1670), under the title *Entremés de Alcolea*. Fernández-Guerra
does not mention this *entremés* or the *Entremés de doña Esquina,*
both of which appeared in *Parnaso nuevo*. He apparently had a
mutilated copy of this volume because he does refer to the
inclusion in it of the *Entremés de los sacristanes burlados* and
the *Baile del cerco de las hembras*, but its title page was obviously missing, and he accurately conjectured that the volume
must have appeared between 1670 and 1675.[4]

Robledo, a pretentious fellow who in public boasts of a
nobility which he does not possess, has hired a *valiente* to accompany him on a night of projected escapades. He plans to
have a complete and licentious fling, doing whatever strikes his
fancy, including "handling" (*manoseando*) any women who
appeal to him, and even mixing it up with the law. He counts

on his ferocious *valiente* to remove any obstacle to the full satisfaction of his will.

Alcolea, the *valiente*, appears terrifyingly tough in his initial phrases but, when Robledo gets fresh with some females and is beaten by their companions, Alcolea does nothing. When asked by his bruised employer why he did not intervene, Alcolea puts together a string of ridiculous excuses.

A man carrying water approaches. When Robledo tries to take it from him, the man throws it in his face and proceeds to whip first Robledo and then Alcolea. The latter's untruthful excuse for inaction is that the aggressor was his fencing student and that the aggression itself was really a show of affection.

When confronted by the authorities, the master-swordsman relinquishes his weapon instantaneously, because he "very much respects the law." All ends in a song which mocks the false valor of the *valiente* and others of his ilk.

II *Women of Easy Virtue*

The woman of easy virtue is captured in the effervescent gaiety of her wayward life in pieces whose endings are devoid of prudish moral admonitions. Moreto simply exploits the possibilities of light satiric description of this type of woman and the society in which she flourished.

A. Entremés del hijo de vecino (Interlude of the Neighbor's Boy)

First published in *Theatro poético* (Zaragoza: Juan de Ybar, 1658), this *entremés* is one of Moreto's liveliest. The prostitute doña Esnefa paints a very earthy picture of the joys of her profession. She is willing to take on all comers, hoping always to meet the proverbial rich and liberal Genoese who will assure the life of ease to which she aspires.

A poor neighbor boy, the *gracioso*, is a frequent visitor. Doña Esnefa refers to him as an "angel," but becomes infuriated when the maid implies that he would be a good steady man for her mistress. He is too poor, according to doña Esnefa, and could never provide the things she wants. As a result of conversations which Esnefa has had in the Prado the day before, servants of each of two gentlemen come bearing invitations. The first reports that his master, a Milanese, has enough of an extremely fine cloth to make a skirt and blouse. The material, along with a beautiful jewel, will be hers in return for a visit to her benefactor's residence. She accepts and agrees to be picked up by his coach. The other servant conveys the offer of expensive silver bowls for a similar house call. The offer of his master, a precentor, is also accepted.

At this point, the *hijo de vecino*, who had earlier put in a brief appearance, bringing just a few coins to Esnefa before departing to fetch food, returns with some partridges. Esnefa, covetous of the promised riches, attempts to leave, but her indigent admirer refuses to let her go. All of her feigned excuses (a neighborhood wedding, the need to attend Mass, etc.) are to no avail and, what is more, finally irritate the boy to the point that he beats Esnefa with his belt. Her landlord intervenes and asks Esnefa if she wishes to press charges against her aggressor. Her masochistic reply is: "... since he hit me, I love him more than my soul." Esnefa begs the pardon of all women for having discovered "the great virtues of the backhanded slap." Obviously pleased with his handling of the situation, the triumphant *gracioso*'s closing advice to men is that they literally have the solution to such problems in their own hands.

B. Entremés de doña Esquina (Interlude of Miss Streetcorner)

First published in *Primera parte del Parnaso nuevo y amenidades del gusto* (Madrid, 1670), this *entremés* appeared translated into French in 1897,[5] and is available in the modern Spanish editions of Balbín[6] and Felicidad Buendía.[7] Thematically, it is one of the most interesting of Moreto's short pieces. Doña Esquina is liberal in regaling three neighbors of easy virtue with gastronomic delicacies. She has been seeing a wealthy man whom she detests, but whose lavish gifts she does not wish to have discontinued. As she departs to make three calls—on a young blond boy, an *indiano* ("wealthy man from the New World"), and a former lover—she asks her neighbors to do her a favor when her prodigal suitor arrives with the *esportillero* ("errand boy"), laden down with gifts from the market. They are to tell him she left in a rage when she heard that he was seen with another woman in Atocha.

Upon the arrival of the suitor, played by the *gracioso*, he is told in detail by each of the neighbors, who spare no derogatory adjectives in their attempts to defame her, of the three visits planned by doña Esquina. Each also showers the man with praise, ending with the refrain: "Come on in with the *esportillero.*" Upon her return, Esquina is confronted with the justified accusations of the *gracioso*. Thinking quickly, she tells him she instructed her neighbors to tell him those lies to make him rage. She calls her neighbors and, before they have a chance to speak, presents them with a chicken, a box of preserves, and a side of bacon, and asks them if they did not, in effect, lie under her instructions. Self-interest prompts all to cooperate, and Esquina ends the piece by scratching the face of her embarrassed suitor.

C.   Entremés del cerco de las hembras (Interlude of the Siege of the Women)

The only known published version is found in *Parnaso nuevo*. There is only minimal action and movement in this treatment of the theme of self-interest, specifically the financial demands always made by women. The combat terminology of the title is extended in the work to military, and especially naval, analogies.

III   *Social Climbers*

Social climbing is exposed in areas in which its pretentiousness and absurdity are emphasized but, as is customary in the genre, the exposition is lighthearted. Moreto does not close with heavy moralizing dicta, but rather on a joyful note or with a dance, joined in by all: the climbers, their deceivers—the tricksters and the tricked.

A.   Entremés del aguador (Interlude of the Water Vendor)

First published in *Rasgos del ocio* (Madrid: Joseph Fernández de Buendía, 1661), this *entremés* exploits the comic possibilities of the names of its protagonists, don Desperdicio ("Mr. Waste") and doña Estafa ("Miss Swindle").

Don Desperdicio complains bitterly to his friend, don Maula ("Mr. Lazy Loafer"), that doña Estafa, having become wealthy through swindling him, now wants to marry a man of nobility. Having consumed don Desperdicio's fortune in jewels and other fineries, her vanity attains the ridiculous point of demanding that her servants address her as "Señoría" ("Ladyship") or, as she adds, "syncopating the word ... *Sía* is enough." Don Maula suggests a trick. He has a French lackey who formerly was a water vendor and for whom he arranges a visit with doña Estafa. An old woman attempting to pass the water vendor off as a wealthy French nobleman seeking a wife wins Estafa immediately by the flattering use of three "Your ladyships" in four lines. Completely taken in, she gives her hand to the French ex-water vendor. When Don Desperdicio rushes in, Estafa, most anxious to put an end to his pretensions, reports that she is married. As Maula enters and extends his best wishes to the newlyweds, a constable arrives with an irate tax collector, who identifies the Frenchman as a water vendor who owes three years of delinquent income taxes. The lackey admits to his past profession, but puts the tax collector at ease by saying that his new wife is rich and will pay whatever he owes. The tools of his former trade are brought on stage and the group begins to dance. The old woman closes the action with the moral note that in this way vanity is punished.

B. Entremés de la Mariquita (Interlude of Little Mary)

First published in *Flor de entremeses* (Zaragoza: Diego Dormer, 1676), this *entremés* also exists in a manuscript version and in *Entremeses varios* (Zaragoza, 1676). It is one of the few works which contain unfavorable reference to priests.[8]

The *graciosa*, Quiteria, as a means to escape poverty, plans to hoax Lorenzo, imbecilic nephew of a doctor, into thinking that he has married her. With the aid of two accomplices, she enters Lorenzo's house. As the victim approaches his house, the uncle is trying to convince him that he should marry and suggests four possible brides: the daughters of the lawyer, the barber, the blacksmith, and the mayor. To each suggestion Lorenzo has an objection, including a claim, atypical of Moreto's theater, that the lawyer's daughter is involved with a priest.

As Lorenzo enters his house, he is congratulated on his marriage by Quiteria's "accomplices." His confusion increases as Quiteria tells him of all the good things she is cooking for him. When the gullible nitwit asks if they have had any children yet, Quiteria responds that as soon as she has finished cooking she will bear three: Juanico, Sanchico, and Mariquita (whose name serves as the play's title). Music interrupts the uncle's objections, and Quiteria's prey is securely caught.

IV   *Picaresque Backgrounds*

The seamy side of life is not a significant part of Moreto's full-length theater. If treated occasionally, as in the case of scenes from *San Franco de Sena*, where it is portrayed merely to underscore the impressiveness of the ultimate redemption of the protagonist, it is never central to the action. To readers acquainted only with Moreto's *comedias*, the picaresque and underworld atmosphere of the following plays will be surprising, and will probably appear not unworthy of the pens of the consecrated names associated with the literature of the antihero.

A.   Entremés de los gatillos (Interlude of the Little Pickpockets)

First published in *Verdores del Parnaso* (Madrid: Domingo García Morrás, 1668), this work features *pícaros* of both sexes. Its plot consists of thwarted attempts of the males, Tejoletas ("Broken Tiles") and Poca Ropa ("Little Clothing"), to attempt thievery to pay for a meal. They are first upstaged by Manuela, a female counterpart who steals from their first prey a handkerchief laden with money. The victim, a witless old man, goes home for a second handkerchief which he plans to use as a decoy to catch the thief. His wife and niece are then accosted by Tejoletas and Poca Ropa, who steal a purse, only to discover inside nothing but some beans, blue cloth, coal, and dirt. When the old man returns, Manuela beats the boys to the handkerchief again. They next turn up following Escamilla, who has put a doubloon in his mouth for safety. Tejoletas and Poca Ropa despair, but the artful Manuela proclaims that Escamilla has stolen a doubloon from her and put it in the unlikely hiding place of his mouth. The police officer who has come upon the scene finds the doubloon, believes Manuela, and is about to lead everyone to jail, including the wife, because the strange contents of her purse make him think she is a witch. Manuela then offers the doubloon to buy lunch for all, and sprightly music closes the action.

Tejoletas, in one of his opening speeches, gives the typical rationalization of the *pícaro*'s condition:

> Fortunate is the lazy fellow, since he rests
> without the two little cares
> about possessions and honor.

B.   Entremés de las brujas (Interlude of the Witches)

Published first in *Autos sacramentales y al nacimiento de Christo* (Madrid: Antonio Francisco de Zafra, 1675), its theme is thievery interpreted as the work of witches.[9] Careful about their larceny for ten days in town, Tringintania, Sarcoso, and Limpadosa, aware of the fact that everyone thinks that witches are to blame, plan to play a trick on the mayor. Tringintania, dressed in a black cape, tells him that Pluto will call off the witches if the mayor himself will purchase a protective dispensation for the town. When he delivers the money, they feign to be witches and invite him to become one, too. One of the conditions is to disrobe. They depart with his clothes, and he is found by two town officials to whom he swears he is a warlock. The priest sprinkles him with Holy Water, and the mayor attacks, driving them all from the stage in a lively dance.

C.   Entremés del hambriento (Interlude of the Hungry Boy)

First published in *Autos sacramentales y al nacimiento de Christo* (Madrid, 1675), this short piece, which is available in two modern editions,[10] features the traditional wily and always hungry student. He is following three women who, with their lunch in a basket carried by a Galician *esportillero*, are trying to shake him from their trail. He obviously has frequently been successful in sponging food from them. One stops him to ask that he serve as a witness to a deed of sale, another hands him a bundle of rags, claiming that it is a baby, and another stops him to ask the time. The persistent student is about to continue the pursuit when cries of "stop, thief" are heard. The "thief" is the *esportillero* who has refused to relinquish the contents of his basket until he is paid. He declares in his Galician dialect that the student is his master, and the latter exits with all the food.

D. Entremés del Mellado (Interlude of Snaggle-Tooth)

Published first in *Tardes apacibles* (Madrid: Andrés García de la Iglesia, 1663), this portrayal of underworld characters, judicial proceedings, and the bonanza of royal clemency, was written to celebrate the birthday of the young Princess Margarita (born July 12, 1651).

La Chaves and La Escalanta are respectively the molls of the imprisoned criminals El Zurdo ("Lefty") and El Mellado ("Snaggle-Tooth"). They have come to the jail with baskets of food because they have heard that their men, convicted murderers, are to be taken through the streets on muleback, a customary procedure of the times as a part of a criminal's punishment. El Mellado has been sentenced to be hanged in the plaza the next day and El Zurdo to ten years in the galleys. Even the women admit to having criminal records. La Chaves has had her ear cut, a punishment inflicted to make it easy to recognize convicted criminals, and La Escalanta is reminded of the time she had all of her hair cut off while under sentence to the galleys. The play is filled with picturesque underworld vocabulary, descriptions of tortures used on prisoners, and the impressive dignity with which El Mellado brags he will meet his end on the scaffold: "My spirit is good, thanks to God, and I know that I will strike a fine posture in the plaza; and the executioner knows me—he's really first class—and he will want to do a fine job."

Just as the women take food from their baskets for a last meal together, the mayor arrives with news that the criminals have been pardoned because it is the birthday of Princess Margarita. One chuckles at the bravado which the obviously relieved Mellado displays after being notified of his pardon: "In a way I'm sorry, since I had already made my peace with God." This blend of the picaresque and the criminal makes the *Entremés del Mellado* one of the more appealing one-act plays of Moreto's delightful repertory.

E. Baile de la Zamalandrana hermana (Interlude of Sister Zamalandrana)

Published first in *Parnaso nuevo* (Madrid, 1670), this play is considered to be Moreto's by both Fernández-Guerra and Balbín. Cotarelo[11] claims that it was written by Quiñones de Benavente, and it is not edited in Carner's dissertation. The work contains very little action; it merely portrays some of the male brutality that characterizes male-female relationships in the lower echelons of society. Toribio beats María regularly, but her friend Bernarda says that women would rather have that treatment than be ignored. The beating picks up tempo and to the notes of the dance, *Zamalandrana hermana*, joined in by everyone, all is forgiven.

F. Entremés de la bota (Interlude of the Wineskin)

Published first in *Tardes apacibles* (Madrid, 1663), this piece is a light farce. The *gracioso* Botín ("spoils, plunder") meets doña Marina and doña Estefanía, recipients of a lunch sent by don Silvestre. Noting that wine was not included, Botín procures a wineskin, dresses as a girl, and puts it under his clothes so that the neck sticks out right under his mouth. Pretending to be faint and ill, he inveigles first a Portuguese, then a Castilian into giving him a bottle of wine, which he deposits in the wineskin. The wily Portuguese sees the trick played on the Castilian. When Botín returns, he is followed by both of his dupes. Surprised by knocking at the door, the *gracioso* lies down, puts the wineskin on his stomach, and pretends to be a pregnant woman. The Castilian, who suspects another trick, says he will help speed the process and squeezes the protuberance, squirting its contents all over Botín. Everyone takes the tricks as good fun, and the play closes with singing and dancing.

G. Baile entremesado de los oficios (Interlude-like Dance of the Trades)

Published first in *Tardes apacibles* (Madrid, 1663), and by Francisco Rico in 1971,[12] this piece could be cross-referenced as a pale example of the satire of the *valentón*. Borja, Luisa, Luciana, Mariana, and Simón, peddling respectively food, drink, chestnuts, scrap metal, and olives, converge and fight because all want to sell on the same location. At this point, the four *jaques* (synonym for *valientes*), San Juan, Onofre, Mendoza, and Carmona come upon the scene. They watch as Mariana tears out some of Luciana's hair. The latter then asks her *jaque* for his dagger, using the picaresque term *la chica*, and is imitated by the other girls. A minor scuffle ensues, but ends before anyone is hurt. Singing, the group breaks up to return home, nothing having been sold.

V *The Honor Code*

The satire of excessive punctiliousness in the observance of the famous *pundonor* (point of honor—honor code) receives extensive treatment in Moreto's *comedias*. We know of but one of the short plays in which this theme is central, but it unequivocally ridicules the rigid irrationality of the imprisoned slaves of honor. The title is *Entremés de las galeras de la honra (Interlude of Honor's Galleys)* and it first appeared in *Autos sacramentales y al nacimiento de Christo* (Madrid, 1675). It was published in a modern edition by Francisco Rico in 1971.[13] The opening speech is an explicit indictment of those too punctilious in the obeisance shown to the "point of honor":

BORJA. Know ye, ladies and gentlemen,
          that I have come, sent
          against those who, for their honor,
          spend their lives without pleasure.
          Those who attend to their dignity
          without ever departing from it a whit,
          I have come to throw into the galleys
          so they may pay for their ignorance.
          Before me they must appear

and, their guilt established,
the whip of honor
will tan their hides.

Three victims appear separately before Borja:
1. A woman who invites her husband's mistress to the house
to avoid scandal.
2. A man who has accepted the request of an unknown man
to be his second in a duel.
3. A young girl who wants to marry but who is giving in to
her family's wishes that she become a nun.

In each case, Borja cites examples of how other people not
burdened with obsessive punctiliousness would use common
sense to solve the same problems. However, all three of those
on trial are so sensitive to *"el qué dirán"* ("what will they say,"
"gossip"), that they prefer to suffer their respective fates rather
than to abandon their staunch sense of honor. Borja sentences
them all!

VI   *Nonsatiric Portrayals of Society*

In some of Moreto's short plays, not even the slight sting of
mild satire is detected. In the light of the documentary dimension of three of the four plays discussed in this category, it is
necessary to revise Ruth Lee Kennedy's judgment, based on
Moreto's full-length *comedias*: "The author's theatre likewise
gives little direct information concerning theatrical conditions
of the day."[14] This judgment evaporates when we examine three
of Moreto's effervescent short works devoted to contemporary
theater.

A.   Entremés del poeta (Interlude of the Poet)

This *entremés* exists only in manuscript.[15] It deals with a trick
played by the *gracioso* on the members of a theatrical company. He arrives just as a rehearsal is about to begin, passes
himself off as a poet who has composed every conceivable type
of theatrical piece, and brags that his talents extend even into
the area of stage machinery. In short, if the company will only
contract his services, its director will never again need to look
for other poets. When asked if his plays have been produced,

he claims recently to have sold four bizarre-sounding titles to the director Avendaño, in Seville.

During the dance which concludes the hoax, the Poet brags to the audience that he has, subtle student that he is, played pranks on people of all professions and all walks of life. The only people whom he had not yet victimized were actors. Now he has closed the circle and requests the laurel which will crown his achievement!

Although this *entremés* has little movement, it does directly concern itself with the theater and contains a number of interesting contemporary references. The reference to the actor Avendaño, who died in 1637, indicates to Cotarelo[16] that the *entremés* is a work of Moreto's youth if, in truth, it is his.

B. Entremés del vestuario (Interlude of the Dressing Room)

When Balbín published the manuscript of this *entremés* in 1942,[17] he claimed that it was formerly unpublished. He obviously was unacquainted with Carner's edition published ten years earlier.[18] As Balbín points out, Moreto here gives "a vigorous dramatization of a collective psychological state, that of the psychic complex that attends a theatrical première."[19]

The action opens with a conversation in which Blas Carrillo, a presumptuous fop, tries to impress a friend with his knowledge of the theater and, especially, his acquaintance with the actors. As the theater fills, the actors begin to arrive, and amidst the commotion of preparing for a première performance, the dramatist worries that someone will ruin his play. The conversation reveals that nerves are taut and glances are taken to see what kind of crowd will be present. La Quiñones reveals that she does not eat on the day of a première, Olmedo states that the performance will last three hours, last-minute changes in the script are mentioned, there is a spicy dialogue between an actress and the prompter, and the public provides the deprecatory whistling customary as a sign of displeasure. All of the actors mentioned in the cast were real actors, but Carner claims that "Not all the actors whose names appear played together in the same company before 1663"[20]—and he dates the piece 1663–1669.

C. Loa entremesada para la compañía de Pupilo (Interlude-like "loa" for Pupilo's Company)

Published in the rare *Verdores del Parnaso* (Madrid, 1668), this prologue to a play about to be presented by Pupilo's company is a rich document on contemporary theater.

Having just arrived in Madrid from the provinces, Pupilo reveals that three of his male actors have gone mad: Escamilla thinks that he is a choirmaster, Juan de la Calle thinks he is Philip II, and Juan González thinks he is the director of the company. To make Pupilo's situation worse, his first lady, Francisca Verdugo, has been ill. The position of first lady is claimed by Isabel Gálvez. She receives the support of the other actors, but just then a fully recuperated Francisca appears on horseback and, in a parody of Diego Ordóñez's challenge from the siege of Zamora ballads, claims her rightful position as first lady. The actors calm down and return to their senses as Pupilo reminds them that "the great Madrid" is awaiting their performance. The company then directs itself to the dreaded *mosqueteros* (groundlings) and to the several sections of the theater: the *grada* (orchestra), *aposentos* (boxes), *desvanes* (seats in houses overlooking the stage), and *cazuela* (gallery for women only), soliciting indulgence for the play which is to follow.

This *loa* is rich in documentation on the personnel in Pupilo's company and the spirit and language which must have characterized contemporary theatrical life.

Critics of Moreto's *teatro menor* are lavish in their praise. Balbín[21] lauds Moreto's satiric genius and his handling of comic situations, and Hannah Bergman[22] feels that his *comedias* and *entremeses* assure him a place among the first-ranking dramatists of his generation. According to Cotarelo, "After Cervantes and Quiñones de Benavente, Moreto is the best writer of *entremeses* of the seventeenth century."[23] Juliá Martínez[24] rates Moreto as the best of his contemporaries. Any view of Moreto which does not take into account his *teatro menor* can be but partial. We know little enough concerning his life, and his presence is anything but obtrusive in his full-length plays.

New insights into the earthy, jovial, irrational dimensions of Moreto's personality are available in his one-act plays. J. H. Parker perceptively notes that "Moreto gives assurance to the members of the audience that their foibles and little vices are not too serious, and he provides them with a sort of for-giveness—absolution by laughter."[25] Acquaintance with the de-lightful components of his *teatro menor* adds new and significant dimensions to our knowledge and appreciation of Moreto and his art.

CHAPTER 9

Nondramatic Poetry

MORETO'S muse was almost exclusively dramatic. We know but fourteen poems and some *villancicos* (popular carols)[1] independent of his theater.[2] Most of these incidental pieces are occasional and should not be expected to reveal poetic quality comparable to that of the genre to which Moreto devoted his literary life.

Just as his *entremeses* and other short pieces manifest facets of Moreto which are not prominent in his full-length plays, the extant poems also contribute to the completion of his portrait. The facile wordplay and affected imagery of his earliest efforts are not surprising in the poetry of a young student nineteen or twenty years of age, and it is interesting to see in some of his poems the gongoristic and *conceptista* temptations to which he readily succumbed when not writing for the stage.

In 1639, when Moreto was a twenty-year-old student at the University of Alcalá, his first two poems were published. One was included among many panegyric contributions of well-known poets to commemorate the death in the preceding year of the poet, dramatist, and theologian, Juan Pérez de Montalbán.[3] It is a sonnet, "Este, a quien con su pena premió el hado"[4] ("This man, whom fate rewarded with grief"), containing wordplay and concepts which will not be found in the serious expression of Moreto's later years. The other poem published in this same year was a laudatory sonnet, "Con grave admiración, con verdad pura" ("With grave admiration, with pure truth"), in the prefatory pages of a genealogical volume, honoring its author.[5] Although there is little literary value in these first two poems, Moreto's collaboration in such volumes attests to his nascent fame in literary circles.

One year later there appears another elegiac sonnet, "Yace

aquí: ¿quién diré para decirle?" ("Here lies—whom shall I say to describe him?"), in a volume dedicated to the memory of the Portuguese commander, Nuño Alvarez Pereyra.[6]

In 1644 Moreto was one of several poets who contributed compositions to a volume commissioned by Philip IV to honor the soldiers who died in the Battle of Lérida.[7] His sonnet, "Si a la valiente sangre derramada" ("If to the valiant spilled blood"),[8] rather unpoetically shifts emphasis from the valiant soldiers to Spain's monarch, about whom Moreto obsequiously asks: "Who wouldn't die for you?"

Emilio Orozco Díaz has published a *romance* by Moreto of three hundred lines, "Poder de Dios, fulanica" ("The power of God, little girl"), on the events of a celebrated bullfight which took place on July 6, 1648.[9]

The study of Orozco Díaz is the most complete one we know of any of Moreto's nondramatic poems. A clear distinction is noted between the restrained poetry of his dramatic writing and the clearly more learned, even gongoristic traits of this account written to be read or recited rather than declaimed from the stage. The imagery of colors and movement makes an impressive sensory appeal and complements well the wit and conceits which titillate the intellect. This poem represents a significant step forward in comparison with Moreto's first nondramatic efforts.

In 1650, along with Calderón and other important literary figures, Moreto dedicated a laudatory sonnet, "Si en las airosas muestras desta suma" ("If in the resplendent models of this treatise"),[10] to Joseph de Casanova, author of a style manual.

Simón Díaz[11] refers to a sonnet, "¿Qué es esto? Tomás, pobre en muerte y vida" ("What is this? Thomas, poor in death and life"), which Moreto contributed to Fray Benito de Aste's volume on the canonization of Tomás de Villanueva, the celebration of which took place in Toledo in 1659.[12] In addition to the sonnet, which is uninspired, Moreto is declared to be the author of the *villancicos* which are scattered throughout the book.[13]

Although other of the undated poems of Moreto may well fall within the period 1640–1670, it is not until the latter date, the year following Moreto's death, that another dated piece is published, this time an ambitious 340-line version of the mythological story of Atalanta, "Esquiva Atalanta siempre"[14] ("Always aloof Atalanta").

Moreto retells the Boeotian version of the story of the Greek mythological heroine who, warned by an oracle against marriage, challenged all suitors to a foot race. She defeated and killed all of her challengers until Hippomenes, counseled by Venus, dropped three golden apples in her path during the race. For having stopped to pick them up, she lost the race. Angered at not being shown the proper deference and gratitude, Venus converts the couple into lions. In his total faithfulness to the myth, Moreto has written a sound poem. His vocabulary and images are mildly gongoristic, but the quality of poetic expression is infinitely superior to that of his youthful sonnets.

In the same volume there is another *romance* of forty-four lines dedicated to the eyes of a beautiful woman, "Ya no mata amor, zagales"[15] ("Love doesn't kill any more, young men").

Guillén y Buzarán publishes five of an unstated total of *quintillas* (five-line stanzas of octosyllabic verses with two rhymes) which form a burlesque, satiric composition attributed to Moreto entitled *Defensa de don Serafín*, "Si queréis echar un bando"[16] ("If you want to issue a proclamation"). The poem treats a contemporary theme, but its precise date is not given.

Historically, don Serafín de Mosquera, Corregidor of San Clemente, was so addicted to dancing that he became the subject of generally unfavorable poetic jibes in Madrid. From the excerpt and comments on the whole poem published by Guillén y Buzarán, we see that Moreto has given the satire a new twist. After citing a succession of severe and feared judges and magistrates sent to implement the reforms ordered by the powerful favorite, the Count-Duke of Olivares, Moreto applauds the appointment in La Mancha of one who uses his feet to dance merrily rather than his pen to govern oppressively.

In the letter of Joaquín Manuel de Alba which Fernández-Guerra publishes,[17] there is included the text of another poem "Canto fiestas de San Juan" ("I sing the St. John's celebrations"), composed of twenty-five *coplas de pie quebrado* (stanzas of six verses, varying in length from eight to four syllables, with rhyme abc abc). Written in honor of don Isidro Bandrés de Abarca (Knight of the Order of Santiago and treasurer of don

Juan de Austria) for his heroic exploits as a *rejoneador* (equestrian bullfighter) in the plaza of Madrid during the festivities of St. John's Day, the poem does not seem very inspired.[18] It recounts the valor of don Isidro in saving an inept *espontáneo* (spectator who jumps into the ring to fight the bull) and in avenging on foot the death of his horse. Although no date has been assigned to the poem, a trite comparison made in the next-to-last strophe ("gallantry goes with valor like eggs with bacon") speaks for an early date. Moreto has injected a comic image in the rescue of the *espontáneo*. Don Isidro "saved him so quickly, / that he spared his rump / from more eyes."

The last of the poems cited by Fernández-Guerra is a twenty-four line ballad, "Lleve el compás mi llanto"[19] ("Let my weeping carry the beat"). On the subject of the captivity inherent in love, the poem's ease and consistent lyrical expression indicate it to be the work of a mature Moreto.

Each of the two poems published by Entrambasaguas[20] is a burlesque portrait of a woman. The first, "Nise, por lo que condena mi gusto tu rostro" ("Nise, for the way in which your face condemns my pleasure"), in nine *coplas de pie quebrado* paints a grotesque picture of a woman named Nise. The other, "Pintura que hizo un amante" ("Portrait done by a lover"), in nine *quintillas*, is in the same vein, but the woman is unnamed. As Entrambasaguas remarks, although these little poems do not have the literary value of Moreto's dramatic works, they are not inferior to his other nondramatic poems.

CHAPTER 10

Moreto's Significance and Popularity

SUCCEEDING periods reveal, in their appraisals of literary works, something about themselves as well as something about the objects of their criticism. Recently, problems relating to the orientation, goals, and feasibility of different critical approaches with specific reference to Spanish Golden Age theater have been brought into focus by A. A. Parker,[1] Reichenberger,[2] Wade,[3] Gilman,[4] Hesse,[5] and Bentley.[6] Whichever particular focus Moreto's twentieth-century readers choose to employ in attaining their own interpretive goals, their understanding of this dramatic poet and the succeeding periods in literary history cannot help but be enhanced by knowledge of the patterns of his reputation and popularity through the years.

During his lifetime Moreto shared the dramatic spotlight with Calderón. He subsequently maintained a consistently high repute throughout the eighteenth century and into the first part of the nineteenth, generally ranking third behind Calderón and Cañizares, but decisively ahead of Lope de Vega and Tirso de Molina.

Moreto, as we are reminded by Romera-Navarro,[7] was the only dramatist mentioned by the great contemporary moralist and prose stylist, Baltasar Gracián (1601–1658) who, in *El Criticón*, refers to him as the "Spanish Terence."[8]

One of the first critical assessments of Moreto's dramaturgy was registered by Francisco Bances Candamo in 1689–1690 in his *Theatro de los Theatros*, a work considered by Edward Wilson[9] to be one of the best early studies of Golden Age theater. According to Bances: "Don Agustín Moreto was the one who corrupted the purity of the theater, with imprudent witticisms, letting himself be dragged down by the vulgar applause of the common people."[10]

Luzán, in 1737,[11] voiced high praise for *El desdén con el desdén,* in spite of the neoclassical proclivities which led him to an antipathy for Golden Age drama. Moreto's acceptance by neoclassic scholars is founded on the high priority which he gave to balance, proportion, structural cohesiveness, and reason.

In 1838 Martínez de la Rosa stated: "Moreto placed himself in front of the other dramatists of his time, and I doubt that he has ever had an equal in Spain."[12] Mesonero Romanos, in 1851,[13] claimed that eight to ten plays of Moreto were the favorite plays of the theatergoing public. Gil y Zárate, commenting in the same year that Moreto's works "will always be the richest jewels in our dramatic crown,"[14] cited the regularity of Moreto's plays, his easy, natural style, devoid of gongoristic extravagances, as the reason for his lasting popularity.

A recent echo of Moreto's popularity is found in the words of Margaret Wilson: "One sees in Moreto a slighter and a less critical Alarcón. He too appealed to French taste... and his plays continued popular with his own countrymen when a new century and cultural influences from across the Pyrenees were starting to bring the old *comedia* into disfavour."[15]

We have also discovered two independent testimonies to popularity of another sort. Scattered through several numbers of the comic review *La carcajada* (*"The Cackle of Laughter"*) in 1844 are many humorous compositions facetiously attributed to Moreto's pen.[16] Ugarte, in 1932, published prose adaptations for children of six of Moreto's plays.[17]

Notwithstanding the indictments of Moreto's "plagiaristic" tendencies, the popularity he has enjoyed in his own time and through the years, and the impact exercised by his theater on the subsequent work of Spanish and foreign dramatists amply attest to the appeal of his dramaturgy. Even as we remind ourselves of Cervantes's sage dictum, *toda comparación es odiosa*[18] ("all comparisons are hateful"), we must cite the case of Calderón, whose most "successful" efforts are reworkings of older plays, on the surface apparently slavishly close to their sources but, when examined closely and with great regard for detail, revealing the subtle changes of a master craftsman which confer both high dramatic quality and "originality" on the adaptation. The point at issue is simply that, in spite of a certain

evident parallelism in the manner in which Moreto and Calderón spent large portions of their careers reworking and per-
fecting the plays of other dramatists or efforts of their own
younger years, criticism has been much more ready to condone
the appropriation, adaptation, and use of source material in
the case of Calderón than in the case of Moreto. Ruth Lee
Kennedy, who is really the first word on virtually everything
connected with Moreto and still the last word on many points,
indicates in her succinct analyses of Moreto's work the improve-
ments wrought by the changes, some substantial, some minimal,
in his adaptations of earlier plays. The comprehensive nature of
her study of Moreto precludes, however, the minute analysis
required to demonstrate the specific dramatic techniques, philos-
ophy, and devices employed by Moreto to produce the effects
realized in his adaptations. Following, and indeed patterning
his work after that of Sloman,[19] Frank Casa[20] has used close
analysis to demonstrate the obvious superiority in dramatic
technique which imbued Moreto's theater with a lasting appeal,
based in large part on the modernity, or universality, of his
homage to order and reason.

The new priorities of Romanticism eventually brought about
a decline in Moreto's popularity. It is interesting to note, however, that Viel-Castel, in 1840, was able to attest to the fact
that "Moreto's glory has never perished among his countrymen,
neither has it suffered, as in the case of Lope de Vega, a
temporary eclipse."[21]

The exportation of the Spanish *comedia* to the New World,
both in the form of printed texts and stage presentations, is
documented well enough to attest to the veracity of statements
such as that made by Dorothy Schons: "Mexicans were fond
of the drama. During the colonial period they imported large
numbers of plays from Spain. They read Lope de Vega, Calderón,
Moreto and minor dramatists."[22] There is record of the exportation of *comedias* by Moreto to New Spain specifically in 1665,
1678, 1686, 1690, 1692, 1712, and 1732. Dorothy Schons also
documents a performance of *El lindo don Diego* in the Viceroy's
palace as early as November of 1676.[23]

Irving A. Leonard, who, in several publications, has studied
the shipment of books to the New World, speaks of royal pro-

hibitions against the dissemination of secular literature: "By command of the kings of Spain the colonists of America were forbidden under the severest penalties from reading what were called books of fiction, poetry, novels, plays, etc. It was not possible to read Cervantes, [Lope de] Vega, Quevedo, Moreto."[24] Leonard's theory, however, is that, in spite of the prohibition, works by these authors were imported and widely read. He speaks of "the flood of dramatic works which poured into the colonies in the seventeenth and eighteenth centuries, and far exceeded in quantity any other single class of profane litera-ture,"[25] and he has discovered a document which indicates that by 1683 Moreto's *Partes* of 1671 [*sic*], 1676, and 1681 had already been imported for sale into Mexico.[26] Elsewhere, he indicates eleven titles of Moreto which were shipped to the Indies[27] and he gives performance dates for several of Moreto's plays in Lima, 1790–1793.[28] Guillermo Lohmann Villena documents the presentation of forty-one plays attributed to Moreto during the viceroyalty in Peru.[29] José Juan Arrom[30] provides documenta-tion on the performance of several of Moreto's plays in Ha-vana in 1791.

Primero es la honra was performed in San Juan, Puerto Rico,[31] in 1747, as part of the celebration of the coronation of Ferdi-nand VI. In 1789, in Salta, *La fuerza del natural* was similarly produced to celebrate the coronation of Charles IV.[32]

In addition to other plays performed in Argentina, Trenti Rocamora documents performances of *El desdén con el desdén* (1777–1778) in Chile, of *No puede ser* (1731) in Guayaquil, Ecuador, and of several *comedias* and the *Entremés del corta-caras* in Peru, on dates ranging from 1713 to 1792. Ortega Ricaurte[33] reports 1797 productions of *No puede ser* and *Hasta el fin nadie es dichoso* in Bogotá, and alludes to twentieth-century performances of *El desdén con el desdén*. Amunátegui ranks Moreto among the five most important Golden Age drama-tists, and cites performances of *El desdén con el desdén* and *El valiente justiciero* in Chile on February 22 and October 4, 1816, respectively.[34] Pedro Henríquez Ureña states that the plays most frequently produced in eighteenth-century Santo Domingo were those of Calderón and Moreto.[35] J. R. Spell[36] has discovered three of Moreto's plays which were performed in Mexico City

in the period 1805–1806. Everett W. Hesse has provided a brief
survey of Moreto's plays presented in the New World from 1659
when *La adúltera penitente* was performed in Lima, to March 17,
1953, when *El lindo don Diego* was presented at the University
of Wisconsin.[37]

Moreto is one of the three leaders in popularity according to
all of the available statistics. For the period 1791–1792 in Mexico
City, Leonard discovered that our playwright ranked third
behind Calderón and Cañizares.[38] Moreto's fame was even
carried to Brazil where in 1729, in Bahía, *El desdén con el
desdén* and *La fuerza del natural* were performed as part of
royal Luso-Spanish wedding ceremonies.[39]

The frequency of representation of several of Moreto's plays
in Latin America during the eighteenth and nineteenth centuries
attests to the high and wide-ranging esteem enjoyed and maintained by his theater. Surprisingly complete documentation
is also available on the plays of Moreto which have been produced in several cities of Spain almost down to the present
day. Ada Coe has catalogued the plays announced in Madrid's
newspapers from 1661 to 1819.[40] Alonso Cortés documents the
plays produced in Valladolid from 1681 to 1798.[41] There is a
heavy representation of Moreto titles, led by *No puede ser*
with forty-nine performances, and *El desdén con el desdén*
with thirty-three.

Among the ambitious scholars who provide statistical evidence of the popularity of Golden Age dramatists, Juliá Martínez[42] attests to the fact that Moreto ranked second only to
Calderón with Valencia's theatergoers in the first half of the
eighteenth century. Of the total of 458 entries, Juliá claims
18.45% to be Calderón's and 7.15% to be Moreto's; in third place,
with 6.59%, is Cañizares. His study of ticket receipts reveals
that Moreto's *El desdén con el desdén*, *Antíoco y Seleuco*, and
No puede ser were among the leaders in attracting large
audiences.

Theatrical performances in Barcelona during the period 1719–
1794 are documented by Alfonso Par.[43] The use of variant
titles and the absence of authors' names makes a statistical
analysis difficult, but an abundance of Moreto's *comedias* are
included.

Cotarelo, in his book on Isidoro Máiquez,[44] Madrid's leading actor from 1783 to 1819, includes many of Moreto's titles in a catalogue of plays performed in the capital during that period.

In Madrid, during the period 1820–1850, based upon 273 performances of fourteen of his plays, Moreto ranks fourth in popularity behind Tirso de Molina, Lope de Vega, and Calderón, according to the study published by Nicholson B. Adams.[45] Sterling A. Stoudemire attests to Moreto's indirect popularity at the turn of the nineteenth century in the form of Dionisio Solís's adaptation of *El valiente justiciero.*[46]

In a study of plays produced in Madrid's three theaters during the War of Independence and the return of Absolutism with Ferdinand VII, Charlotte M. Lorenz[47] finds that Moreto ranked fourth, behind Lope, Cañizares, and Calderón, but far ahead of Tirso de Molina.

In addition to the translations and adaptations which we have studied, there exist several others in English, French, German, Italian, and Hungarian.[48] The biannual *Bulletin of the Comediantes* frequently carries news of current productions of Golden Age plays. We even find evidence as recent as 1946 of translations into Russian of three titles, *El valiente justiciero, El desdén con el desdén,* and the charming *entremés, El retrato vivo.*[49]

In recent years there has been a surge of interest in making available catalogues of Spanish plays found in the collections of institutional or private libraries. Ada M. Coe, in 1933,[50] cites *sueltas* of thirty-nine different titles attributed to Moreto which are found either in the Ticknor Collection in the Boston Public Library, in the private collection of Buchanan, or in her personal library. Paul P. Rogers, in 1940,[51] catalogued thirty-five entries on Moreto which are found in the Oberlin College Library. In 1959, J. A. Molinaro, J. H. Parker, and Evelyn Rugg[52] catalogued eighty-three Moreto entries in the University of Toronto Library. In 1965, two more important catalogues appeared: in B. B. Ashcom's,[53] eighty entries on Moreto were given for the Wayne State University Library and the private library of the author; and, lastly, William A. McKnight, with the collaboration of Mabel Barrett Jones,[54] catalogued 116 Moreto titles in the collection of the University of North Carolina Library.

The decline of Moreto's great popularity coincided with the

enthronement by Romanticism of novelty, uniqueness, inventiveness, and other such aesthetic virtues. But the regularity, order, reasoned approach, and the overall consummate dramatic art and craftsmanship which maintained the high appeal of Moreto's dramaturgy for close to two centuries, unpopular in a romantic age, can still charm and promise rich rewards to all who wish to become better acquainted with one of Spain's most accomplished dramatists.

Notes and References

Chapter One

1. Contemporary documents gave several variant forms of the poet's maternal surname: Cavaña, Cabaña, Cavana, Cabana. Among later scholars, Fernández-Guerra, Ruth Lee Kennedy, and Frank Casa use the spelling "Cabaña"; Entrambasaguas, in "Doce documentos inéditos relacionados con Moreto y dos poesías suyas desconocidas," *Revista de la Biblioteca, Archivo y Museo,* VII (1930), 341, n. 1, argues convincingly for the form Cavana, which is also used by La Barrera, *Catálogo bibliográfico y biográfico del teatro antiguo español* (1860), p. 275; by Pérez Pastor, *Bibliografía madrileña,* III, 434; and by Alonso Cortés, *Moreto—teatro (Clásicos Castellanos,* XXXII). For full names and titles, see the Selected Bibliography.

2. Fernández-Guerra, *Don Juan Ruiz de Alarcón y Mendoza* (Madrid, 1871), p. 340, claims that the poet's father was from Monferrato and his mother from Mantua. Emilio Cotarelo y Mori, "Testamento de una hermana de Moreto," *Boletín de la Real Academia Española,* I (1914), 67–68, publishes the will, dated December 14, 1704, of Moreto's youngest sister, Angela Manuela, in which it is stated that both parents were Milanese. Entrambasaguas, "Doce documentos," p. 344, is nevertheless inclined to believe that the father was from Florence, home of the sculptors Juan de Moreto and Pedro de Moreto, to whom he was perhaps related.

3. Fernández-Guerra, *Comedias escogidas de Don Agustín Moreto y Cabaña,* in *Biblioteca de Autores Españoles,* XXXIX (1950), viii. Hereafter, this collection will be referred to as the *BAE.*

4. Fernández-Guerra, *Don Juan Ruiz de Alarcón y Mendoza,* p. 340.

5. La Barrera, p. 275.

6. Entrambasaguas, "Doce documentos," p. 342.

7. *The Dramatic Art of Moreto. Smith College Studies in Modern Languages,* XIII (1931–1932), 3.

8. *Ibid.*

9. Entrambasaguas, "Doce documentos," p. 345, stated that the family had a total of eight children. E. V., "Sobre la familia de

Agustín Moreto (1657)," *Correo erudito*, I (1940–1941), 101, cites a document which refers to another sister, Margarita, who was twenty-three years old in 1657.

10. Alain-René Lesage, *Histoire de Gil Blas de Santillane*, ed. Maurice Bardon, II (Paris: Editions Garnier Frères, 1955), 65.

11. Ramón de Mesonero Romanos, "Rápida ojeada histórica sobre el teatro español," *Revista de Madrid*, IV (1842), 157.

12. *BAE*, XXXIX, xvii–xviii.

13. "Escritores del siglo XVII. Literatura dramática española, Don Agustín Moreto," *Revista de Ciencias, Literatura y Artes*, I (Sevilla, 1855), 396–404, 445–67, 508–23, 577–93, and 656–73.

14. *Ibid.*, p. 398.

15. Ruth Lee Kennedy, "Moreto's Span of Dramatic Activity," *Hispanic Review*, V (1937), 170–72.

16. Cristóbal Pérez Pastor, *Bibliografía madrileña. Parte tercera—1621–1625* (Madrid, 1907), pp. 433–34.

17. *BAE*, XXXIX, xi.

18. Pérez Pastor, *Bibliografía madrileña*, III, 434.

19. *The Dramatic Art of Moreto*, pp. 4–5.

20. *BAE*, XXXIX, xxviii.

21. Jerónimo de Barrionuevo, *Avisos (1654–1658)*, ed. Paz y Melia (Madrid, 1892–1893), III, Carta CLXXVI, 201.

22. Emilio Cotarelo y Mori, ed., *Colección de entremeses, loas, bailes, jácaras y mojigangas desde fines del siglo XVI a mediados del XVIII. Nueva Biblioteca de Autores Españoles*, XVII (1911), xciv, n. 2.

23. José Sánchez Arjona, *El Teatro en Sevilla en los Siglos XVI y XVII* (Madrid, 1887), p. 229.

24. Antonio de Jesús María, *D. Baltasar de Moscoso y Sandoval* ... (Madrid, 1680), *Libro VII, Capítulo V, Item* 2132.

25. *Ibid.*

26. *Catálogo*, p. 276.

27. Nicolás Antonio, *Bibliotheca hispana nova* (Madrid, 1783) I, 177.

28. "Moreto's Span of Dramatic Activity," p. 172.

29. The *vejamen* may be read in *Poetas líricos de los siglos XVI y XVII*, ed. Adolfo de Castro, *BAE*, XLII, 435–37.

30. *Ibid.*, p. 437.

Chapter Two

1. Notably *La Celestina* (1499), with its twenty-one acts, and Lope de Vega's *La Dorotea* (1632).

2. See several indexed references in Hugo Albert Rennert, *The Spanish Stage in the Time of Lope de Vega* (New York, 1909).

3. This problem is carefully studied and discussed by James O. Crosby in his edition of Quevedo's *Política de Dios* (Urbana, 1966), pp. 329–30.

4. See J. P. Wickersham Crawford, *Spanish Drama before Lope de Vega*. A Revised Edition (Philadelphia, 1937).

5. See N. D. Shergold, *A History of the Spanish Stage from Medieval Times Until the End of the Seventeenth Century* (Oxford, 1967), pp. 153–57.

6. Rennert, *The Spanish Stage*, pp. 26–27.

7. Shergold, *A History of the Spanish Stage*, p. 177.

8. Both Rennert and Shergold provide excellent accounts on the theaters of this period, based largely on studies such as Casiano Pellicer's *Tratado histórico sobre el origen y progresos de la comedia y del histrionismo en España*, I (Madrid, 1804).

9. José Sánchez Arjona, *El teatro en Sevilla*, p. 141.

10. See Shergold, Chaps. 7 and 8.

11. Cotarelo y Mori, *Bibliografía de las controversias sobre la licitud del teatro en España* (Madrid, 1904), pp. 622–25.

12. *Ibid.*, pp. 632–33.

13. Cotarelo, *Bibliografía de las controversias*, pp. 622–27.

14. For a vivid description of the wide range of theatrical groups in Spain at the turn of the seventeenth century, see Agustín de Rojas Villandrando, *El viaje entretenido*, ed. Menéndez y Pelayo, in *Nueva Biblioteca de Autores Españoles*, XXI (1915), 497–99.

15. Shergold, p. 187.

16. *Ibid.*, p. 278.

17. *Ibid.*, p. 527.

18. Cotarelo, *Bibliografía de las controversias*, pp. 619–20.

19. Rennert, p. 139.

20. Cotarelo, *Bibliografía de las controversias*, p. 620.

21. *Ibid.*, p. 621.

22. *Ibid.*, p. 626.

23. *Ibid.*, p. 632.

24. *Ibid.* Cotarelo's study and bibliography are the most comprehensive treatment of this controversy.

25. Pellicer, p. 161.

26. Rennert, p. 246.

27. *Ibid.*, pp. 247–49; see also Sánchez Arjona, pp. 383–86.

28. Cotarelo, *Bibliografía de las controversias*, p. 635.

29. Ruth Lee Kennedy, "The Theme of 'Stratonice' in the Drama

of the Spanish Peninsula," *Publications of the Modern Language Association,* LV (1940), 1022, n. 44.

30. Barrionuevo, *Avisos,* I, CARTA XLIX, 212–13.

31. *Ibid.,* II, CARTA CXXXII, 303.

32. *Ibid.,* IV, CARTA CCXXI, 199-200.

33. The most ambitious study and anthology of these short pieces is Cotarelo's *Colección de entremeses, loas, bailes, jácaras y mojigangas,* in *Nueva Biblioteca de Autores Españoles,* XVII–XVIII (1911).

34. Studied comprehensively by Hannah E. Bergman, *Luis Quiñones de Benavente y sus entremeses* (Madrid, 1965). See also Professor Bergman's later book, *Luis Quiñones de Benavente* (New York: Twayne, 1972).

35. M. Romera Navarro, "Sobre la duración de la comedia," *Revista de Filología Española,* XIX (1932), 417–21.

36. On the actors and their companies, see Rennert, particularly Chapters VII, VIII, and IX and the valuable appendices and list of Spanish actors and actresses.

37. Pellicer, p. 214.

38. Lope de Vega, *Obras escogidas,* II (Madrid: Aguilar, 1953), 887.

39. Luis Vélez de Guevara, *El diablo cojuelo.* Reproducción de la edición príncipe de Madrid, 1641, por Adolfo Bonilla y San Martín (Vigo, 1902), p. 5.

Chapter Three

1. S. Griswold Morley, "Studies in Spanish Dramatic Versification of the *Siglo de Oro,*" *University of California Publications in Modern Philology,* VII (1918), 131–73.

2. S. Griswold Morley and Courtney Bruerton, *The Chronology of Lope de Vega's 'Comedias'* (New York: The Modern Language Association; London: Oxford University Press, 1940). An updated, revised, and corrected edition appeared in Spanish translation in 1968 (Madrid: Gredos), *Cronología de las comedias de Lope de Vega.*

3. "Studies in Spanish Dramatic Versification," p. 164.

4. *Ibid.*

5. *Ibid.,* p. 166. (Cf. James Fitzmaurice Kelly, *Histoire de la littérature espagnole,* 3rd edition [Paris: C. Klincksieck, 1928], p. 428).

6. Pedro Henríquez Ureña, *La versificación irregular en la poesía castellana.* Publicaciones de la *Revista de Filología Española,* IV (Madrid, 1920), 243–44.

7. *The Dramatic Art of Moreto,* pp. 60–69.

8. Lucile K. Delano, "The *Gracioso* Continues to Ridicule the Sonnet," *Hispania,* XVIII (1935), 383–400.

9. Hymen Alpern, "Jealousy as a Dramatic Motive in the Spanish *Comedia*," *Romanic Review,* XIV (1923), 276-85, is not able to cite a single reference to Moreto's theater.

10. Sturgis E. Leavitt, "Some Aspects of the Grotesque in the Drama of the *Siglo de Oro,*" *Hispania,* XVIII (1935), 77–86.

11. Carlos Ortigoza, *Los móviles de la "comedia" en Lope, Alarcón, Tirso, Moreto, Rojas, Calderón* (Mexico, 1954), p. 42.

12. *The Dramatic Art of Moreto,* p. 115; *Los móviles de la comedia,* p. 64.

13. M. Romera Navarro, "Las disfrazadas de varón en la comedia," *Hispanic Review,* II (1934), 269–86; Carmen Bravo Villasante, *La mujer vestida de hombre en el teatro español, Siglos XVI y XVII* (Madrid: Revista de Occidente, 1955).

14. J.-C.-L. Simonde de Sismondi, *De la littérature du midi de l'Europe,* IV, 2nd edition (Paris: Crapelet, 1819), 212.

15. Ortigoza, *Los móviles de la comedia,* pp. 169–71.

16. Ermanno Caldera, *Il teatro di Moreto* (Pisa: Goliardica, 1960).

17. Daniel Poyán Díaz, "Sin desdén para el desdén. Notas al margen de un libro sobre el teatro de Moreto," *Segismundo,* I (1965), 311–23.

18. *Il teatro di Moreto,* pp. 167–68.

19. *The Dramatic Art of Moreto,* p. 122.

20. Several virtually identical observations on Moreto may be found in the following of Valbuena's publications, arranged chronologically: *Literatura dramática española* [1st edition, 1930] (Barcelona: Editorial Labor, 1950), pp. 260–67; "Sobre el tono menor y el estilo en la escuela de Calderón," *Homenatge a Antoni Rubió i Lluch,* I (Barcelona, 1936), 627–49; *Historia de la literatura española* [1st edition, 1937] 4th edition (Barcelona: G. Gili, 1953), II, 590–609; *Historia del teatro español* (Barcelona: Noguer, 1956), pp. 8–9, 72–73; and *El teatro español en su Siglo de Oro* (Barcelona: Planeta, 1969), pp. 377–84.

21. "Sobre el tono menor," p. 628.

22. Adolphe Friedrich von Schack, *Historia de la literatura y del arte dramático en España,* V, 118, 124–37.

23. Vicente García de la Huerta, *Theatro hespañol,* III (Madrid: Imprenta Real, 1785), 159.

24. Anna Marie Lottman, "The Comic Elements in Moreto's *Comedias*" (Unpublished Ph.D. dissertation, The University of Colorado, 1958), p. 136.

25. Louis de Viel-Castel, "Moreto," *Revue des Deux Mondes*, XXI (1840), 787.

26. Adolphe de Puisbusque, *Histoire comparée des littératures espagnole et française*, II (Paris: G.-A. Dentu, 1843), 514–15.

27. Adolf Schaeffer, *Geschichte des spanischen Nationaldramas*, II (Leipzig: F. A. Brockhaus, 1890), 185. Hereafter this volume will be referred to as *Geschichte*.

28. Frank Casa, *The Dramatic Craftsmanship of Moreto* (Cambridge: Harvard University Press, 1966).

29. *Histoire comparée*, II, 30.

30. Ramón de Mesonero Romanos, "Teatro de Moreto," *Semanario pintoresco español* (1851), p. 323.

31. Antonio Gil y Zárate, *Resumen histórico de la literatura española* (Madrid: Gaspar y Roig, 1851), pp. 376–77.

32. George Ticknor, *History of Spanish Literature* [1st edition, 1849], II (Boston: Houghton Mifflin, 1891), 489.

33. "Moreto," p. 756.

34. *Historia*, V, 96.

35. Edward M. Wilson and Duncan Moir, *A Literary History of Spain—The Golden Age: Drama 1492–1700* (London: Ernest Benn, 1971), pp. 125–29.

36. Charles Vincent Aubrun, *La Comédie espagnole, 1600–1800* (Paris: Presses Universitaires de France, 1966), pp. 77–78.

37. *The Dramatic Art of Moreto*, pp. 37–112.

38. Casa, *op. cit.*, pp. 146–47.

39. "Manuscripts Attributed to Moreto in the Biblioteca Nacional," *Hispanic Review*, IV (1936), 312–32.

40. "Moreto's Span of Dramatic Activity," p. 170.

41. *Parte XXXVI* of the *Escogidas* (Madrid: Joseph Fernández de Buendía, 1671), p. 1.

42. *Comedias nuevas escogidas de los mejores ingenios de España* [Published in 48 *Partes*, in Madrid, from 1652 to 1704].

43. *Primera parte de comedias de D. Agvstín Moreto y Cabana* (Madrid: Diego Díaz de la Carrera, 1654).

44. *Segunda parte de las comedias de Don Agvstín Moreto* (Valencia: Benito Macé, 1676). Although they have identical bibliographic entries and contain the same plays, the printings are different.

45. *Tercera parte de comedias de D. Agvstín Moreto y Cavaña* (Madrid: Antonio de Zafra, 1681).

46. Emilio Cotarelo, "La bibliografía de Moreto," *Boletín de la Real Academia Española*, XIV (1927), 458–66.

47. Francisco Medel de Castillo, *Indice general alfabético de todos los títulos de comedias que se han escrito por varios autores, antiguos*

y modernos y de los autos sacramentales y alegóricos (Madrid: Alfonso de Mora, 1735); Reprint with appendix published by John M. Hill, *Revue Hispanique*, LXXV (1929), 144–369.

48. "Catálogo alphabético," *Theatro hespañol*, XVI.

49. A typical catalogue is that of Mesonero Romanos, "Teatro de Moreto," *Semanario pintoresco español* (1851), pp. 323–25. It lists seventy-nine *comedias* and seven *sainetes* and *entremeses* attributed to Moreto. Mesonero is aware of the tentative nature of his catalogue and expresses hope that it will be improved by future scholars.

50. *BAE*, XXXIX.

51. *Ibid.*, xxix-xliv.

52. *Catálogo*, pp. 276–81.

53. George Tyler Northup, "The Imprisonment of King García," *Modern Philology*, XVII (1919), 393–411, casts doubt on Moreto's authorship of *La lindona de Galicia* in one of the few attribution studies prior to the work of Miss Kennedy.

54. *BAE*, XXXIX, xlvii.

55. "La bibliografía de Moreto," pp. 488–91.

56. Ruth Lee Kennedy, "Concerning Seven Manuscripts Linked with Moreto's Name," *Hispanic Review*, III (1935), 295–316.

57. *"La milagrosa elección de San Pío V,"* The Modern Language Review, XXXI (1936), 405–8.

58. "Manuscripts Attributed to Moreto," pp. 312–32. The six excised titles are: *La cautela en la amistad, Merecer para alcanzar, Empezar a ser amigos, En el mayor imposible nadie pierda la esperanza, El parecido,* and *La princesa de los montes y satisfacer callando.*

59. *"La renegada de Valladolid,"* The Romantic Review, XXVIII (1937), 122–34.

60. "Sin honra no hay valentía," *Smith College Studies in Modern Languages*, XXI (1939–1940), 110–21.

61. "Moretiana," *Hispanic Review*, VII (1939), 225–36.

62. *"La gala del nadar*—Date and Authorship," *Modern Language Notes*, LIV (1939), 514–17.

63. *"Escarramán* and Glimpses of the Spanish Court in 1637–38," *Hispanic Review*, IX (1941), 110–36.

64. Fernández-Guerra, *BAE*, XXXIX, xlvii-xlviii, had proposed a different set of categories, which Ruth Lee Kennedy has reclassified in *The Dramatic Art of Moreto*, pp. 13–16.

Chapter Four

1. Francisco Martínez de la Rosa, *Obras literarias*, II (London, 1838), 425.

2. *San Franco de Sena* and *Caer para levantar*, in *BAE*, XXXIX.

3. *The Dramatic Art of Moreto*, p. 37.

4. *Ibid.*, pp. 40–41.

5. *Ibid.*, p. 25, n. 51; "The Theme of 'Stratonice,' " p. 122, n. 44; "*La renegada de Valladolid*," p. 133.

6. *The Dramatic Art of Moreto*, p. 42.

7. Angel Valbuena Prat, *Historia de la literatura española*, II, 606. See also *Historia del teatro español*, pp. 248–53.

8. *The Dramatic Craftsmanship of Moreto*, pp. 6–29.

9. *The Dramatic Art of Moreto*, p. 38.

10. We use the abbreviated reference to the *Comedias nuevas escogidas de los mejores ingenios de España*, published in Madrid, 1652–1704.

11. See Guillermo Lohmann Villena, *El arte dramático en Lima durante el virreinato* (Madrid, 1945), pp. 245–46, and Everett W. Hesse, "Moreto en el nuevo mundo," *Clavileño*, V, No. 27 (May-June, 1954), 15.

12. Kennedy, *The Dramatic Art of Moreto*, p. 124.

13. *Escogidas*, IX, 281: *Es la vida una jornada / que haze el hombre para el cielo, / andamos quando vivimos, / partimos quando nacemos, / quando morimos llegamos, / y descansamos muriendo.*

14. *BAE*, XXXIX, 583–600.

15. *Le Théâtre espagnol. 'San Gil de Portugal' de Moreto* (Paris, 1898).

16. Earliest-known edition is found in *Tercera parte de las comedias de Lope de Vega y otros autores . . .* (Barcelona: Sebastián de Cormellas, 1612); see also the edition and introduction of Angel Valbuena Prat, *Clásicos Castellanos*, LXX (Madrid: "La Lectura," 1926).

17. James A. Castañeda, "*El esclavo del demonio y Caer para levantar*: reflejos de dos ciclos," *Studia Hispanica in Honorem R. Lapesa*, II (Madrid: Editorial Gredos, 1974), 181–88.

18. *The Dramatic Art of Moreto*, p. 155.

19. *BAE*, XXXIX, 121–42.

20. *Historia del teatro español*, pp. 248–53.

21. *The Dramatic Craftsmanship of Moreto*, pp. 7–29.

22. *Ibid.*, p. 7.

23. Alexander A. Parker, "Santos y bandoleros en el teatro español del Siglo de Oro," *Arbor*, XII (1949), 395–416, concludes that the bandit of Spanish Golden Age Drama differs from the stock figure of his exalted and idealized prototype in other literatures in that he is paradoxically devoid of intention to reform society. Melveena McKendrick, "The Bandolera of Golden Age Drama: A Symbol of

Feminist Revolt," *Bulletin of Hispanic Studies*, XLVI (1969), 1–20, discusses *Caer para levantar* and *San Franco de Sena* as variations on the theme of guilt and responsibility.

24. *Geschichte*, pp. 183–84.

25. Generally attributed to Tirso de Molina. See the edition of Américo Castro, *Clásicos Castellanos*, I.

26. *The Dramatic Art of Moreto*, p. 195.

27. *The Dramatic Craftsmanship of Moreto*, pp. 7–8.

28. *Ibid.*, p. 29.

29. *Parte XXXVI* of the *Escogidas* (Madrid: Joseph Fernández de Buendía, 1671), p. 1.

30. *The Dramatic Art of Moreto*, pp. 151–52.

31. Cotarelo, "Actores famosos del siglo XVII: Sebastián de Prado y su mujer Bernarda Ramírez," *Boletín de la Real Academia Española*, II (1915), 602, n. 2.

32. Pérez Pastor, *Documentos para la biografía de D. Pedro Calderón de la Barca* (Madrid: Fortanet, 1905), p. 245.

33. *Avisos*, II, letters of October 30 and November 3, 1655.

34. *The Dramatic Art of Moreto*, p. 152.

35. *Geschichte*, p. 286.

36. Guillén de Castro, *Obras*, ed. Eduardo Juliá Martínez, III (Madrid: "Revista de Archivos," 1927), 393–425.

37. *The Dramatic Art of Moreto*, p. 154.

38. *BAE*, XXXIX, xxx.

39. *The Dramatic Art of Moreto*, pp. 149–50, 154.

40. *Ibid.*, p. 102.

41. *Ibid.*, p. 150.

42. *Ibid.*, p. 17.

43. The eleventh of twelve *sueltas* bound together in *Comedias antiguas*, X [Biblioteca Nacional—call number T 14963].

44. *The Dramatic Art of Moreto*, p. 201.

45. *Ibid.*, pp. 40–41.

46. *Ibid.*, pp. 185–86.

47. "Manuscripts Attributed to Moreto," pp. 320–23.

48. *BAE*, XXXIX, xxxviii.

49. *The Dramatic Art of Moreto*, p. 136.

50. *Ibid.*, p. 151.

51. "*La renegada de Valladolid*," pp. 122–34.

52. "*La renegada de Valladolid*," *Boletín de la Real Academia Española*, XVI (1929), 672–79.

53. Narciso Alonso Cortés, *Miscelánea vallisoletana*, Quinta serie (Valladolid: E. Zapatero, 1930).

54. *BAE*, XLV, 347–66.

Chapter Five

1. Kennedy, *The Dramatic Art of Moreto,* p. 24, n. 50: "All of Moreto's well-known plays of intrigue may be placed before 1652."

2. *Ibid.,* pp. 115–16.

3. *Ibid.,* p. 116.

4. P. 144.

5. Ms. 1087.

6. *Hispanic Review,* I (1933), 353.

7. "Concerning Seven Manuscripts," pp. 297–99.

8. *Geschichte,* pp. 166–67.

9. *BAE,* XXXIX, xxxiv.

10. *BAE,* XIV, 537–56.

11. *The Dramatic Art of Moreto,* p. 131. See also her article, "Moretiana," *Hispanic Review,* VII (1939), 225–36, in which she is less certain of Moreto's collaboration.

12. "Actores famosos," III, 154.

13. *Geschichte,* p. 284.

14. *The Dramatic Art of Moreto,* p. 171.

15. "Actores famosos," III, 11.

16. *Documentos para la biografía de Calderón,* p. 266.

17. *Geschichte,* p. 161.

18. *The Dramatic Art of Moreto,* pp. 173–75.

19. Guillén de Castro, *Obras,* III, edition of Eduardo Juliá Martínez (Madrid, 1927), 1–38.

20. *The Dramatic Art of Moreto,* pp. 173–75.

21. *Geschichte,* p. 281. Lope's play is published in the Royal Academy Edition, XIII.

22. *The Dramatic Art of Moreto,* p. 183.

23. *Ibid.,* p. 16, n. 46.

24. Biblioteca Nacional Ms. 15242.

25. "Concerning Seven Manuscripts," pp. 308–11.

26. La Barrera, *Catálogo,* p. 276.

27. Ms. Res. 81.

28. *BAE,* XXXIX, xl.

29. *The Dramatic Art of Moreto,* p. 139. The play is studied, along with its Lopean source, by N. I. Balashov in a 1963 article summarized in French by A. Zviguilsky, *Bulletin Hispanique,* LXIX (1967), 148–53.

30. *BAE,* XXXIX, 391–406.

31. *The Dramatic Art of Moreto,* p. 118.

32. See Chapter 8, p. 120; also Harvey L. Johnson, "The Model Used by Moreto in the Legal Consultation Scene of *Las travesuras de Pantoja,*" *Hispania,* XXV (1942), 444–45.

33. *The Dramatic Art of Moreto*, pp. 101, 115–16.

34. See Harry W. Hilborn, "The Calderonian *gracioso* and Marriage," *Bulletin of the Comediantes*, III, No. 2 (1951), 2–3.

35. *The Dramatic Art of Moreto*, p. 206.

36. *Ibid.*, p. 142.

37. *Ibid.*, p. 197; cf. also p. 142: "It is the only instance in the theatre of Moreto where there is a death that takes place on the stage. A collaborating hand would explain the retention of a scene which must have struck Moreto as repugnant."

38. *BAE*, XXXIX, 289–309.

39. *Ibid.*, xxx.

40. *The Dramatic Art of Moreto*, p. 15.

41. "Moretiana," *Hispanic Review*, VII (1939), 225–36.

42. *BAE*, XXXIX, 511–26.

43. *Ibid.*, xxxi.

44. *The Dramatic Art of Moreto*, pp. 142–43.

45. Juan Hurtado y J. de la Serna and Angel González Palencia, *Historia de la literatura española*, 2nd ed. (Madrid, 1925), p. 733.

46. P. 16, n. 46.

47. *BAE*, XXXIX, xxxv–xxxvi.

48. Ms. 1-35-5.

49. "Concerning Seven Manuscripts," pp. 300–303. Miss Kennedy's comparison of the manuscript with Beneito's play of the same title revealed that the works were not related.

50. *Ibid.*, p. 302.

51. *BAE*, XXXIX, x, xxxix.

52. *Geschichte*, p. 165.

53. Ruth Lee Kennedy, *The Dramatic Art of Moreto*, p. 189, and "Manuscripts Attributed to Moreto," p. 325, n. 75, cites *Suelta* No. 96 (Madrid: Antonio Sanz, 1741); Cotarelo, "La bibliografía de Moreto," p. 34, mentions another by Juan Sanz (d. 1729).

54. *BAE*, XXXIX, 311–30.

55. *Parte XXIII* of the *Escogidas* (Madrid: Joseph Fernández de Buendía, 1665); *Segunda parte* of Moreto's comedias (Valencia: Benito Macé, 1676).

56. Agustín Moreto, *El parecido en la corte*, edición de Juana de José Prades (Madrid: Anaya, 1965), pp. 10–11.

57. *BAE*, XXXIX, xxxix.

58. *Ibid.*, XXXIX, 143–65; Cotarelo, "Actores famosos," II, 586, refers to a performance in 1651.

59. *The Dramatic Art of Moreto*, p. 116.

Chapter Six

1. *The Dramatic Art of Moreto*, p. 116.
2. *BAE*, XXXIX, 39–55.
3. *The Dramatic Craftsmanship of Moreto*, pp. 53–83.
4. "The Theme of 'Stratonice,' " pp. 1010–32.
5. Casa, *op. cit.*, pp. 53–59.
6. *Ibid.*, p. 62.
7. *Ibid.*, p. 64.
8. "The Theme of 'Stratonice,' " p. 1029.
9. Casa, *op. cit.*, p. 83.
10. Carlos Ortigoza-Vieyra, "Aniquilamiento del móvil honor en *Antíoco y Seleuco* de Moreto respecto *El castigo sin venganza* de Lope," *Los móviles de la comedia*, III (Bloomington, 1969).
11. *BAE*, XXXIX, 427–42, xxxi.
12. *Ibid.*, pp. 491–510.
13. *Ibid.*, pp. 57–79.
14. *The Dramatic Art of Moreto*, p. 160.
15. *BAE*, XXXIX, 1–19.
16. *Clásicos Castellanos*, XXXII (Madrid: Ediciones de "La Lectura," 1916).
17. Agustín Moreto, *El desdén, con el desdén, Las galeras de la honra, Los oficios*. Edición, introducción y notas de Francisco Rico (Madrid: Castalia, 1971).
18. Ignacio de Luzán, *La poética, o reglas de la poesía*. Ed. Luigi de Filippo (Barcelona, 1956), II, 83, 311.
19. Eugenio de Ochoa, *Tesoro del teatro español* (Paris: Dramard-Baudry, 1838–1867) IV, 249.
20. Adolphe de Puibusque, *Histoire comparée*, II, 480.
21. Bruce W. Wardropper, "Moreto's *El desdén con el desdén*: The *Comedia* Secularized," *Bulletin of Hispanic Studies*, XXXIV (1957), 9.
22. Roger Bauer, "Les Métamorphoses de Diane," *Wort und Text—Festschrift für Fritz Schalk* (Frankfurt am Main, 1963), pp. 294–314.
23. Molière, *Œuvres complètes*, I, *Bibliothèque de la Pléiade* (1956), 619–68. See also E. Martinenche, *Molière et le théâtre espagnol* (Paris: Hachette, 1906), pp. 142–51.
24. In Carlo Gozzi, *Opere edite ed inedite*, VII (Venezia, 1802). Mario Ottavi, "Carlo Gozzi, imitateur de Moreto: *El desdén con el desdén* et *La principessa filosofa*," in *Mélanges de philologie, d'histoire et de littérature offerts à Henri Hauvette* (Paris, 1934), pp. 471–79, refutes Gozzi's claim that he had in no way been influenced by Molière and that the structure and dialogue of his adaptation did not closely follow his Spanish source.
25. Schreyvogel's play was first published under the pseudonym

C. A. West, *Donna Diana*, Lustspiel in drei Akten nach dem Spanischen des don Agustín Moreto, in *Almanach für Privatbühnen*, III (Leipzig, 1819), 3–188.

26. George Hyde, *Love's Victory* or *The School for Pride*. A Comedy, in Five Acts. Founded on the Spanish of Don Agustín Moreto . . . (London, Edinburgh, 1825).

27. Ludmilla Buketoff Turkevich, *Spanish Literature in Russia and in the Soviet Union, 1735–1964* (Metuchen: The Scarecrow Press, 1967), p. 141.

28. Dwain Edward Dedrick, *A Critical Edition of Moreto's "El poder de la amistad,"* Estudios de Hispanófila, VIII (Garden City, 1968), xxi.

29. Casa, *op. cit.*, p. 145.

30. "The Relation of Moreto's *El desdén con el desdén* to Suggested Sources," *Indiana University Studies*, XI (1924), 1–109.

31. *BAE*, XXXIX, 82–100.

32. *Geschichte*, pp. 174–75.

33. Cotarelo, "Actores famosos," II, 586.

34. *Geschichte*, pp. 174–75.

35. Lucile K. Delano, "The *Gracioso* Continues to Ridicule the Sonnet," pp. 386–87, cites Gregüesco's parody of the form and its gongoristic users and tendencies.

36. "The Theme of 'Stratonice,' " p. 1022, n. 43.

37. Pp. 70, 92.

38. "Sin honra no hay valentía," p. 115, n. 12.

39. *BAE*, XXXIX, 209–28.

40. *Ibid.*, XLVII, xxviii.

41. "The Sources of *La fuerza del natural*," *Modern Language Notes*, LI (1936), 369–72.

42. *The Dramatic Art of Moreto*, p. 220.

43. *Ibid.*, p. 161.

44. *Parte XI* of the *Escogidas*, 38v.

45. *BAE*, XXXIX, 269–88.

46. *Geschichte*, p. 170.

47. Carole E. Christian, "La originalidad de Moreto en su uso de comedias anteriores" (Unpublished M.A. thesis, Rice University, 1973).

48. *BAE*, XXXIX, 463–89.

49. "Actores famosos," II, 455, n. 3.

50. *Geschichte*, p. 175.

51. Lope de Vega, Royal Academy Edition, XIII.

52. *The Dramatic Art of Moreto*, p. 114, n. 2.

53. *"Los jueces de Castilla,"* Revista de Filología Hispánica, VI (1944), 285–86.

54. BAE, XXXIX, 249–68.

55. *The Dramatic Craftsmanship of Moreto*, pp. 30–52.

56. BAE, XXXIX, 351–72.

57. Among which the best is still that of Narciso Alonso Cortés, *Clásicos Castellanos*, XXXII (Madrid: Ediciones de "La Lectura," 1916).

58. Guillén de Castro, *Obras*, III, 77–115. For a convenient edition containing both plays, see Guillén de Castro, *El narciso en su opinión*; Agustín de [sic] Moreto, *El lindo don Diego*. Edición e introducción de A. V. Ebersole. *Temas de España*, No. 73 (Madrid: Taurus, 1968).

59. Casa, *op. cit.*, pp. 117–44.

60. *Ibid.*, p. 129; Alborg, *Historia de la literatura española*, II (Madrid: Gredos, 1967), 798–99.

61. Milton A. Buchanan, "Notes on the Spanish Drama: Lope, Mira de Amescua and Moreto," *Modern Language Notes*, XX (1905), 38–41, considers mention of a "Lindo don Diego" in *La ventura de la fea*, cited by Lope in 1612, to be the earliest recorded use of the phrase later used as the title of Moreto's play. See also Gerald Wade's "Two Anecdotes," *Bulletin of the Comediantes*, XXIV (Spring, 1972), 5–6, for a description of "A Real-Life 'Lindo.'"

62. Edwin B. Place, "Notes on the Grotesque: The *comedia de figurón* at Home and Abroad," *Publications of the Modern Language Association*, LIV (1939), 412–21.

63. BAE, XXXIX, 167–86.

64. Kennedy, *The Dramatic Art of Moreto*, p. 178, notes 90 and 91.

65. Ms. 15540.

66. Kennedy, "Concerning Seven Manuscripts," p. 308.

67. We have examined No. 76 (Valencia: Viuda de Joseph de Orga, 1764), and No. 133 (Sevilla: Viuda de Francisco de Leefdael, s. a.).

68. *Geschichte*, pp. 284–85.

69. "Concerning Seven Manuscripts," p. 308.

70. BAE, XXXIX, xxxvii. The play is also published in this same volume, 601–21.

71. *The Dramatic Art of Moreto*, p. 181.

72. *Geschichte*, p. 166.

73. BAE, XXXIX, 101–20.

74. *Geschichte*, p. 166.

75. BAE, XXXIX, 187–208.

76. Thomas St. Serfe, *Tarugo's Wiles: or, The Coffee House* (London: Printed for Henry Herringman, 1668).

77. John Crowne, *Sir Courtly Nice.* A Critical Edition by Charlotte Bradford Hughes (The Hague: Mouton & Co., 1966).

78. *Ibid.,* p. 37.

79. *Ibid.,* p. 39.

80. *BAE,* XXXIX, xxxix.

81. *The Dramatic Art of Moreto,* p. 138.

82. Designated Ms. Vitr.ᵃ 7–4 by Paz y Melia, *Catálogo de las piezas de teatro que se conservan en el departamento de manuscritos de la Biblioteca Nacional,* I (Madrid, 1934), 438; but as Ms. 2898 by Dedrick, *ed. cit.,* p. ix. Although discussed throughout Miss Kennedy's *The Dramatic Art of Moreto,* this play was accidentally omitted from the lists of Moreto's works, pp. 14–16, as noted by W. L. Fichter in his review, *Hispanic Review,* I (1933), 356.

83. *BAE,* XXXIX, 21–38.

84. Dwain Edward Dedrick, *A Critical Edition of Moreto's "El poder de la amistad,"* Estudios de Hispanófila, VIII (Garden City, 1968).

85. See Mabel Harlan, "The Relation of Moreto's *El desdén con el desdén* to Suggested Sources," pp. 92–99; and Ruth Lee Kennedy, *The Dramatic Art of Moreto,* pp. 163–65.

86. *BAE,* XXXIX, 229–47.

87. *Geschichte,* pp. 170–71.

88. Raúl Moglia, "*Primero es la honra* en Buenos Aires," *Revista de Filología Hispánica,* VIII (1946), 147–48, also detects traces of Garcilaso's first eclogue, in addition to the sonnet which had already been noted by Kennedy, *The Dramatic Art of Moreto,* p. 103.

89. P. 140.

90. A. Paz y Melia, *Catálogo,* I, 479.

91. Listed by Paz y Melia, *op. cit.,* and by Ruth Lee Kennedy, "Manuscripts Linked with Moreto's Name," p. 311, as Ms. 15.543. In *The Dramatic Art of Moreto,* it is listed as Ms. 2903.

92. "Manuscripts Linked with Moreto's Name," pp. 311–16.

93. *Ibid.,* p. 313.

94. *Ibid.,* p. 314.

95. *BAE,* XXXIX, 331–49.

96. Claude H. Britt, Jr., "A Variorum Edition of Moreto's *El valiente justiciero*" (Unpublished Ph.D. Dissertation, Northwestern University, 1966).

97. *Biblioteca Anaya,* XIX (Madrid, 1971).

98. See, for example, Eugenio de Ochoa, *op. cit.,* IV, 279, where the play is termed *un plagio escandaloso.*

99. Antonio Gil y Zárate, *Resumen histórico de la literatura*

española, 4ª edición (Madrid, 1851), p. 383, contradicts his contemporary with high praise for the play.
100. *The Dramatic Art of Moreto,* p. 197.
101. Casa, *op. cit.,* pp. 84–116.
102. *The Dramatic Art of Moreto,* p. 198.
103. Casa, *op. cit.,* p. 105.
104. Sterling A. Stoudemire, "Dionisio Solís's *refundiciones* of Plays, 1800–1834," *Hispanic Review,* VIII (1940), 307.
105. *BAE,* XXXIX, 373–90.
106. "The Relation of Moreto's *El desdén con el desdén* to Suggested Sources," pp. 99–101.
107. *BAE,* XXXIX, xliv.
108. *The Dramatic Art of Moreto,* p. 161, n. 64.
109. Castañeda, "La 'brava mina' de Moreto," in *Homenaje a William L. Fichter* (Madrid: Castalia, 1971), p. 145.
110. See *BAE,* XXXIX, xliv.

Chapter Seven

1. Samuel A. Wofsy, "A Critical Edition of Nine Farces of Moreto" (University of Wisconsin, 1927), and R. J. Carner, "The *Loas, Entremeses,* and *Bailes* of D. Agustín Moreto" (Harvard, 1940).
2. *BAE,* XXXIX, xlv–xlvi.
3. *Catálogo,* pp. 276–81.
4. *Colección de entremeses,* XVI, xciv, n. 1, and "La bibliografía de Moreto," pp. 491–94.
5. *Auto de la gran casa de Austria y divina Margarita,* in *BAE,* LVIII, 551–63.
6. *Harvard Studies and Notes in Philology and Literature,* XIV (1932), 187–96. *El entremés de las brujas* and *El hambriento* appeared with *El desdén con el desdén* in the undated Volume 25 of the series, *Las cien mejores obras de la literatura española* (Madrid: Compañía Ibero-Americana de Publicaciones, [1928?]).
7. "Tres piezas menores de Moreto, inéditas," *Revista de Bibliografía Nacional,* III (1942), 80–116, and "*Entremés de Doña Esquina,*" *Segismundo,* I (1965), 95–109.
8. *Las brujas* and *El hambriento,* in *El teatro español—historia y antología,* III (Madrid: Aguilar, 1943), 1047–65.
9. *Entremés para la noche de San Juan,* in *Piezas teatrales cortas* (Madrid: Consejo Superior de Investigaciones Científicas, 1944), pp. 247–59.
10. *El aguador* and *Doña Esquina* in *Antología del entremés (desde Lope de Rueda hasta Antonio de Zamora) Siglos XVI y XVII* (Madrid: Aguilar, 1965), pp. 807–38.

11. *Verdores del Parnaso,* Edición de Rafael Benítez Claros (Madrid: Consejo Superior de Investigaciones Científicas, 1969), pp. 219–38, 287–305.

12. *Ramillete de entremeses y bailes nuevamente recogido de los antiguos poetas de España–Siglo XVII* (Madrid: Castalia, 1970).

13. *El desdén, con el desdén, Las galeras de la honra, Los oficios,* ed. Francisco Rico (Madrid: Castalia, 1971).

14. "Notas sobre el teatro menor de Moreto," *Homenaje a Fritz Krüger,* II (Mendoza, 1954), 603.

15. *The Dramatic Art of Moreto,* pp. 106–7.

16. Vol. LVIII [First published in 1865], 551–63.

17. "The Source of Moreto's only *Auto sacramental,*" *Bulletin of the Comediantes,* XXIV (Spring, 1972), 21–22.

18. Jaime Mariscal de Gante, *Los autos sacramentales desde sus orígenes hasta mediados del siglo XVIII* (Madrid, 1911), 352–54.

19. *BAE,* LVIII, 551.

20. Shallow bibliographic knowledge leads Mariscal de Gante, pp. 333–34, to the unfounded assumption that Moreto was the author of several *autos.*

21. *El teatro en Sevilla,* p. 230.

22. *Colección de entremeses,* XVI, xxvii.

23. In "Tres piezas menores," pp. 80–116.

24. See numbers 362 and 363 of the Durán collection, *BAE,* X.

25. Francisco de Rojas Zorrilla, *Lucrecia y Tarquino.* Edited with an Introduction and Notes by Raymond R. MacCurdy, together with a Transcription of Agustín Moreto y Cabaña, *Baile de Lucrecia y Tarquino* (Albuquerque, 1963).

26. For biographical data on Cosme Pérez see Rennert, *The Spanish Stage in the Time of Lope de Vega,* pp. 553–54; Cotarelo, *Colección de entremeses,* XVI, clvii–clxiii; Hannah E. Bergman, *Luis Quiñones de Benavente y sus entremeses, con un catálogo biográfico de los actores citados en sus obras* (Madrid, 1965), pp. 519–23.

27. Hannah E. Bergman, "Juan Rana se retrata," *Homenaje a Rodríguez-Moñino,* I (Madrid: Castalia, 1966), 65–66.

28. *Colección de entremeses,* XVI, clxi.

29. *Ibid.,* clvii–clxiii.

30. *Ramillete,* pp. 323–33.

31. "Actores famosos," III, 13.

32. *Ramillete,* p. 324.

33. "Actores famosos," III, 152.

34. *Ramillete,* p. 430.

35. Cotarelo, "Actores famosos," III, 175–76, notes the accuracy of the description of the beautiful but irascible María de Prado.

36. "Notas sobre el teatro menor de Moreto," p. 603.

37. "La bibliografía de Moreto," p. 493.

38. *BAE*, XXXIX, xlvi.

39. *Colección de entremeses*, XVI, xcii.

40. *Catálogo*, p. 281, n. 1.

41. See Harvey L. Johnson, "The Model Used by Moreto in the Legal Consultation Scene of *Las travesuras de Pantoja*," *Hispania*, XXV (1942), 444–45.

42. For descriptions of the festivities, see Jerónimo de Barrionuevo, *Avisos*, III, carta CXCVI, Dec. 5, 1657; Cotarelo, "Actores famosos," II, 607–21, and *Colección de entremeses* XVI, xciii–xciv.

43. *Colección de entremeses*, XVI, xciii.

44. *Ibid.*, xxxvi.

Chapter Eight

1. *Colección de entremeses*, XVI, xci.

2. *Ibid.*, xcii.

3. "La bibliografía de Moreto," p. 493.

4. Fernández-Guerra, *BAE*, XXXIX, xlv.

5. Léo Rouanet, *Intermèdes Espagnols (Entremeses) du XVIIe siècle* (Paris: A. Charles, 1897), pp. 103–13.

6. "Entremés de Doña Esquina," *Segismundo*, I (1965), 95–109.

7. *Antología del entremés*, pp. 824–38.

8. It is not, however, as claimed by Carner, the only such reference; recall doña Esnefa's involvement with a precentor in the *Entremés del hijo de vecino*.

9. Mario N. Pavia, *Drama of the Siglo de Oro—A Study of Magic, Witchcraft, and Other Occult Beliefs* (New York: Hispanic Institute, 1959), pp. 145–46, cites *Las brujas* as the only reference to witchcraft in Moreto's theater.

10. Published with the *Entremés famoso de las brujas* and *El desdén con el desdén* (Madrid: Compañía Ibero-Americana de Publicaciones [1928?]), pp. 145–53, and Sainz de Robles, *El teatro español*, III (Madrid, 1943), 1059–65.

11. "La bibliografía de Moreto," p. 494.

12. *Ed. cit.*, pp. 188–202.

13. *Ibid.*, pp. 117–29.

14. *The Dramatic Art of Moreto*, p. 104.

15. Manuscript 17.034, Biblioteca Nacional.

16. *Colección de entremeses*, XVI, xciii.

17. "Tres piezas menores de Moreto, inéditas," pp. 30–36.

18. *Harvard Studies and Notes in Philology and Literature,* XIV (1932), 187–96.
19. "Tres piezas menores," p. 12.
20. *"El vestuario,"* pp. 187–88.
21. "Notas sobre el teatro menor de Moreto," p. 612.
22. *Ramillete,* p. 323.
23. *Colección de entremeses,* XVI, xci.
24. *Piezas teatrales cortas,* p. 193.
25. J. H. Parker, "Some Aspects of Moreto's *Teatro Menor,"* *Philological Quarterly,* LI (1972), 217.

Chapter Nine

1. Fernández-Guerra, *BAE,* XXXIX, vi–vii, cites the eight which were known to him; Joaquín de Entrambasaguas, "Doce documentos," p. 352, repeats Fernández-Guerra's list and then publishes two more poems from a Biblioteca Nacional manuscript; Emilio Orozco Díaz, "Moreto y la poesía taurina—Comentario a un romance inédito," *Studia Philologica. Homenaje ofrecido a Dámaso Alonso . . .,* II (Madrid: Editorial Gredos, 1961), 541–55, studies and publishes the text of another of Moreto's poems; and the last which we have found available for inspection are noted in Simón Díaz, *Bibliografía de la Literatura Hispánica,* VI, 101–2; VII, 569; and IX, 751. José María de Cossío, *Los toros en la poesía castellana,* I (Madrid: Compañía Ibero-Americana de Publicaciones, 1931), 181, mentions a sonnet by Moreto published as one of thirteen on an undated single page which we have not been able to consult. Gallardo, *Ensayo,* III, 915, "presumes" Moreto's authorship to another on the unconvincing ground that it was commissioned in Toledo and signed by "el Licenciado Vidriera."
2. See, however, the study of Lucile K. Delano, "The *Gracioso* Continues to Ridicule the Sonnet," *Hispania,* XVIII (1935), 383–400, for a treatment of dramatic satires of the sonnet and its gongoristic uses and tendencies.
3. *Lágrimas panegíricas a la tenprana* [sic] *muerte del gran poeta y teólogo insigne Doctor Juan Pérez de Montalbán . . . Lloradas y vertidas por los más ilustres ingenios de España.* Recogidas y publicadas por . . . don Pedro Grande de Tena (Madrid: En la Imprenta del Reino, 1639).
4. *Ibid.,* fol. 48r.
5. Rodrigo Méndez Silva, *Catálogo real genealógico de España* (Madrid: Diego Díaz de la Carrera, 1639), hoja 11.
6. Rodrigo Méndez Silva, *Vida y hechos heroicos del gran*

Condestable de Portugal D. Nuño Alvarez Pereyra ... (Madrid: Juan Sánchez, 1640), fol. 79r.

7. *Exequias reales que Felipe el Grande, quarto deste nombre, rey de las Españas, que Dios guarde, mandó hazer en San Felipe de Madrid a los soldados que murieron en la batalla de Lérida* (Madrid: Diego Díaz de la Carrera, 1644).

8. *Ibid.*, fols. 9r–9v.

9. "Moreto y la poesía taurina," pp. 552–55.

10. *Primera parte del Arte de escrivir todas formas de letras.* Escrito y tallado por José de Casanova (Madrid: Diego Díaz de la Carrera, 1650). Moreto's sonnet is on the sixth of seven unnumbered folios which precede the main text.

11. José Simón Díaz, *Bibliografía de la Literatura Hispánica*, VI, 100.

12. *El glorioso y diuino triumpho en la canonización del padre de los pobres* ... *S. Thomás de Villanueua* (Toledo: Francisco Calvo, 1660). Moreto's sonnet is on the *verso* of the fifteenth unnumbered folio of the prefatory material.

13. The *villancicos* are found on folios 29r, 30v–31r, 33v, 42r, 42v, 52v, 52v–53r, 64v, 64v–65r, 80r, 80v, 98v, 111r, 111v, and 126r–126v.

14. *Delicias de Apolo, recreaciones del Parnaso por las tres musas Urania, Euterpe y Caliope. Hechas de varias poesías de los mejores ingenios de España.* Recogidas y dadas a imprimir por Don Francisco la Torre y Sevil (Madrid: Por Melchor Alegre, 1670), pp. 114–18.

15. *Ibid.*, p. 176.

16. J. Guillén y Buzarán, "D. Agustín Moreto," *Revista de Ciencias, Literaturas y Artes*, I, 454.

17. *BAE*, XXXIX, xviii. The Biblioteca Nacional designation given by Joaquín Manuel de Alba is M. 14. The modern designation on the manuscript which we have consulted is 3.922.

18. Its lack of poetic qualities leads Orozco Díaz, *op. cit.*, 541–42, to doubt that it was penned by Moreto.

19. *BAE*, XXXIX, vii.

20. "Doce documentos," pp. 352–56.

Chapter Ten

1. A. A. Parker, *The Approach to the Spanish Drama of the Golden Age* (London: The Hispanic and Luso-Brazilian Councils, 1957). Reprinted in the *Tulane Drama Review* IV (1959), 42–59; revised in *The Great Playwrights*, I, ed. Eric Bentley (New York: Doubleday, 1970), pp. 679–707.

2. Arnold G. Reichenberger, "The Uniqueness of the *Comedia*," *Hispanic Review*, XXVII (1959), 303–16.

3. Gerald E. Wade, "The Interpretation of the *Comedia*," *Bulletin of the Comediantes*, XI (Spring, 1959), 1–6.

4. Stephen Gilman, "The *Comedia* in the Light of Recent Criticism, Including the New Criticism," *Bulletin of the Comediantes*, XII (Spring, 1960), 1–5.

5. Everett W. Hesse, *Análisis e interpretación de la comedia* (Madrid: Editorial Castalia, 1968).

6. Eric Bentley, "The Universality of the *Comedia*," *Hispanic Review*, XXXVIII (1970), 147–62. See also Reichenberger's reply to Bentley, which immediately follows (163–73), and for which Reichenberger again uses the title "The Uniqueness of the *Comedia*."

7. M. Romera Navarro, "Góngora, Quevedo y algunos literatos más en *El Criticón*," *Revista de Filología Española*, XXI (1934), 248–73.

8. Baltasar Gracián, *El Criticón*, ed. Arturo del Hoyo, in *Obras completas* (Madrid: Aguilar, 1960), *Parte* III, Crisi VIII, 949.

9. Edward M. Wilson, "Nuevos documentos sobre las controversias teatrales: 1650–1681," *Actas del Segundo Congreso Internacional de Hispanistas*, II (Nimega, 1965), 170.

10. Francisco Bances Candamo, *Theatro de los theatros de los passados y presentes siglos*. Prólogo, edición y notas de Duncan W. Moir (London: Támesis, 1970), p. 30.

11. Ignacio de Luzán, *La poética, o reglas de la poesía* (Barcelona, 1956), II, 311.

12. *Obras literarias*, II, 425.

13. "Teatro de Moreto," *Semanario pintoresco español*, p. 323.

14. *Resumen histórico de la literatura española*, p. 375.

15. *Spanish Drama of the Golden Age* (London: Pergamon Press, 1969), p. 191.

16. Wenceslao Ayguals de Izco, *La carcajada* (Madrid: Sociedad Literaria, 1844), I, (no. 7), 54; (no. 10), 78; (no. 11), 84; and (no. 15), 118.

17. Julio de Ugarte, *Agustín Moreto. Sus mejores obras al alcance de los niños* (Madrid: Juan Ortiz [1932]).

18. *Don Quijote*, edition of Francisco Rodríguez Marín (Madrid: Ediciones Atlas 1948), IV, 52, line 13; V, 178, line 2.

19. Albert E. Sloman, *The Dramatic Craftsmanship of Calderón* (Oxford: The Dolphin Book Co., Ltd., 1958).

20. *The Dramatic Craftsmanship of Moreto*.

21. Louis de Viel-Castel, "Moreto," *Revue des Deux Mondes*, XXI (1840), 788.

22. Dorothy Schons, "Alarcón's Reputation in Mexico," *Hispanic Review*, VIII (1940), 139.

23. *Ibid.*, p. 140, n. 4.

24. Irving A. Leonard, *Books of the Brave. Being an Account of Books and of Men in the Spanish Conquest and Settlement of the Sixteenth Century New World* (Cambridge: Harvard University Press, 1949), p. 79.

25. "A Shipment of *Comedias* to the Indies," *Hispanic Review*, II (1934), 41.

26. "On the Mexican Book Trade, 1683," *Hispanic American Historical Review*, XXVII (1947), 403–35.

27. "A Shipment of 'Comedias' to the Indies," pp. 39–50.

28. "El teatro en Lima, 1790–1793," *Hispanic Review*, VIII (1940), 93–112.

29. Guillermo Lohmann Villena, *El arte dramático en Lima durante el virreinato* (Madrid: Estades, Artes Gráficas, 1945).

30. José Juan Arrom, *Historia de la literatura dramática cubana.* Yale Romanic Series, XXIII (New Haven: Yale University Press; London: Oxford University Press, 1944), 21–26.

31. Emilio Julio Pasarell, *Orígenes y desarrollo de la afición teatral en Puerto Rico* (Río Piedras: Editorial Universitaria, 1951), pp. 7, 392.

32. J. Luis Trenti Rocamora, *El teatro en la América colonial* (Buenos Aires: Editorial Huarpes, 1947), p. 217.

33. José Vicente Ortega Ricaurte, *Historia crítica del teatro en Bogotá* (Bogotá: Ediciones Colombia, 1927), pp. 38, 265.

34. Miguel Luis Amunátegui, *Las primeras representaciones dramáticas en Chile* (Santiago: Imprenta Nacional, 1888), pp. 36, 38.

35. Pedro Henríquez Ureña, *La cultura y las letras coloniales en Santo Domingo* (Buenos Aires: Imprenta de la Universidad de Buenos Aires, 1936), p. 141, n. 3.

36. J. R. Spell, "The Theater in Mexico City, 1805–1806," *Hispanic Review*, I (1933), 55–65.

37. Everett W. Hesse, "Moreto en el nuevo mundo," *Clavileño*, V, No. 27 (mayo–junio, 1954), 15–18.

38. Leonard, "The Theater Season of 1791–92 in Mexico City," *Hispanic American Historical Review*, XXXI (1951), 349–64.

39. Lafayette Silva, *Historia do teatro brasileiro* (Rio de Janeiro: Serviço grafico do ministerio de educaçao e saude, 1938), p. 18.

40. Ada M. Coe, *Catálogo bibliográfico y crítico de las comedias anunciadas en los periódicos de Madrid desde 1661 hasta 1819* (Baltimore: The Johns Hopkins Press, 1935).

41. Narciso Alonso Cortés, *El teatro en Valladolid* (Madrid: Revista de Archivos, 1923).

42. E. Juliá "Preferencias teatrales del público valenciano en el siglo

XVIII," *Revista de Filología Española*, XX (1933), 113–59. Juliá's study is limited to the first half of the century.

43. Alfonso Par, "Representaciones teatrales en Barcelona durante el siglo XVIII," *Boletín de la Real Academia Española*, XVI (1929), 326–46, 492–513, and 594–614.

44. Cotarelo, *Isidoro Máiquez y el teatro de su tiempo* (Madrid: José Perales y Martínez, 1902).

45. Nicholson B. Adams, "*Siglo de Oro* Plays in Madrid, 1820–1850," *Hispanic Review*, VII (1936), 342–57.

46. Sterling A. Stoudemire, "Dionisio Solís's *refundiciones* of Plays, 1800–1834," *Hispanic Review*, VIII (1940), 305–10.

47. Charlotte M. Lorenz, "Seventeenth Century Plays in Madrid from 1808–1818," *Hispanic Review*, VI (1938), 324–31.

48. See Kennedy, *The Dramatic Art of Moreto*, pp. 118–19; the *Catalogue* of the British Museum; and Margaret Wilson, *Spanish Drama of the Golden Age*, pp. 194–95.

49. Ludmilla Buketoff Turkevich, *Spanish Literature in Russia and in the Soviet Union, 1735–1964* (Metuchen, N. J.: The Scarecrow Press, 1967), p. 141; and Jack Weiner, "Translations of Spanish Golden Age Drama in Tsarist Russia," *Theatre Documentation*, I (1968), 31–34.

50. "Additional Bibliographical Notes on Moreto," *Hispanic Review*, I (1933), 236–39.

51. *The Spanish Drama Collection in the Oberlin College Library—A Descriptive Catalogue. Author List* (Oberlin, 1940).

52. *A Bibliography of 'Comedias Sueltas' in the University of Toronto Library* (Toronto, 1959).

53. *A Descriptive Catalogue of the Spanish 'Comedias Sueltas' in the Wayne State University Library and the Private Library of Professor B. B. Ashcom* (Detroit, 1965).

54. *A Catalogue of 'Comedias Sueltas' in the Library of the University of North Carolina* (Chapel Hill, 1965).

Selected Bibliography

PRIMARY SOURCES

Collections

Primera parte de comedias de D. Agvstín Moreto y Cabana. Dedicada a D. Francisco Fernández de la Cueva, Duque de Albuquerque, Marqués de Cuellar, Marqués de Cadereita . . . Con licencia. En Madrid, por Diego Díaz de la Carrera. Año M. DC.LIV. A costa de Mateo de la Bastida, Mercader de libros, frontero de S. Felipe.

Primera parte de comedias de D. Agvstín Moreto y Cabaña [2nd edition—contains the same plays as the 1st edition]. Dedicado a don Ioseph de Cañizares, procurador de los Reales Consejos de su Magestad. Año 1677. Con licencia. En Madrid, por Andrés García de la Iglesia.

Segunda parte de las Comedias de Don Agvstín Moreto (Valencia: Benito Macé, 1676).

Segunda parte de las Comedias de Don Agvstín Moreto [2nd edition—the plays it contains are the same as those in the 1st edition, but the book has been newly set. Cotarelo postulates that the publication of the 2nd edition is later than the date it bears.] (Valencia: Benito Macé, 1676).

Tercera parte de Comedias de D. Agvstín Moreto y Cavaña (Madrid: Antonio de Zafra, 1681).

Comedias nuevas escogidas de los mejores ingenios de España [Published in 48 *Partes*, in Madrid, from 1652 to 1704; referred to normally in the abbreviated form, *Escogidas*]. Moreto's *San Franco de Sena* was included in the *Primera parte* and his plays appeared frequently in subsequent volumes.

García de la Huerta, Vicente. *Theatro hespañol.* I–XVII (Madrid: Imprenta Real, 1785). Contains editions of several of Moreto's plays. Volume XVI provides a catalogue of Spanish plays which represents, as García de la Huerta admits, a revision and expansion of the Medel list.

Moreto y Cabaña, Don Agustín. *Comedias escogidas,* edited by Luis Fernández-Guerra y Orbe. *Biblioteca de Autores Españoles,*

XXXIX (Madrid: M. Rivadeneyra, 1856; reprinted, 1950). Contains thirty-three *comedias* attributed to Moreto and a valuable preliminary study which deals with biography, bibliography, and criticism.

Teatro selecto y moderno, nacional y extranjero. Coleccionado e ilustrado con una introducción, notas, observaciones críticas y biográficas de los principales autores, por Don Francisco José Orellano. I—VI (Barcelona: Establecimiento Tipográfico Editorial de Salvador Manero, 1866–1868). The second volume contains a biographic sketch, a list of dramatic attributions, and eleven plays, two of which, *El defensor de su agravio* and *La traición vengada* have subsequently been removed from Moreto's canon.

MORETO. *Teatro* [*El lindo don Diego* and *El desdén con el desdén*]. Edición y notas de Narciso Alonso Cortés (Madrid: Ediciones de "La Lectura," 1916: *Clásicos Castellanos*, XXXII, 2nd edition, Madrid: Espasa-Calpe, S.A., 1937).

UGARTE, JULIO DE. *Agustín Moreto. Sus mejores obras al alcance de los niños.* "Collección Ortiz—Los clásicos castellanos al alcance de los niños" (Madrid: Juan Ortiz, [1932]). Six plays retold as prose stories.

Individual Plays

El desdén con el desdén, Edited with Notes, Questions, and Vocabulary, by Willis Knapp Jones (New York: Henry Holt and Company, 1935).

El desdén con el desdén, ed. Jack H. Parker. *Biblioteca Anaya,* IV (Madrid, 1970).

El desdén, con el desdén, Las galeras de la honra, Los oficios. Edición, introducción y notas de Francisco Rico. *Clásicos Castalia,* XXXIII (Madrid: Editorial Castalia, 1971). Excellent critical edition of Moreto's masterpiece, along with two previously unpublished works from his *teatro menor.*

El lego del Carmen, San Franco de Sena, ed. Florián Smieja. *Biblioteca Anaya,* XVIII (Madrid, 1970).

El lindo don Diego (published with Guillén de Castro's *El narciso en su opinión*). Edición e introducción de A. V. Ebersole. *Temas de España,* No. 73 (Madrid: Taurus Ediciones, S.A., 1968).

El parecido en la corte, ed. Juana de José Prades. *Biblioteca Anaya,* LX (Madrid, 1965).

El poder de la amistad, A Critical Edition by Dwain Edward Dedrick. *Estudios de Hispanófila,* 8 (Valencia: Artes Gráficas Soler, 1968).

El valiente justiciero, "A Variorum Edition of Moreto's . . ." by Claude

Henry Britt, Jr. (Unpublished Ph.D. dissertation, Northwestern University, 1966).

El valiente justiciero, ed. Frank P. Casa. *Biblioteca Anaya,* XIX (Madrid, 1971).

Teatro Menor

Autos sacramentales con cuatro comedias nuevas y sus loas, y entremeses. Primera parte (Madrid: María de Quiñones, 1655). Contains first known printing of Moreto's *Baile entremesado del Rey Don Rodrigo y la Cava.*

Theatro poético. Repartido en veinte y un entremeses nuevos, escogidos de los mejores ingenios de España (Zaragoza: Juan de Ybar, 1658). Contains, although without attribution, the first known printings of Moreto's *El hijo de vecino* and *La reliquia.*

Rasgos del ocio, en diferentes bailes, entremeses y loas. De diversos autores (Madrid: Joseph Fernández de Buendía, 1661). Contains the first known printings of *El aguador, Loa para los años del Emperador de Alemania,* and *El retrato vivo.*

Tardes apacibles de gustoso entretenimiento, repartidas en varios entremeses y bailes entremesados, escogidos de los mejores ingenios de España (Madrid: Andrés García de la Iglesia, 1663). Contains first known printings of *El alcalde de Alcorcón, Las fiestas de palacio, Los galanes, La bota, La Perendeca, El Mellado,* and *Los oficios.*

Rasgos del ocio, segunda parte (Madrid, 1664). The title page is stuck to the inside of the cover and the first six pages are badly motheaten; the Biblioteca Nacional has it withdrawn from circulation, but special permission to read it revealed that its first known printings of the *Entremés de los órganos y el reloj* and *La loa de Juan Rana* are in perfect condition.

Navidad y Corpus Christi festejados por los mejores ingenios de España (Madrid, 1664). Contains the first printing of Moreto's only known *auto.*

Verdores del Parnaso, en veinte y seis entremeses, bayles, y saynetes de diversos autores (Madrid: Domingo García Morrás, 1668). Only one copy is known to exist. There is a modern edition by Rafael Benítez Claros, Instituto "Miguel de Cervantes," Serie A, Volumen XXX (Madrid: Consejo Superior de Investigaciones Científicas, 1969). Contains the first printings of *Los gatillos* and the *Loa entremesada para la compañía de Pupilo.*

Primera parte del Parnaso nuevo y amenidades del gusto, en veinte y ocho entremeses, bailes, y sainetes, de los mejores ingenios de España (Madrid: Andrés García de la Iglesia, 1670). Contains the first known printings of six *entremeses* attributed to Moreto: *Doña Esquina, El cortacaras, Los sacristanes burlados, El cerco de las hembras, La Zamalandrana hermana,* and *La noche de San Juan.*

Autos sacramentales y al nacimiento de Christo, con sus loas y entremeses, recogidos de los mayores ingenios de España (Madrid: Antonio Francisco de Zafra, 1675). Contains first known printings of *Las galeras de la honra, Las brujas, El hambriento,* and *La burla de Pantoja y el doctor.*

Vergel de entremeses, y conceptos del donaire, con diferentes bailes, loas y mojigangas, compuesto por los mejores ingenios destos tiempos (Zaragoza: Diego Dormer, 1675). Contains the *Loa sacramental para la fiesta del Corpus, representada en Valencia.*

Flor de entremeses, bailes y loas. Escogidos de los mejores ingenios de España (Zaragoza: Diego Dormer, 1676). Contains the first known printing of *La Mariquita,* and two *entremeses* which Balbín considers falsely attributed to Moreto, *Los muertos vivos* and *Los cinco galanes.* (Also includes *El hijo de vecino* and *La reliquia.*)

Floresta de entremeses, y rasgos del ocio, a diferentes asuntos, de bailes, y mojigangas (Madrid: Antonio de Zafra, 1691). Contains the first known printing of *La campanilla.*

Autos sacramentales desde su origen hasta fines del siglo XVII, edited by Eduardo González Pedroso. *Biblioteca de Autores Españoles,* LVIII (Madrid: M. Rivadeneyra, 1865; reprinted 1916). Contains *La gran casa de Austria y divina Margarita.*

ROUANET, LÉO. *Intermèdes Espagnols (Entremeses) du XVIIe siécle. Traduits, avec une préface et des notes, par* ... (Paris: A. Charles, Editeur, 1897). Preface contains only one incidental mention of Moreto. His *Entremés de doña Esquina* (pp. 103–13) is the only one translated in this volume.

WOFSY, SAMUEL ABRAHAM. "A Critical Edition of Nine Farces of Moreto." (Unpublished doctoral dissertation, University of Wisconsin, 1927.) Contains *La loa de Juan Rana, Las brujas fingidas, Los órganos y el reloj, La reliquia, El hijo de vecino, La Mariquita, Doña Esquina, Los galanes,* and *El cortacaras.*

MORETO, AGUSTÍN. *El desdén con el desdén* [and *Entremés famoso de las brujas* and *Entremés famoso del hambriento*] (Madrid: Compañía Ibero-Americana de Publicaciones, [1928?]). The *entremeses* are the first we have found published in Spanish since 1691.

CARNER, ROBERT J. "*El vestuario*: An Unpublished *Entremés* of Moreto," *Harvard Studies and Notes in Philology and Literature,*

XIV (1932), 187–96. Published from seventeenth-century Biblioteca Nacional manuscript 14856.

―――――. "The *Loas, Entremeses* and *Bailes* of D. Agustín Moreto." (Unpublished doctoral dissertation, Harvard University, 1940.) Critical edition of thirty-one works with short introductions primarily bibliographic in nature.

BALBÍN, RAFAEL DE. "Tres piezas menores de Moreto, inéditas." *Revista de Bibliografía Nacional,* III (1942), 80–116. Texts and perceptive analyses of the *Baile del Conde Claros,* the *Baile de Lucrecia y Tarquino,* and the *Entremés del vestuario.*

SAINZ DE ROBLES, FEDERICO CARLOS. *El teatro español—historia y antología (Desde sus orígenes hasta el Siglo XIX),* III (Madrid: Aguilar, 1943). In addition to *El desdén con el desdén* and *El lindo don Diego,* contains *La confusión de un jardín* and two *entremeses: Las brujas* and *El hambriento.* The brief biographic account is characteristically imaginative and undocumented.

Piezas teatrales cortas. Selección, observaciones preliminares y notas por Eduardo Juliá Martínez (Madrid: Consejo Superior de Investigaciones Científicas, 1944). Contains a modern edition of Moreto's *Entremés para la noche de San Juan.*

ROJAS ZORRILLA, FRANCISCO DE. *Lucrecia y Tarquino.* Edited with an Introduction and Notes by Raymond R. MacCurdy, together with a Transcription of Agustín Moreto y Cabaña, *Baile de Lucrecia y Tarquino* (Albuquerque: The University of New Mexico Press, 1963).

BUENDÍA, FELICIDAD (ed.), *Antología del entremés (desde Lope de Rueda hasta Antonio de Zamora) Siglos XVI y XVII* (Madrid: Aguilar, 1965). Short defective bibliographic section precedes editions of *El aguador* and *Doña Esquina.*

MORETO, AGUSTÍN. "Entremés de Doña Esquina. Edición y estudio de Rafael de Balbín." *Segismundo—Revista Hispánica de Teatro,* I (1965), 95–109. Scenic division and versification are emphasized in the accompanying study.

Ramillete de entremeses y bailes nuevamente recogido de los antiguos poetas de España—Siglo XVII. Edición de Hannah E. Bergman. "Clásicos Castalia," No. 21 (Madrid: Castalia, 1970). Modern edition of *El retrato vivo* and *La loa de Juan Rana.*

SECONDARY SOURCES

ANTONIO, NICOLÁS. *Bibliotheca hispana nova,* I (Madrid: J. de Ibarra, 1783). Bibliographic account by a contemporary of Moreto.

ANTONIO DE JESÚS MARÍA. *D. Baltasar de Moscoso y Sandoval . . .* (Madrid: Bernardo de la Villa-Diego, 1680). Claims Moreto was appointed chaplain of the Hospital de San Nicolás, refuge for the poor, which was added to the Hermandad del Refugio, in Toledo (*Libro* VII, *Cap.* V, *Item* 2132).

BALBÍN, RAFAEL DE. "Notas sobre el teatro menor de Moreto," in *Homenaje a Fritz Krüger*, II (Mendoza: Ministerio de Educación –Universidad Nacional de Cuyo, 1954), 601–12. List of thirty-four works considered authentic and a study of the characteristics of Moreto's *teatro menor*.

BARRERA, CAYETANO ALBERTO DE LA. "Agustín Moreto." In *Catálogo bibliográfico y biográfico del teatro antiguo español, desde sus orígenes hasta mediados del siglo XVIII* (Madrid: M. Rivadeneyra, 1860; Edición facsímil–Madrid: Editorial Gredos, 1969), pp. 275–81. Brief biography, based largely on Fernández-Guerra's, and an improvement on the latter's catalogue of Moreto's works.

BAUER, ROGER. "Les Métamorphoses de Diane." *Wort und Text—Festschrift für Fritz Schalk* (Frankfurt am Main: Vittorio Klostermann, 1963), pp. 294–314. A perceptive study of three theatrical adaptations of *El desdén con el desdén*: by Molière (1664), Gozzi (1772), and Schreyvogel (1816).

BENNHOLDT-THOMSEN, UWE CARL. *Das idealisierte Weltbild des Theaters im Siglo de Oro. Eine Studie zum dramatischen Werk Moretos.* Published Dissertation, Universität zu Köln (Köln, 1966). A brief biography is followed by a study of Moreto's dramatic technique, structure, and character delineation.

BUCHANAN, MILTON A. "Notes on the Spanish Drama: Lope, Mira de Amescua and Moreto," *Modern Language Notes*, XX (1905), 38–41. Considers mention of a "Lindo don Diego" in *La ventura de la fea*, cited by Lope in 1612, to be the earliest recorded use of the phrase which later became the title of Moreto's play.

————. "Short Stories and Anecdotes in Spanish Plays," *Modern Language Review*, IV (1908–1909), 178–84; V (1910), 78–89. Three references to plays of Moreto in Volume V.

BUSTILLO, EDUARDO, and EDUARDO DE LUSTONÓ. *Galas del ingenio. Cuentos, pensamientos y agudezas de los poetas dramáticos del Siglo de Oro*, I–II (Madrid: A. de San Juan, 1879). Volume II contains selections from eighteen *comedias* attributed to Moreto.

CALDERA, ERMANNO. *Il teatro di Moreto* (Pisa: Editrice Libreria Goliardica, 1960). A perceptive study of several aspects of Moreto's dramaturgy. Emphasis is placed on the importance of reason to Moreto and on his close correspondence to Gracián.

CASA, FRANK P. *The Dramatic Craftsmanship of Moreto* (Cambridge: Harvard University Press, 1966). Vindication of Moreto from alleged plagiarism on the basis of close analysis of five of his plays and their sources.

CASTAÑEDA, JAMES A. "La brava mina de Moreto." In *Homenaje a William L. Fichter. Estudios sobre el teatro antiguo hispánico y otros ensayos*. Editado por A. David Kossoff y José Amor y Vázquez (Madrid: Editorial Castalia, 1971), pp. 139–49. General comments on the unjustified charges of plagiarism leveled at Moreto and specific reference to *El desdén con el desdén*.

————. "*El esclavo del demonio y Caer para levantar*: reflejos de dos ciclos." In *Studia Hispanica In Honorem R. Lapesa*, II (Madrid: Editorial Gredos, 1974), 181–88. A study of the adaptation made by Matos, Cáncer, and Moreto of Mira de Amescua's masterpiece, *El esclavo del demonio*. Emphasis is given to the characteristic differences of the two periods in which the works were written.

CHRISTIAN, CAROLE E. "La originalidad de Moreto en su uso de comedias anteriores." (Unpublished M.A. thesis, Rice University, 1973). Perceptive study of *El mejor amigo el rey* and *Industrias contra finezas*.

COE, ADA M. "Additional Bibliographical Notes on Moreto," *Hispanic Review*, I (1933), 236–39. *Sueltas* of thirty-nine different titles attributed to Moreto and found in the Ticknor Collection and the private collections of Buchanan and the author supplement Cotarelo's 1927 "Bibliografía de Moreto."

————. *Catálogo bibliográfico y crítico de las comedias anunciadas en los periódicos de Madrid desde 1661 hasta 1819*. The Johns Hopkins Studies in Romance Literatures and Languages. Extra Volume IX (Baltimore: The Johns Hopkins Press, 1935). In number of titles and total performances, Moreto appears to rank behind Calderón and Tirso and substantially ahead of Lope.

COTARELO Y MORI, EMILIO. *Colección de entremeses, loas, bailes, jácaras y mojigangas desde fines del siglo XVI a mediados del XVIII*. *Nueva Biblioteca de Autores Españoles*, XVII, XVIII (Madrid: Bailly Baillière, 1911). Still the most ambitious study of the genre. Useful comments on several of Moreto's works, none of which is published in the collection.

————. "Testamento de una hermana de Moreto," *Boletín de la Real Academia Española*, I (1914), 67–68. Dated December 14, 1704, the will mentions no close relatives, leading Cotarelo to conclude that the Moreto line died with Agustín and this sister, María Angela.

————. "Actores famosos del siglo XVII: Sebastián de Prado y su mujer Bernarda Ramírez," *Boletín de la Real Academia Española*, II (1915), 251–93, 425–57, 583–621; III (1916), 3–38, 151–85.

Published as a book, *Sebastián de Prado y su mujer Bernarda Ramírez* (Madrid: Tip. de la Revista de Arch., Bibl. y Museos, 1916). Contains several aids to the dating of performances of Moreto's plays.

––––––. "La bibliografía de Moreto," *Boletín de la Real Academia Española*, XIV (1927), 449–94. Indispensable bibliographic aid with regard to early editions of Moreto.

CROWNE, JOHN. *Sir Courtly Nice*. A Critical Edition by Charlotte Bradford Hughes (The Hague: Mouton & Co., 1966). A 1685 English adaptation of *No puede ser*. The Introduction discusses Moreto's play and compares the Spanish *comedia* to English Restoration Comedy.

DELANO, LUCILE K. "The *Gracioso* Continues to Ridicule the Sonnet," *Hispania*, XVIII (1935), 383–400. Evidence from *La fuerza de la ley* and *Amor y obligación* that Moreto followed Lope's lead in using sonnets spoken by *graciosos* to parody the form and its gongoristic users and tendencies.

DE PUIBUSQUE, ADOLPHE. *Histoire comparée des littératures espagnole et française*, I–II (Paris: G.-A. Dentu, 1843). Repetition of errors related to Moreto's testamentary request to be buried among criminals. De Puibusque predates Schaeffer in supposing a dramatic source for all of Moreto's plays, but praises the perfection of his adaptations.

ENTRAMBASAGUAS Y PEÑA, JOAQUÍN DE. "Doce documentos inéditos relacionados con Moreto y dos poesías suyas desconocidas," *Revista de la Biblioteca, Archivo y Museo*, Año VII, No. 28 (Octubre, 1930), 341–56. Documents found in the parochial archives of San Ginés, in Madrid, throw light on formerly unknown members of the poet's immediate family. Moreto was evidently one of eight brothers and sisters, rather than three, as had previously been thought. The two poems are burlesque portraits of women.

E.V., "Sobre la familia de Agustín Moreto (1657)," *Correo erudito*, I (1940–1941), 101. Documentary reference to a previously unmentioned sister of Moreto, named Margarita, 23 years old in 1657.

GALLARDO, BARTOLOMÉ JOSÉ. *Ensayo de una biblioteca española de libros raros y curiosos*, III (Madrid: Imprenta y Fundición de Manuel Tello, 1888). A posthumous edition of Gallardo's (d. 1852) biographic and bibliographic notes, which actually antedate Fernández-Guerra's published work (1856) on Moreto.

GASSIER, ALFRED. *Le Théatre espagnol—'San Gil de Portugal' de*

Moreto (Paris: Paul Ollendorff, 1898). Contains a study of Moreto's theater and a translation of *Caer para levantar*.

GIL Y ZÁRATE, ANTONIO. *Resumen histórico de la literatura española*, segunda parte del *Manual de Literatura*, 4ª edición, corregida y aumentada (Madrid: Imprenta y Librería de Gaspar y Roig, 1851), 374–89. Brief biographical sketch which perpetuates several inaccuracies. One of the earliest and most eloquent defenses of Moreto against the charge of plagiarism.

GOZZI, CARLO. *La principessa filosofa, o sia Il controveleno*. In *Opere edite ed inedite*, VII (Venezia, 1802). Italian adaptation of *El desdén con el desdén*.

GUILLÉN Y BUZARÁN, JUAN. "Escritores del siglo XVII. Literatura dramática española, Don Agustín Moreto," *Revista de Ciencias, Literatura y Artes*, I (Sevilla, 1855), 396–404, 445–67, 509–23, 577–93, and 656–73. Contains highly imaginative biographic accounts and favorable comments on several plays.

HARLAN, MABEL. "The Relation of Moreto's *El desdén con el desdén* to Suggested Sources," *Indiana University Studies*, XI (1924), 1–109. A study of the twenty *comedias* which have been proposed as sources for Moreto's masterpiece.

HENRÍQUEZ UREÑA, PEDRO. "Los jueces de Castilla," *Revista de Filología Hispánica*, VI (1944), 285–86. Confirmation, based on *redondilla* and *romance* percentages, that Moreto's version is heavily indebted to Lope's lost play.

HESSE, EVERETT W. "Moreto en el nuevo mundo," *Clavileño*, Año V, Núm. 27 (mayo–junio 1954), 15–18. A brief survey of Moreto's plays presented in the New World from 1659 in Lima to March 17, 1953 in Madison, Wisconsin.

HYDE, GEORGE. *Love's Victory* or *The School for Pride*. A Comedy, in Five Acts. Founded on the Spanish of Don Agustín Moreto, first performed at the Theatre Royal, Covent Garden, on Wednesday, November 16, 1825 (London: Printed for Hurst, Robinson & Co., and A. Constable and Co., 1825). Prose adaptation of *El desdén con el desdén*.

JIMÉNEZ Y HURTADO, MANUEL. *Cuentos españoles contenidos en las producciones dramáticas de Calderón de la Barca, Tirso de Molina, Alarcón y Moreto. Con notas y biografías* (Sevilla: Biblioteca Científico-Literaria, [1881]). Twenty *cuentos*, all related by the *gracioso* or a servant, and 103 plays are ascribed to Moreto. One of the former and several of the latter are false attributions.

JOHNSON, HARVEY L. "The Model Used by Moreto in the Legal Consultation Scene of *Las travesuras de Pantoja*," *Hispania*, XXV

(1942), 444–45. Brief further comment on Menéndez Pelayo's indication that the lively *Entremés del letrado*, published in 1644, seems to have served as the source of inspiration for the comic scene in Act III between Guijarro and the *Letrado*, the episode also performed and printed separately as the *Entremés de la burla de Pantoja*.

JONES, JAMES ATKINS. "The Satire in the Comedies of Moreto." (Unpublished M.A. thesis, The University of Oklahoma, 1930). A superficial treatment which is erroneous in several instances.

JOUISSE, CHRISTIANE. "Moreto transposant Lope de Vega." (Mémoire pour l'obtention du diplôme d'études supérieures, Université de Paris, 1954). Comparative study of five of Moreto's *comedias* and their Lopean sources.

JULIÁ MARTÍNEZ, EDUARDO. *"La renegada de Valladolid,"* Boletín de la Real Academia Española, XVI (1929), 672–79. Concludes that the printed version, attributed to Belmonte, is a revision of the manuscript version of Belmonte, Moreto, and Martínez de Meneses.

KENNEDY, RUTH LEE. *The Dramatic Art of Moreto*. Northampton, Massachusetts (*Smith College Studies in Modern Languages*, Volume XIII, Nos. 1–4, October, 1931–July, 1932. Reprinted, Philadelphia, 1932). The most important single study of Moreto. A monumental accomplishment which has never been surpassed. Review of W. L. Fichter, *Hispanic Rieview*, I (1933), 352–56. An important, essentially favorable, evaluation with valuable supplemental information.

————. "Concerning Seven Manuscripts Linked with Moreto's Name," *Hispanic Review*, III (1935), 295–316. Four years after the publication of her monumental book, Miss Kennedy excludes from Moreto's canon one work which, although she had not at the time seen, she had accepted as unquestionably authentic (*Antes morir que pecar*); reverses her stand on a manuscript version of *El Eneas de Dios*, while continuing to exclude the printed version; claims for Moreto works excluded by Fernández-Guerra (*El hijo obediente*) and Cotarelo (*No puede mentir el cielo*); rejects a play attributed to Matos, Cáncer, and Moreto which was not even treated in her book (*El hijo pródigo*); and discusses Moreto's part in two works consistently considered collaborations (*La mejor luna africana* and *El rey don Enrique el Enfermo*).

————. "The Sources of *La fuerza del natural*," *Modern Language Notes*, LI (1936), 369–72. Amplification of her theory that Leyva's *Cuando no se aguarda y príncipe tonto* was inspired by

La fuerza del natural and not vice versa, as claimed by Mesonero Romanos. Moreto's sources are Mira's *Examinarse de rey* and Lope's *La dama boba.* Bretón de los Herreros's *El príncipe y el villano* is added to Leyva's play as another work inspired by *La fuerza del natural.*

—————. "Manuscripts Attributed to Moreto in the Biblioteca Nacional," *Hispanic Review,* IV (1936), 312–32. After refuting the Moretian attribution of six of nine plays studied, Miss Kennedy lists a total of sixteen titles which she would definitely exclude from Moreto's theater. She then proposes a canon of thirty-three plays written by Moreto alone, nineteen collaborative efforts, and six of doubtful authenticity.

—————. *"La milagrosa elección de San Pío V,"* The Modern Language Review, XXXI (1936), 405–8. Concludes that the play should definitely be removed from Moreto's theater and tentatively added to Montalbán's.

—————. "Moreto's Span of Dramatic Activity," *Hispanic Review,* V (1937), 170–72. Sufficiently important in the first half of the forties to be collaborating with such well-known dramatists as Belmonte and Martínez de Meneses, Moreto probably wrote no secular play after Philip IV's death in December, 1665.

—————. *"La renegada de Valladolid,"* The Romanic Review, XXVIII (1937), 122–34. A summation of studies on this collaboration in which Moreto wrote the second act. The original manuscript version, dated around February, 1637, from a contemporary reference in Act II, was substantially revised by a second-rate writer for publication in the *Parte I* of the *Escogidas,* 1652.

—————. "Moretiana," *Hispanic Review,* VII (1939), 225–36. Observations on *El caballero* and *La fingida Arcadia,* and identification of *El mejor esposo,* attributed to Moreto, as Guillén de Castro's *El mejor esposo, San José.*

—————. *"La gala del nadar*—Date and Authorship," *Modern Language Notes,* LIV (1939), 514–17. The play, first published in 1672 under Moreto's name, considered a questionable attribution in *The Dramatic Art of Moreto,* is here definitely removed from Moreto's canon by Miss Kennedy. She convincingly indicates that it was written before 1628 and that it is either by Lope or at least by a member of the Lopean school.

—————. *"Sin honra no hay valentía,"* Smith College Studies in Modern Languages, XXI (1939–1940), 110–21. A doubtful attribution in Miss Kennedy's *The Dramatic Art of Moreto,* the play is here definitely removed from his theater. It is considered a reworking,

accomplished between January, 1643, and February, 1644, of
a play belonging to the Lopean period.

—————. "The Theme of 'Stratonice' in the Drama of the Spanish
Peninsula," *Publications of the Modern Language Association*,
LV (1940), 1010–32. Good documentation on the classical
sources of the theme and on Moreto's adaptation of Lope's *El
castigo sin venganza*.

—————. "*Escarramán* and Glimpses of the Spanish Court in 1637–38,"
Hispanic Review, IX (1941), 110–36. Although testimony of a
1715 Dutch translation ascribed *Escarramán* to Moreto, Miss
Kennedy, basing her conclusions on internal evidence and contemporary allusions to Manuel Cortiços de Villasante, opines not
only that Luis Vélez de Guevara was the author of at least the
last scenes—and possibly of the whole work—but that it was
presented before the court on Thursday, February 13, 1638.

LEAVITT, STURGIS E. "Some Aspects of the Grotesque in the Drama of
the *Siglo de Oro*," *Hispania*, XVIII (1935), 77–86. Leavitt
notes with pleasure that Moreto and Rojas are among the very
few major playwrights of the Golden Age who "have little or
nothing to contribute to this assembly of gruesome exhibits."

LESAGE, ALAIN-RENÉ. *Histoire de Gil Blas de Santillane*, I–II. Ed.
Maurice Bardon (Paris: Editions Garnier Frères, 1955). Book
VII, Chapter XIII (1724) contains a brief and unfounded
description of Moreto as a talented but foppish young courtier.

LEY, CHARLES DAVID. *El gracioso en el teatro de la península—Siglos
XVI–XVII* (Madrid: Revista de Occidente, 1954). A superficial
study in which it is noted that the *gracioso* was given very important roles by Moreto.

LOTTMANN, ANNA MARIE. "The Comic Elements in Moreto's
Comedias." (Unpublished Ph.D. Dissertation, The University of
Colorado, 1958). A perceptive study of nine comic devices employed in the twenty-three plays of the Fernández-Guerra edition
which are indisputably Moreto's.

MARISCAL DE GANTE, JAIME. *Los autos sacramentales desde sus
orígenes hasta mediados del siglo XVIII* (Madrid: Biblioteca
Renacimiento, 1911). The pages on Moreto (331–54) reflect
shallow bibliographic knowledge which permits the unfounded
assumption that he wrote several *autos*. *El auto de la gran casa
de Austria* is praised as a poetic jewel but rejected as a theological
work because of its portrayal of "brutal and horrendous sacrilege."

MARTINENCHE, E. *Molière et le théâtre espagnol* (Paris: Hachette,
1906). Of special interest is the study of *La Princesse d'Élide*
as an adaptation of *El desdén con el desdén* (pp. 142–51).

MARTÍNEZ DE LA ROSA, FRANCISCO. *Obras literarias*, II (London: Imprenta de Samuel Bagster, menor, 1838), 424–28. Moreto judged superior to Calderón in several areas and specially praised for his models of the *comedia de carácter* and *comedia de figurón*. Perpetuates erroneous attribution of *El marqués del Cigarral* to Moreto.

MATULKA, BARBARA. "The Feminist Theme in the Drama of the Siglo de Oro," *Romanic Review*, XXVI (1935), 191–231. Two of the several plays discussed are Moreto's *El desdén con el desdén*, "replete with traditional feminism," and *Hacer remedio el dolor*.

McCREADY, WARREN T. *Bibliografía temática de estudios sobre el teatro español antiguo* (Toronto: University of Toronto Press, 1966). Indispensable for research in Golden Age theater.

McKENDRICK, MELVEENA. "The *Bandolera* of Golden-Age Drama: A Symbol of Feminist Revolt," *Bulletin of Hispanic Studies*, XLVI (1969), 1–20. *Caer para levantar* and *San Franco de Sena*, both of which received inspiration from Mira de Amescua's *El esclavo del demonio*, are discussed as variations on the theme of guilt and responsibility.

MESONERO ROMANOS, RAMÓN DE. *Nuevo manual histórico-topográfico-estadístico, y descripción de Madrid* (Madrid: Imprenta de la Viuda de D. Antonio Yenes, 1854). Brief biographic account (pp. 118–20), containing some erroneous dates, which perpetuates the false notion that Moreto was a soldier and that he requested to be buried in the *Pradillo de los Ahorcados*.

————. "Rápida ojeada histórica sobre el teatro español," *Revista de Madrid*, IV, Tercera serie (Madrid: Imprenta de D. Fernando Suárez, 1842), 157–58. Contains favorable comment on Moreto's theater but also some biographic inaccuracies which have been accepted at face value by many scholars.

————. "Teatro de Moreto," *Semanario pintoresco español* (1851), pp. 323–25. Repetition of previously expressed erroneous biographic data and a list of works attributed to Moreto which contains many inaccuracies.

MOGLIA, RAÚL. "*Primero es la honra* en Buenos Aires," *Revista de Filología Hispánica*, VIII (1946), 147–48. Moglia deduces from a cast list that an unnamed play presented in 1772 was *Primero es la honra*, in which he finds traces of Garcilaso's first eclogue in addition to others of "Oh dulces prendas por mi mal halladas," already noted by Ruth Lee Kennedy.

M[OREL]-F[ATIO], A. "Simón y ayuda," *Bulletin Hispanique*, V (1903), 186–88. Discussion of the possible meanings of the phrase as used by Polilla in Act I of *El desdén con el desdén*.

186 AGUSTÍN MORETO

MORLEY, S. GRISWOLD. "Studies in Spanish Dramatic Versification of the *Siglo de Oro*. Alarcón and Moreto," *University of California Publications in Modern Philology*, VII (1918), 131–73. The study of strophic data provides objective criteria for help in solving problems of doubtful authenticity. Unfortunately, Morley's sample of thirty *comedias* included one collaboration, one doubtful attribution, and five no longer considered to be Moreto's.

NORTHUP, GEORGE TYLER. "The Imprisonment of King García," *Modern Philology*, XVII (1919), 393–411 (Appended is a note by S. Griswold Morley, pp. 412–13, on *La lindona de Galicia* [*o la ricahembra de Galicia*]). Although Northup leans toward attribution to Montalbán, the versification studies of Morley do not permit a conclusive decision between Montalbán and Moreto, to both of whom, as well as to Lope, the play has been attributed.

OCHOA, EUGENIO DE. *Tesoro del teatro español*, I–V. (Paris: Dramard-Baudry, 1838–1867). Volume IV contains editions of *El desdén con el desdén*, *El valiente justiciero*, and *El lindo don Diego*, accompanied by prefatory remarks.

OROZCO DÍAZ, EMILIO. "Moreto y la poesía taurina—comentario a un romance inédito." In *Studia Philologica. Homenaje ofrecido a Dámaso Alonso por sus amigos y discípulos con ocasión de su 60º anniversario*, II (Madrid: Editorial Gredos, 1961), 541–55. Important distinction is made between the restrained, clear poetry of Moreto's *comedias* and the more learned tone of his poems.

ORTIGOZA-VIEYRA, CARLOS. *Los móviles de la "comedia" en Lope, Alarcón, Tirso, Moreto, Rojas, Calderón [pretextos para el estudio 10,000]* (Mexico: C.U., 1954). In attempting to refute the theory that only love, jealousy, and honor motivate Golden Age protagonists, Ortigoza perceptively identifies several other motives in Moreto's plays.

————. "Aniquilamiento del móvil honor en *Antíoco y Seleuco* de Moreto respecto *El castigo sin venganza* de Lope," *Los móviles de la comedia*, III (Bloomington, 1969). Because of its departure from the mold of the honor code, *Antíoco y Seleuco* is considered the first manifestation of a theater which is neither like Lope's nor like Calderón's.

OTTAVI, MARIO. "Carlo Gozzi, imitateur de Moreto: *El desdén con el desdén* et *La principessa filosofa*." In *Mélanges de philologie, d'histoire et de littérature offerts à Henri Hauvette* (Paris: Les Presses Françaises, 1934), pp. 471–79. A refutation of Gozzi's claim that he had in no way been influenced by Molière and that the structure and dialogue of his adaptation of *El desdén con el desdén* did not closely follow his Spanish source.

PARKER, J. H. "Una nota comparada: el gracioso de Molière." In *Homenaje a William L. Fichter. Estudios sobre el teatro antiguo hispánico y otros ensayos.* Editado por A. David Kossoff y José Amor y Vázquez (Madrid: Editorial Castalia, 1971), pp. 575–80. A comparison between Moron of *La Princesse d'Élide* and Moreto's Polilla leads to other reflections on the inspirational value of the Spanish *gracioso* in Molière's theater.

————. "Some Aspects of Moreto's *Teatro Menor*," *Philological Quarterly*, LI (1972), 205–17. Perceptive analyses of eleven works.

PÉREZ PASTOR, CRISTÓBAL. *Bibliografía madrileña. Parte tercera: 1621 al 1625* (Madrid: Tipografía de la Revista de Archivos, Bibliotecas y Museos, 1907). Seven documents related to Moreto are included in the appendix.

————. *Documentos para la biografía de D. Pedro Calderón de la Barca,* I (Madrid: Establecimiento Tipográfico de Fortanet, 1905). A document dated July 7, 1645 refers to a play by Moreto, along with others by Calderón and Martínez, as having been provided to Antonio García de Prado, whose company was to perform at court on October 24 of that year.

PLACE, EDWIN B. "Notes on the Grotesque: the *comedia de figurón* at Home and Abroad," *Publications of the Modern Language Association,* LIV (1939), 412–21. Questions the accuracy of the traditional classification of *El lindo don Diego* as a *comedia de figurón.*

POYÁN DÍAZ, DANIEL. "Sin desdén para el desdén. Notas al margen de un libro sobre el teatro de Moreto," *Segismundo,* I (1965), 311–23. Primarily an article written in praise of Caldera's *Il teatro di Moreto.* Caldera's comparison of Moreto with Gracián is considered to be most felicitous, marking Moreto as a true man of his epoch. Many comparisons are noted between Moreto, Calderón, Gracián, Descartes; all refuse to trust their senses and pursue rational motivation.

RENNERT, HUGO ALBERT. *The Spanish Stage in the Time of Lope de Vega* (New York: The Hispanic Society of America, 1909). The best work on the Spanish stage prior to Shergold's monumental study. Still the best single source of biographic data on Golden Age actors and actresses. Reprinted in 1963 by Dover Publications, Inc. (New York), without the appendix containing this biographic data.

REYNOLDS, JOHN J. "The Source of Moreto's only *Auto Sacramental,*" *Bulletin of the Comediantes,* XXIV (Spring, 1972), 21–22. Moreto's *La gran casa de Austria y divina Margarita* is shown to be an adaptation of Mira de Amescua's *auto* entitled *La fe de Hungría*, of which Reynolds is preparing an edition.

ROMERA NAVARRO, M. "Las disfrazadas de varón en la comedia," *Hispanic Review*, II (1934), 269–86. Reference is made to *San Franco de Sena*, *La negra por el honor*, *La ocasión hace al ladrón*, and *La adúltera penitente*, all of which have at one time been attributed to Moreto.

—————. "Góngora, Quevedo y algunos literatos más en *El Criticón*," *Revista de Filología Española*, XXI (1934), 248–73. Moreto, whom Gracián labels "the Spanish Terence," is the only playwright named in *El Criticón*.

—————. "Sobre la duración de la comedia," *Revista de Filología Española*, XIX (1932), 417–21. Several references from seventeenth-century authors and critics, supported by verse counts (Moreto: average length, 2,750; shortest, 2,068—*Las travesuras de Pantoja*; longest, 3,154—*Los jueces de Castilla*), indicate a variance from two to three hours.

ST. SERFE, THOMAS. *Tarugo's Wiles: or, The Coffee-House. A Comedy*. As it was acted at His Highness's, the Duke of York's Theater (London: Printed for Henry Herringman, 1668). Prose adaptation in five acts which closely follows its source, *No puede ser*.

SAINZ DE ROBLES, FEDERICO. "Agustín Moreto y Cabaña." In *Historia general de las literaturas hispánicas*, III (*Renacimiento y Barroco*), (Barcelona: Editorial Barna, S.A., 1953), 472–77. The imaginative biographic anecdotes and the frequently erroneous critical comment reveal but slight acquaintance with current scholarship.

SÁNCHEZ ARJONA, JOSÉ. *El teatro en Sevilla en los siglos XVI y XVII* (Madrid: Establecimiento tipográfico de A. Alonso, 1887). Includes a document found in the Ayuntamiento of Seville which states that Moreto, in 1656, was a resident in that city and that he presented the *loas* and *sainetes* for the Corpus Christi celebrations of that year.

SCHACK (ADOLPHE FRIEDRICK VON), COUNT. *Historia de la literatura y del arte dramático en España*, I–V. Translation of E. de Mier (Madrid, 1885–1887). Published originally in 1845–1846, it contains false biographic legends. Criticism is harsh for Moreto's religious plays, but extremely favorable with respect to his comic vein.

SCHAEFFER, ADOLF. *Geschichte des spanischen Nationaldramas*, I–II. (Leipzig: F. A. Brockhaus, 1890). Analyses of forty-seven plays, many of which have subsequently been removed from Moreto's canon, include pioneer work in the discovery of sources.

SHERGOLD, N. D. *A History of the Spanish Stage from Medieval Times until the End of the Seventeenth Century* (Oxford: The Clarendon Press, 1967). An indispensable compendium of knowledge concerning all aspects of the Spanish stage through the Golden Age.

SISMONDI, J.-C.-L. SIMONDE DE. *De la littérature du midi de l'Europe.* Seconde édition, revue et corrigée, IV (Paris: Imprimerie de Crapelet, 1819), 212–14. Mistakenly considers *El marqués del Cigarral* as a work of Moreto's and singles out for praise *No puede ser,* Molière's source for *L'École des maris.*

VALBUENA PRAT, ÁNGEL. "Sobre el tono menor y el estilo en la escuela de Calderón." *Homenatge a Antoni Rubió i Lluch—Miscellània d'estudis literaris, històrics i lingüístics,* I (Barcelona, 1936), 627–49. Views on Moreto which are repeated in expanded form in Valbuena's *Historia de la literatura española.*

—————. *Historia de la literatura española* [1st edition, 1937]. 4th edition, I–III (Barcelona: Editorial Gustavo Gili, 1953). Classifies Moreto as "the Alarcón of the second dramatic cycle," and detects "a tone of dance, an air of minuet" which announce the theater of Marivaux, the painting of Watteau, and the music of Mozart.

VIEL-CASTEL, LOUIS DE. "Moreto," *Revue des Deux Mondes,* XXI (1840), 749–88. A product of the Romantic period, this favorable and perceptive evaluation of Moreto is one of the earliest studies of his theater to be published outside of Spain. Contains plot summaries and extensive translation of passages from nine plays then attributed to Moreto.

WARDROPPER, BRUCE W. "Moreto's *El desdén con el desdén*: The *Comedia* Secularized," *Bulletin of Hispanic Studies,* XXXIV (1957), 1–9. A provocative study which concludes that "Moreto is the first Spanish dramatist to achieve a fully disciplined art."

WEST, C. A. *Donna Diana,* Lustspiel in drei Akten nach dem Spanischen des don Agustín Moreto. In *Almanach für Privatbühnen,* III (Leipzig: Georg Joachim Goschen, 1819). First publication of Joseph Schreyvogel's adaptation of *El desdén con el desdén* under the pseudonym of C. A. West.

Index

191

Index

Index